Teaching, Learning and Education in Late Modernity

In the **World Library of Educationalists**, international scholars themselves compile career-long collections of what they judge to be their finest pieces – extracts from books, key articles, salient research findings, major theoretical and practical contributions – so the world can read them in a single manageable volume. Readers will be able to follow the themes and strands of their work and track their contribution to the development of a field, as well as the development of the field itself.

Peter Jarvis has spent over 30 years researching, thinking and writing about some of the key and enduring issues in education. He has contributed well over 30 books and 200 papers and chapters in books on learning theory, adult education and learning, continuing professional education, nurse education, primary school education, distance education and third age education.

In *Teaching, Learning and Education in Late Modernity*, he brings together 19 key writings in one place. Beginning with a specially written Introduction, which gives an overview of Peter's career and contextualises his selection within the progression of the field, the chapters cover:

- learning
- learning and religion/spirituality
- learning and doing
- teaching
- late modernity
- learning in later life.

This book showcases Peter's substantial contribution to the fields of learning and education while also exhibiting how his thinking has developed during his long and distinguished career. It also gives an insight into the development of the fields in which he is involved.

Peter Jarvis is Professor Emeritus of Continuing Education at the University of Surrey, UK.

Contributors to the series include Richard Aldrich, Stephen J. Ball, John Elliott, Elliot Eisner, Howard Gardner, John Gilbert, Ivor F. Goodson, David Labaree, John White and E.C. Wragg.

World Library of Educationalists series

Other books in the series:

Lessons from History of Education
The selected works of Richard Aldrich
Richard Aldrich

Education Policy and Social Class
The selected works of Stephen J. Ball
Stephen J. Ball

In Search of Pedagogy Volume I
The selected works of Jerome Bruner, 1957–1978
Jerome S. Bruner

In Search of Pedagogy Volume II
The selected works of Jerome Bruner, 1979–2006
Jerome S. Bruner

Reimagining Schools
The selected works of Elliot W. Eisner
Elliot W. Eisner

Reflecting Where the Action Is
The selected works of John Elliot
John Elliot

Constructing Worlds through Science Education
The selected works of John K. Gilbert
John K. Gilbert

Learning, Curriculum and Life Politics
The selected works of Ivor F. Goodson
Ivor F. Goodson

Teaching, Learning and Education in Late Modernity
The selected works of Peter Jarvis
Peter Jarvis

Education, Markets, and the Public Good
The selected works of David F. Labaree
David F. Labaree

The Curriculum and the Child
The selected works of John White
John White

The Art and Science of Teaching and Learning
The selected works of Ted Wragg
E.C. Wragg

Educational Philosophy and Politics
The selected works of Michael A. Peters
Michael A. Peters

A Life in Education
The selected works of John Macbeath
John Macbeath

Teaching, Learning and Education in Late Modernity

The selected works of Peter Jarvis

Peter Jarvis

Routledge
Taylor & Francis Group

LONDON AND NEW YORK

First published 2012
by Routledge
2 Park Square, Milton Park, Abingdon, Oxon OX14 4RN

Simultaneously published in the USA and Canada
by Routledge
711 Third Avenue, New York, NY 10017

Routledge is an imprint of the Taylor & Francis Group, an informa business

British Library Cataloguing in Publication Data
A catalogue record for this book is available
from the British Library

Library of Congress Cataloging in Publication Data
A catalog record for this book has been requested

ISBN: 978–0–415–68473–6 (hbk)
ISBN: 978–0–415–68474–3 (pbk)
ISBN: 978–0–203–80294–6 (ebk)

Typeset in Sabon
by RefineCatch Limited, Bungay, Suffolk

Dedicated
to
Maureen,
and Frazer and Kierra
with love and thanks for making
so much possible

CONTENTS

ACKNOWLEDGEMENTS

Learning

Chapter 1 originally published as 'Towards a Theory of Learning' in K. Illeris (ed.) (2009), *Contemporary Theories of Learning*, London: Routledge, pp. 21–34.

Chapter 2 originally published as 'It Is the Person who Learns' in D. Aspin, J. Chapman, K. Evans and R. Bagnall (eds) (forthcoming), *The International Handbook of Lifelong Learning*, second edition, Springer.

Chapter 3 originally published as 'Experience' in P. Jarvis (2009), *Learning to Be a Person in Society*, London: Routledge, pp. 55–68.

Chapter 4 originally published as 'Meaning' in P. Jarvis (2009), *Learning to Be a Person in Society*, London: Routledge, pp. 69–78.

Chapter 5 originally published as 'Being and Having' in P. Jarvis (1992), *Paradoxes of Learning*, San Francisco: Jossey-Bass, pp. 143–54.

Learning and religion/spirituality

Chapter 6 originally published as 'Learning as a Religious Phenomenon?' in P. Jarvis and N. Walters (eds) (1993), *Adult Education and Theological Interpretations*, Malabar, FL: Krieger, pp. 3–16.

Chapter 7 originally published as 'The Spiritual Dimension of Human Learning' in R. Mark *et al.* (eds) (2007), *Proceedings of SCUTREA Conference*, Belfast: School of Education, pp. 238–45.

Learning and doing

Chapter 8 originally published as 'Learning to Be an Expert and Competence Development' in K. Illeris (2009), *International Perspectives on Competence Development*, London: Routledge, pp. 99–109.

Chapter 9 originally published as 'Practitioner Research and the Learning Society' in P. Jarvis (1999), *The Practitioner-Researcher*, San Francisco: Jossey-Bass, pp. 159–68.

Teaching

Chapter 10 originally published as 'Ethics and Teaching: Exploring the Relationship between Teacher and Taught' in P. Jarvis (ed.) (2006), *The Theory and Practice of Teaching*, second edition, London: Routledge, pp. 39–52.

Chapter 11 originally published as 'Teaching: An Art or a Science (Technology)?' in P. Jarvis (ed.) (2006), *The Theory and Practice of Teaching*, second edition, London: Routledge, pp. 16–27.

Chapter 12 originally presented as 'Transforming Asian Education through Open and Distance Learning: Through Thinking' (2004), unpublished paper delivered at the Chinese Distance Education and Hong Kong OU Research in Distance Education Conference, Hong Kong.

Late modernity

Chapter 13 originally published as 'The Changing Educational Scene' in P. Jarvis (ed.) (2001), *The Age of Learning: Education and the Knowledge Society*, London: Routledge, pp. 27–38.

Chapter 14 originally published as 'Infinite Dreams, Infinite Growth, Infinite Learning: The Challenge of Globalisation in a Finite World' in P. Jarvis (2007), *Globalisation, Lifelong Learning and the Learning Society: Sociological Perspectives*, London: Routledge, pp. 203–13.

Chapter 15 originally published as 'Beyond the Learning Society' in the *International Journal of Lifelong Learning* (2006), Vol. 25 Nos 3–4, pp. 201–11.

Chapter 16 originally presented as 'The End of a Sensate Age – What Next?' (2009), unpublished paper delivered as the 40th Sorokin Lecture at the University of Saskatchewan.

Chapter 17 originally presented as 'Globalisation, Knowledge and the Need for a Revolution in Learning' (2007), unpublished paper revised from *Democracy, Lifelong Learning and the Learning Society: Active Citizenship in a Late Modern Age* (2008), London: Routledge, and delivered at the Danish Pedagogical University.

Learning in later life

Chapter 18 originally published as 'Learning Meaning and Wisdom' in P. Jarvis (2001), *Learning in Later Life*, London: Kogan Page, pp. 97–110.

Chapter 19 originally published as 'Learning to Retire' in P. Jarvis (2001), *Learning in Later Life*, London: Kogan Page, pp. 60–9.

INTRODUCTION

Being asked to select some of my own writings to make up an edited book was a great surprise to me; it is also a great honour. At the same time, it constituted a major problem because I really did not know what to put into the book and so I had to take advice about the matter. There seemed to be three major ways of compiling it: the first was to work sequentially through my publications since the first one in 1972 to try to reflect the way that my thoughts have changed and developed, but I rejected this since I am not sure that many of my early papers are relevant, or even of interest to people today; secondly, to reflect on my career and try to choose papers to represent every aspect of it, and to some extent I have done this although I hesitated about this approach because I feel that it is my work rather than me which may be of interest; to reflect on my current philosophy and research interests and try to capture some of these in the later papers and chapters that I have published – which is what I have also done. However, this latter approach also created its own problems because I am still working on many of the issues and these current thoughts may be more interesting, especially to me, than some of the material that I have already published. In this Introduction, I will try to reflect on my career and my current work as I present my selection. However, as I have already intimated, the selection is not entirely my own since I consulted two of my ex-doctoral students, both of whom used some of my work in their own research (Alison le Cornu and Michelle Camilleri) and one good friend who has done me the honour of translating some of my work into Greek (George Koulaouzides). I am most grateful to them for giving their time to look again at some of my work and make suggestions to me – there were a number of similarities between their suggestions which, fortunately, also coincided with some of my own preferences.

At the same time, I realised that the selection only makes sense as a whole if it is related to my own academic development and while I do not relish discussing my background, I have included a few biographical references in order to make sense of the diversity of pieces that I have chosen. I eventually selected the nineteen pieces that are in the book and they are organised into six sections which reflect some of my major interests as well as my background: learning, learning and religion/spirituality, learning and doing, teaching, education and late modernity, and learning in later life.

Learning: Since I wrote my first book on learning, *Adult Learning in the Social Context,* the processes of learning have never been far from my mind because I have long thought that many of the theories over-simplify and de-personalise the learning processes. I think that this is best illustrated in an edited book that should be published within a few months of this one (Jarvis with Watts, in press) in which learning is examined from nearly sixty different perspectives. I have not selected anything specifically from my first book on learning, although the original diagram appears in the opening chapter of this book, despite the fact that it was among the first studies to examine the learning process from a sociological perspective and that it won the Houle Award of the American Association of Adult and Continuing Education. I am delighted, however, that Routledge is going to re-issue it again in 2012. I have re-visited some of its major themes, however, many times since, some of which appear in the first section of this book, such as personhood, experience meaning and being. I shall revisit them yet again in the next book that I am currently writing – on philosophical perspectives on learning.

The first chapter, however, reflects the way that my ideas about human learning have changed in the twenty years since I first undertook the research for and wrote *Adult Learning*. Over the years I have continued to conduct different versions of the research workshop that formed the basis of the original research, most often now in Denmark. I owe the opportunity to do this to Lis Hemmingsen from the Danish Pedagogical University who has consistently invited me to teach at the University and offer the workshop since the time when I was a visiting professor there. This has enabled me to keep on testing the relevance of the model and adapting it where necessary. Consequently, I have continued this research and conducted this same workshop many times over a period of about twenty-five years which is rather longer than many of the currently funded research projects last. I still regard my study of learning as an on-going process! The second chapter reflects my current thinking about the need for philosophical analyses of learning, especially from the perspective of the philosophy of mind. I have subsequently prepared a paper on teaching from the same perspective. I am not a professional philosopher and so I acknowledge that my forays into this field might be regarded as dangerous undertakings and yet it is one that I believe profoundly that educators should undertake and I am currently writing a book from this perspective. As experiential learning has grown in popularity I have feared that we would not conduct the types of in-depth analyses that have been necessary to explore the richness of experience in the learning processes but I have been delighted to read the work of scholars whose philosophical background has been much more extensive than my own. However, the third and the fourth chapters – about experience and meaning on which I have written for many years, and both taken from one of my latest books – also reflect the need for a philosophy of mind in order to enlighten our understanding of human learning. Finally in this section, I include a chapter of an existential nature, which has been reprinted in a number of my books, in which I explore the process of being and learning in relation to the social system of education and having certificates.

Learning and religion/spirituality: The second section of religion and spirituality reflects my own past and my way into the academic life. I left school without sufficient qualifications to enter university and so I joined the Royal Air Force for three years. During that time and in the following year which I spent in a college in Derbyshire – rather like a folk high school – I prepared and offered myself for the Ministry of the Methodist Church: I then spent four years studying for the Ministry at Richmond College – then a constituent college of the University of London. During that time I also gained sufficient qualifications to embark and complete a degree course in Divinity, specialising in the history of the Church. I have always regarded learning, consequently, as a spiritual exercise and this is reflected in both chapters published in this section. The first comes from *Adult Education and Theological Interpretations*, which I edited with my colleague Nicholas Walters, and in which we tried to draw relationships between the practices of adult education and contemporary theology, and the second is a chapter that I prepared for a SCUTREA pre-conference on learning and spirituality. I have subsequently written a number of other papers on this topic and hope to return to it yet again in the near future.

Learning and doing: I have been tempted to include in this book material that I am still working on and this was especially strong in the third section where I have just finished a paper entitled 'Learning to Do: Learning Professional Practice', various drafts of which I have given in a number of recent seminars and conferences. The process of learning to do has become more important to me as I have become convinced that doing is at least as significant as thinking in the process of learning. However, I decided not to include it here but to offer two other chapters – one on expertise and the other on practitioner research. I personally regard expertise as a more important human development than competence development. Competence development does not make such demands on practitioners since the technological society does not appear to require as many experts and it has tended to regard education and training as a process of generating human 'cogs-in-the-wheels' of the system of production – functionaries that are replaceable in the production processes rather than unique human beings. The second chapter is on practitioner research which I regard as a much more democratic research process than many other forms of research, and one that firmly locates it into a learning paradigm, although it has other limitations. Indeed, all my research on human learning has been through a process of practitioner research but the book was actually written when some of my students were studying their own practice as part of their research for their doctorates.

Teaching: The six years that I spent in pastoral ministry of the church was also a teaching ministry; although a great deal of my ministry was spent in pastoral work, I was always happy as a teacher. All my academic life I have believed in the high ideals of the teaching profession and my second book was a textbook, *Adult and Continuing Education: Theory and Practice* (Jarvis 1983) and to my continued satisfaction the fourth edition of that book is still in print almost thirty years later. My first commercial book was *Professional Education* – published in the same year – which reflects some of the work that I did for my doctorate in the sociology of the professions and focuses on the service-nature of the professions. Consequently, two of the three chapters that I have included here are concerned about the ethics and the art of teaching. Being a professional demands from its practitioners an ethic or service primarily to the learners, despite the frequent depiction of teachers as authoritarian practitioners. Teaching is always a relationship of taught and teachers but it is only in relationship that the highest moral values can be manifest – love, care, concern. Teaching, to my mind, demands such as ethical practice. The second of these chapters suggests that teaching is primarily an art rather than a science/technique because it is primarily about the human skill in the practice of relationships. It is something that is learned and each teaching situation is unique: human beings cannot be programmed (hard-wired) to sustain a teaching and learning relationship (see Donald, 2001) – the act of teaching is, therefore, a matter of a learned skill and sensitivity in appreciating the other although we – especially mothers but not exclusively so – may seek to teach our children and members of our family instinctively. In this sense teaching professionally requires morality and learned skills rather than just instinct.

In addition, I was lucky enough to teach part-time for the Open University for its first thirty years in a number of different roles. After thirty years I was informed that my services were no longer required as I was unable to attend a job interview to teach on a new module that was replacing the one on which I taught, and for the only time in my life I received a redundancy payment. However, I was also responsible for the University of Surrey's Master's degree in Continuing Education by distance in the 1980s which I believe to have been the first Master's degree by distance in any form of the study of the education of adults anywhere in the world. Over the years, consequently, I have written a few things about distance teaching and learning and so I am including one chapter on it here in which I try to illustrate my philosophy of teaching and learning within the context of distance learning. Throughout my career I have been lucky enough to visit Eastern Asia many times and to learn a very little about the wonderfully rich cultures of that part of the world and which I only wish I understood better: I have also had the great privilege of speaking at a number of Asian conferences – including distance learning conferences – and the paper that I have included here has used the title of the Conference at which it was presented, *Transforming Asian Education through Open and Distance Education*.

Late modernity: When I was a pastoral minister I quickly learned that reading for a classical divinity degree had not really equipped me in any way to be an effective minister in urban society and that I needed to study the social sciences for this. I was most fortunate that the Faculty of Social Sciences at the University of Sheffield where I was practising my ministry had an enlightened Dean at that time and when I approached the University with the request that I be allowed to sit in some lectures whilst I prepared myself to sit the London University external degree in sociology, the Dean offered me the chance not only to sit in the lectures but to take the examinations as if I were a full-time student. At that time I was minister to four churches having over 400 members and involved in many other activities in the city but the church allowed me to sit in at the lectures when I had the time provided that my full-time ministry was not affected. I was for three years effectively a full-time minister and a part-time/full-time student – not a unique situation today but rarer then – and to everybody's surprise, including my own, I gained a good honours degree in the social sciences. The penultimate section of this book reflects the fact that as a result of these studies I became a sociologist: one of my earliest books was *The Sociology of Adult and Continuing Education* which was one of the earliest sociological studies of adult education but, again I decided that I should use some of my later work in this section. However, I am also pleased to say that Routledge have also decided to re-issue this book in 2012.

The one reading that caused me some doubts about its inclusion was the first one of this section: I wanted to record in some way how the education of adults had changed during my academic life but I have not really written anything from a contemporary history perspective and so I have included a chapter that provides something of an overview. The remaining chapters in this section reflect my views on modernity, globalisation and the learning society.

In 2004, I was invited to deliver a paper at a conference in Uganda, *We Are All One People – Multiple Dreams of a Different World: Transformative Thought, Learning and Action*. I prepared my paper but because I was in the middle of a course of radiotherapy at the time of the conference I was unable to deliver it. Subsequently it appeared in the journal *Lifelong Learning in Europe* – a journal that has its base in Helsinki and which I have been associated with since its foundation, and as an appendix in *Globalisation, Lifelong Learning and the Learning Society: Sociological Perspectives*. This book was the second volume of a trilogy and, like my first sociological study of learning, it was also awarded the Houle Award of the American Association of Adult and Continuing Education. The paper begins to integrate some of my thinking from the various disciplines in which I have written although I soon returned to it as subsequent chapters in this section demonstrate.

One of the things about which I am most proud in my academic career is starting the *International Journal of Lifelong Education*. I certainly could not have done that alone and I was supported throughout that early period by Michael Stephens, and later by Teddy

Thomas, both from the Adult Education Department of the University of Nottingham. However, the journal has been quite successful and when we celebrated the twenty-fifth anniversary with a special issue I wrote a paper in which I tried to look beyond the learning society to a society that was less instrumental and a little more humanistic and to an education that reflected it. This was the first and only paper I have ever published in the journal (although my name appeared amongst the several authors of one other) – apart from the Editorials. The *IJLE* was established as a forum for scholars from around the world and, as such, it has provided a service to the field.

In 2009, during the time of the global economic crisis, the University of Saskatchewan paid me the great honour of asking me to deliver the 40th Sorokin Lecture and I returned to the same theme – because it was one Sorokin had explored many years before. I have included that lecture here since it reflects much in my background: sociology, religion and values. This paper is also similar to one that was prepared for the Danish Pedagogical University at the same time – one that incorporates the argument of the third volume of the trilogy on *Democracy, Lifelong Learning and the Learning Society* and that is the last chapter in this section.

Learning in later life: From the earliest days of my ministry I have enjoyed working with older people and so it is not surprising that I wrote *Learning in Later Life* which was published by Kogan Page, but the book was published at an unfortunate time since Routledge took over Kogan Page's list of educational books very soon after its publication and the book was never really promoted on Routledge's list, although I was actually very pleased with it when I wrote it. I have taken two pieces from it: one on meaning and wisdom, both topics to which I have subsequently returned; the other on an analysis of retirement ritual and learning to retire. Some of my friends say that it is a piece of learning that I do not seem to be able to undertake! Indeed, since there is so much new research about learning that I want to read and write about, I see no reason why I should stop my work provided it is still useful to others.

Over the years I have received support and encouragement from friends and colleagues, too many to name here, but who have often discussed ideas with me, and invited me to speak at conferences and seminars around the world and also to speak to their students. Wherever I go, I feel that I am the learner but I do hope that I can repay just a little of that rich experience and the tremendous opportunities to learn that they have given me in our meeting by my writing.

I have been constantly encouraged to continue my work by Philip Mudd from Routledge: he has frequently listened to some of my ideas and suggested that I produce a book about this or that idea. He encouraged me to write my trilogy when I learned that I had developed a health problem or two: it is also how the two edited versions *The Routledge International Handbook on Lifelong Learning*, published in 2009, and *The Routledge International Handbook on Learning* (forthcoming) emerged. Additionally, he has encouraged me to write *Learning to Be a Person in Society* (2009) from which two of the chapters in the first section were taken and also he is behind the book that I am currently writing on philosophical perspectives on learning. Additionally, I am currently preparing a five-volume major works on learning for Routledge.

Finally, I cannot complete this introduction without reference to my wife, Maureen, and two children, Frazer and Kierra – to whom this book is dedicated: they have put up with me spending hours and hours in my study, spending many days abroad at conferences and never once have they tried to hinder me, although I do get the feeling that they are now beginning to wish that I had begun to learn to retire.

In putting this book together I have been forced to re-read some of my work and I can now see many more of its weaknesses and a few of its strengths and while I have been tempted to alter some things for these chapters, I have left them as they were originally published. I hope, however, that this collection does at least two things: firstly, that it presents both me and my work faithfully and, secondly, that the work proves a useful stimulus to those who do me the honour of reading it.

References

Donald M (2001) *A Mind So Rare* New York: W.W. Norton and Company
Jarvis P (1985) *The Sociology of Adult and Continuing Education* London: Croom Helm
Jarvis P (1987) *Adult Learning in the Social Context* London: Croom Helm
Jarvis P with Watts M (ed) (in press) *The Routledge Handbook on Learning* London: Routledge

LEARNING

CHAPTER 1

LEARNING TO BE A PERSON IN SOCIETY

Learning to be me

Originally published as 'Towards a Theory of Learning' in K. Illeris (ed.) (2009), *Contemporary Theories of Learning*, London: Routledge, pp. 21–34. Cross-references refer to the original publication.

Introduction

Many years ago I used to be invited to speak at pre-retirement courses, and one of the exercises that I asked the participants to undertake was that well-known psychological one on identity. I would put on the flip chart the question, 'Who am I?' and the response which began 'I am (a) . . .'. Then I asked the participants to complete the answer ten times. We took feedback, and on many occasions the respondents placed their occupation high on the list – usually in the top three. I would then ask them a simple question: 'Who will you be when you retire?'

If I were now to be asked to answer that question, I would respond that 'I am learning to be me'. But, as we all know, 'me' exists in society and so I am forced to ask four further questions:

- What or who is me?
- What is society?
- How does the one interact with the other?
- What do I mean by 'learning'?

This apparently simple answer to the question actually raises more profound questions than it answers, but these are four of the questions that, if we could answer them, would help us to understand the person. I want to focus on the 'learning' for the major part of this chapter, but in the final analysis it is the 'me' that becomes just as important. This is also a chapter that raises questions about both 'being' and 'becoming' and this takes us beyond psychology, sociology and social psychology to philosophy and philosophical anthropology and even to metaphysics.

My interest in learning began in the early 1980s, but my concern with the idea of *disjuncture* between me and my world goes back a further decade to the time when I began to focus upon those unanswerable questions about human existence that underlie all religions and theologies of the world. It is, therefore, the process of me interacting with my life-world that forms the basis of my current thinking about human learning, but the quest that I began then is one that remains incomplete and will always be so. I do not want to pursue the religious/theological response to disjuncture (the gap between biography and my current experience) here but I do want to claim that all human learning begins with disjuncture – with either an overt question or with a sense of unknowing. I hope that you will forgive me for making this presentation a little personal – but it will also demonstrate how my work began and where I think it is going, and in this way it reflects the opening chapter of my recent book on learning (Jarvis, 2006). In the process of the chapter, I will outline my developing theory and relate it to other theories of learning. The chapter falls into three parts: developing the theory, my present understanding of learning and learning throughout the lifetime.

Developing my understanding of human learning

As an adult educator I had a number of experiences in the early 1980s that sparked off my interest in learning, but the one which actually began my research was unintentional. I was invited to speak at an adult education workshop about the relationship between teaching and learning. In those days, that was a most insightful topic to choose since most of the books about teaching rarely mentioned learning and most of the texts about learning rarely mentioned teaching. I decided that the best way for me to tackle the topic was to get the participants to generate their own data, and so at the start of the workshop each participant was asked to write down a learning experience. It was a difficult thing to do – but after 20 or 30 minutes, everybody had a story, and I then asked them to pair up and discuss their learning experiences. We took some feedback at this stage, and I then put the pairs into fours and they continued to discuss, but by this time some of their discussion was not so much about their stories as about learning in general. At this point I introduced them to Kolb's learning cycle (1984).

I told the groups that the cycle was not necessarily correct – indeed, I have always maintained that it is too simple to reflect the reality of the complex social process of human learning – and so I asked them to re-draw it to fit their four experiences. We took feedback and produced four totally different diagrams. By

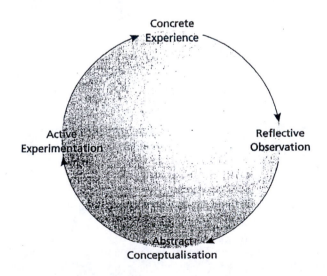

Figure 1.1 Kolb's learning cycle.

good fortune, I had the opportunity over the next year to conduct this workshop in the UK and USA on eight more occasions and, by the third, I realised that I had a research project on adult learning. During all the workshops, I collected all the feedback and, after the second one, I told the participants that I was also using the outcome of their discussions for research. Nobody objected, but rather they started making even more suggestions about my work. By 1986, I had completed the research and wrote it up, and it contained my own model of learning based upon over 200 participants in nine workshops all undertaking this exercise. In 1987, the book *Adult Learning in the Social Context* (Jarvis, 1987) appeared, in which I offered my own learning cycle.

As a sociologist, I recognised that all the psychological models of learning were flawed, including Kolb's well-known learning cycle, in as much as they omitted the social and the interaction. Hence my model included these, and the book discussed the social functions of learning itself, as well as many different types of learning. However, it is possible to see the many routes that we can take through the learning process if we look at the following diagram – I actually mentioned 12 in the book. I tried this model out in many different workshops, including two very early on in Denmark, and over the following 15 years I conducted the workshop many times, and in different books variations on this theme occurred.

However, I was always a little concerned about this model, which I regarded as a little over-simple, but far more sophisticated than anything that had gone before. While I was clear in my own mind that learning always started with experience and that experience is always social, I was moving towards a philosophical perspective on human learning, and so an existentialist study was then undertaken – *Paradoxes of Learning* (Jarvis, 1992). In this, I recognised that, although I had recognised it in the 1987 model, the crucial philosophical issue about learning is that it is the person who learns, although it took me a long time to develop this. What I also recognised was that such concepts as truth and meaning also needed more discussion within learning theory since they are ambiguous and problematic.

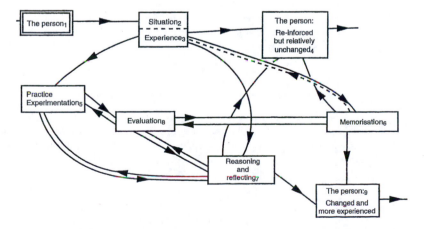

Figure 1.2 Jarvis' 1987 model of learning.

To my mind, the move from experientialism to existentialism has been the most significant in my own thinking about human learning and it occupies a central theme of my current understanding (Jarvis, 2006). It was this recognition that led to another recent book in which Stella Parker and I (Jarvis and Parker, 2005) argued that since learning is human, then every academic discipline that focuses upon the human being has an implicit theory of learning, or at least a contribution to make to our understanding of learning. Fundamentally, it is the person who learns and it is the changed person who is the outcome of the learning, although that changed person may cause several different social outcomes. Consequently, we had chapters from the pure sciences, such as biology and neuroscience, and from the social sciences and from metaphysics and ethics. At the same time, I was involved in writing another book on learning with two other colleagues (Jarvis, Holford and Griffin, 2003) in which we wrote chapters about all the different theories of learning, most of which are still psychological or experiential. What was becoming apparent to me was that we needed a single theory that embraced all the other theories, one that was multi-disciplinary.

Over the years my understanding of learning developed and was changed, but in order to produce such a theory it was necessary to have an operational definition of human learning that reflected that complexity – a point also made by Illeris (2002). Initially, I had defined learning as 'the transformation of experience into knowledge, skills and attitudes' (Jarvis, 1987, p. 32) but after a number of metamorphoses I now define it in the following manner:

> Human learning is the combination of processes throughout a lifetime whereby the whole person – body (genetic, physical and biological) and mind (knowledge, skills, attitudes, values, emotions, beliefs and senses) – experiences social situations, the perceived content of which is then transformed cognitively, emotively or practically (or through any combination) and integrated into the individual person's biography resulting in a continually changing (or more experienced) person.

What I have recounted here has been a gradual development of my understanding of learning as a result of a number of years of research and the realisation that it is the whole person who learns and that the person learns in a social situation. It must, therefore, involve a number of academic disciplines including sociology, psychology and philosophy. These have all come together recently in my current study of learning (Jarvis, 2006, 2007).

Towards a comprehensive theory of human learning

As I have thus far argued, learning is both existential and experiential. In a sense, I would want to argue that learning occurs from before birth – for we do learn pre-consciously from experiences that we have in the womb, as a number of different disciplines indicate – and continues to the point when we lose consciousness before death. However, the fact that the individual is social is crucial to our understanding of learning, but so is the fact that the person is both mind and body. All of our experiences of our life-world begin with bodily sensations which occur at the intersection of the person and the life-world. These sensations initially have no meaning for us as this is the beginning of the learning process. Experience begins with disjuncture (the gap between our biography and our perception of our experience) or a sense of not-knowing, but in the first instance experience is a matter of the body receiving sensations, e.g. sound, sight, smell and so on, which appear to have no meaning. Thereafter, we transform these sensations into the language of our brains and minds and learn to make them meaningful to ourselves – this is the first stage in human learning. However, we cannot make this meaning alone; we are social human beings, always in relationship with us, and as we grow, we acquire a social language, so that nearly all the meanings will reflect the society into which we are born. I depict this first process in Figure 1.3.

Significantly, as adults we live a great deal of our lives in situations which we have learned to take for granted (Box 1), that is, we assume that the world as we know it does not change a great deal from one experience to another similar one (Schutz and Luckmann, 1974), although as Bauman (2000) reminds us, our world is changing so rapidly that he can refer to it as 'liquid'. Over a period of time, however, we actually develop categories and classifications that allow this taken-for-grantedness to occur. Falzon (1998, p. 38) puts this neatly:

> Encountering the world . . . necessarily involves a process of ordering the world in terms of our categories, organising it and classifying it, actively bringing it under control in some way. We always bring some framework to bear on the world in our dealings with it. Without this organisational activity, we would be unable to make any sense of the world at all.

However, the same claim cannot be made for young children – they frequently experience sensations about which they have no meaning or explanation and they have to seek meanings and ask the question that every parent is fearful of: Why? They are in constant disjuncture or, in other words, they start much of their living reflecting Box 2, but as they develop, they gain a perception of the life-world and of the meanings that society gives to their experiences, and so

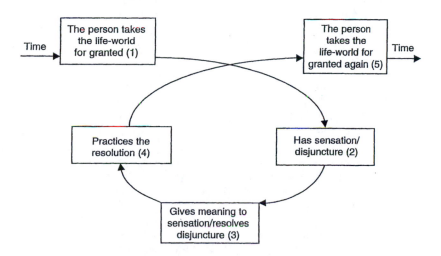

Figure 1.3 The transformation of sensations: learning from primary experience.

Box 1 becomes more of an everyday occurrence. However, throughout our lives, however old and experienced we are, we still enter novel situations and have sensations that we do not recognise – what is that sound, smell, taste and so on? Both adult and child have to transform the sensation to brain language and eventually to give it meaning. It is in learning the meaning, etc. of the sensation that we incorporate the culture of our life-world into ourselves; this we do in most, if not all, of our learning experiences.

Traditionally, however, adult educators have claimed that children learn differently from adults, but the processes of learning from novel situations is the same throughout the whole of life, although children have more new experiences than adults do and this is why there appears to be some difference in the learning processes of children and adults. These are primary experiences and we all have them throughout our lives; we all have new sensations in which we cannot take the world for granted – when we enter a state of disjuncture and immediately we raise questions: What do I do now? What does that mean? What is that smell? What is that sound? and so on. Many of these queries may not be articulated in the form of a question, but there is a sense of unknowing (Box 2). It is this disjuncture that is at the heart of conscious experience – because conscious experience arises when we do not know and when we cannot take our world for granted. Through a variety of ways we give meaning to the sensation and our disjuncture is resolved. An answer (not necessarily a correct one, even if there is one that is correct) to our questions may be given by a significant other in childhood, by a teacher, incidentally in the course of everyday living, through discovery learning or through self-directed learning and so on (Box 3). However, there are times when we just cannot give meaning to primary experiences like this – when we experience beauty, wonder and so on – and it is here that we may begin to locate religious experiences – but time and space forbid us to continue this exploration today (see Jarvis and Hirji, 2006).

When we do get our disjunctures resolved, the answers are social constructs, and so immediately our learning is influenced by the social context within which it occurs. We are encapsulated by our culture. Once we have acquired an answer to our implied question, however, we have to practise or repeat it in order to commit it to memory (Box 4). The more opportunities we have to practise the answer to our initial question, the better we will commit it to memory. Since we do this in our social world, we get feedback, which confirms that we have got a socially acceptable resolution or else we have to start the process again, or be different from those people around us. A socially acceptable answer may be called correct, but here we have to be aware of the problem of language – conformity is not always 'correctness'. This process of learning to conform is 'trial and error' learning – but we can also learn to disagree, and it is in agreeing and disagreeing that aspects of our individuality emerge. However, once we have a socially acceptable resolution and have memorised it, we are also in a position to take our world for granted again (Box 5), provided that the social world has not changed in some other way. Most importantly, however, as we change and others change as they learn, the social world is always changing and so our taken-for-grantedness becomes more suspect (Box 5) since we always experience slightly different situations. The same water does not flow under the same bridge twice and so even our taken-for-grantedness is relative.

The significance of this process in contemporary society, however, is that once we have given meaning to the sensation and committed a meaning to our memories then the significance of the sensation itself recedes in future experiences as the socially acceptable answer (meaning) dominates the process, and when disjuncture then occurs it is more likely because we cannot understand the meaning, we do not know the meaning of the word and so on, than it is about the sensation itself. Naturally the sensation still occurs but we are less conscious of it. In this sense, we carry social meaning within ourselves – whatever social reality is, it is incorporated in us through our learning from the time of our birth onwards. Indeed, this also reflects the thinking of Bourdieu (1992, p. 127) when he describes habitus as a 'social made body' and he goes on in the same page to suggest that '[s]ocial reality exists, so to speak, twice, in things and in minds, in fields and in habitus, outside and inside of agents'. There is a sense then in which we might, unknowingly, be imprisoned behind the bars of our own minds – a phrase which I think was originally termed by Peter Berger. Significantly, this is the type of learning that adult educators have assumed that adults but not children have: these experiences are secondary ones which occur as a result of language or other forms of mediation – secondary experiences are mediated experiences of the world. These always occur in conjunction with primary ones, although we are not always conscious of the primary ones; for instance, when we are listening to someone speak we are not always conscious of how comfortable the chair is, and so on.

We have a continuing ambivalent relationship with our life-world – both in experiencing sensations and in experiencing meaning, both in knowing and not knowing. We have already described the primary experience since it is about experiencing with the senses, and we can continue to have primary experiences throughout our lives so that Figure 1.3 is as relevant for adults as it is for children when the senses are at the heart of the learning. But when the senses are relegated and we are more concerned with the cultural meanings, when we do not know the meanings or words rather than the sounds etc., then we have secondary experiences – these are mediated experiences which are often through speech and the written word, although we are becoming increasingly aware of visual mediation through television and the Web. These are becoming an everyday feature for many of us. Nevertheless, cognition becomes central to learning and while we still have the primary experience, it is relegated to a subsidiary position in the hierarchy of human learning, and in the following diagram I have depicted this secondary process in which we have certain forms of cognitive disjuncture. In Box 1, the whole person is in the life-world and at the point of disjuncture has an experience (Box 2).

Having had an experience (Box 2), which might occur as a result of disjuncture, we can reject it, think about it, respond to it emotionally or do something about it – or any combination of these (Boxes 3–5). But there is a double arrow here since there is always feedback at every point in learning as well as a progressive act. What is important about this observation is that we actually learn from the experience and not from the social situation in which the experience occurs, nor from the sensation once meaning has been attributed to it. As a result of the learning we become changed persons (Box 6) but, as we see, learning is itself a complex process. Once the person is changed, it is self-evident that the next social situation into which the individual enters is changed. And so, we can return to my experiences – I do not need to have a meaning to learn from the experience, although I might want to give meaning to my experiences as I reflect upon them (Box 3). However, my emotions are transformed (Box 4), my beliefs are affected and so are many attitudes and values (Box 3) and so on. I might even want to do something about them (Box 5). Finally, we see that as a result of learning (Box 6), we become changed persons and so only in being can we become and in learning we experience the process of becoming. Indeed, I am changed and so, therefore, is the situation in which I interact. Consequently, we can conclude that learning involves three transformations: the sensation, the person and then the social situation.

In Figure 1.4, I have tried to capture the continuous nature of learning by pointing to the second cycle (Box 1_2). However, this diagram must always be understood in relation to Figure 1.3, since it is only by combining them that we can begin to understand the process of human learning. These two diagrams together depict the complex process of experiencing both sensations and meanings simultaneously; it is also a recognition that both primary and secondary experiences occur simultaneously. However, there is a fundamental issue here about the person becoming more experienced which tells us something more about the nature of the person. For as long as I can continue to learn, I remain an unfinished person – the possibility of more growth, more experience and so on remains – or I am still learning to be me! Philosophically speaking, I only am at the moment 'now' and since I cannot stop time I am always becoming; paradoxically, however, through all that becoming I always feel that I am the

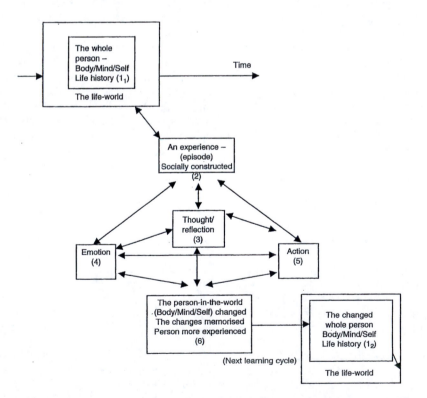

Figure 1.4 The transformation of the person through learning.

same self. Being and becoming are inextricably intertwined, and human learning is one of the phenomena that unite them, for it is fundamental to life itself.

I am now, therefore, confronted with another issue in learning to be me and that is to be found in the nature of the person who learns: I have suggested that the person is about knowledge, skills, attitudes, emotions, beliefs, values, senses and even identity and that through learning each of these can be changed and developed further. But if we look carefully at the literature on learning we find that there is work on personal and cognitive development (Erikson, 1963; Piaget, 1929), work on religious faith development (Fowler, 1981), on moral development (Kohlberg, 1981) and so on. In precisely the same way, there is research in the way that we develop both our personal and social identities, including Mead (Strauss, 1964) and Wenger (1998) in their different ways. If we are to understand how the person learns to become a whole person, then we need to combine all of these theories, and that is where the book that I am just beginning will take us.

A person's lifetime learning

Since learning is an existential phenomenon, my starting point is the whole person – that is, body and mind. We can describe this process as that of the human essence emerging from the human existent, a process that continues throughout the whole of life, and that essence is moulded through interaction with the world. But that essence does not just emerge unaided, as it were – like the physical body needs food in order to mature, so that human existent needs to have experiences and learn if the human essence is to emerge and develop. The stimulus for this learning is our experience of the world – the point at which we intersect with the world (both physical and social). The only way that we can experience these moments of intersection is through our senses – we see, hear, feel, smell and taste. These then are the beginning of every learning experience, so that the bodily sensations are fundamental to the whole of the learning process. Fundamental to our under-standing of learning, therefore, is our understanding of the whole person in the social situation – it is a philosophical anthropology but also a sociology and psychology. Once we recognise that learning is not just psychological and that the exclusive claims of psychology detract from the fullness of our understanding of learning, we can look afresh at human learning.

But before we do, we need to note that the person is both body and mind and that these are not separate entities – they are interrelated. Therefore, once we have recognised the significance of the senses in our learning theory, we need to examine the relationship between body and mind. There have been many volumes written on this topic and so there is no place to review the relationship in depth here. Suffice to note that there are five major sets of theory about the body–mind relationship. Maslin (2001), for instance, suggests five main theories:

- Dualism: the human person is a composite of two completely separate enti-ties: body and mind. However, contemporary brain scanning techniques have demonstrated that brain activity can be seen as a result of the body receiving sensations, which suggests that there is a close interconnection between them;
- Mind–brain identity: a monist theory that claims that only physical substances exist and that human beings are just part of the material world;

therefore, mental states are identical with physical ones, which raises fundamental problems about the nature of culture and meaning;
- Logical or analytical behaviourism: 'statements about the mind and mental
  states turn out, after analysis, to be statements that describe a person's
  actual and potential public behaviour' (Maslin 2001, p. 106). The objections include rejecting the idea that behaviour is the driving force of human
  being, and other forces, such as meaning or even thought itself, are
  significant;
- Functionalism: the mind is a function of the brain. Such a theory rules out
  meaning, intentionality, irrationality and emotion;
- Non-reductive monism: Maslin (2001, p. 163) describes it thus:

> It is non-reductive because it does not insist that mental properties are
> nothing over and above physical properties. On the contrary, it is willing to
> allow that mental properties are different in kind from physical properties,
> and not ontologically reducible to them. It is clusters and series of these
> mental properties which constitute our psychological lives ... property
> dualism dispenses with the dualism of substances and physical events, hence
> it is a form of monism. But these physical substances and events possess two
> very different kinds of property, namely physical properties and, in addi-
> tion, non-physical, mental properties.

Having examined five different ways of looking at the body–mind relationship
we can find no simple theory that allows us to explain it. Exclusive claims
should not logically be made for any single theory, although they are made quite
widely in contemporary society. Some of the theories, however, appear to be
much weaker than others, such as mind–brain identity, behaviourism and functionalism. This is unfortunate since these are the ones most widely cited and
used in contemporary society. We have accepted a form of dualism that may
best be explained as a form of non-reductive monism, although we are less
happy with dualism *per se*. Yet we have to acknowledge that none of the theories can claim universal allegiance and in each there are problems that appear
insurmountable.

From the above brief philosophical discussion we can see immediately that
profound doubt is cast on many contemporary theories of learning as providing
logical understanding of human learning, including behaviourism, information
processing and all forms of cognitive theory. This is not to say that they are not
valid in as far as they go, simply that they do not go far enough: they all have an
incomplete theory of the person. Clearly experientialism comes much closer
because it situates the learning in the social context, but even experiential
learning theories do not go sufficiently far since they also build on an incomplete theory of the person and few of them actually examine the social context
within which the experience occurs. Two theories which offer a great deal of
insight into human learning – in fact to my mind the most comprehensive – are
those of Illeris (2002) and Wenger (1998).

Conclusion

As with many other learning theories, the two last mentioned start from the
psychological and the sociological angle, respectively. Each of them provides

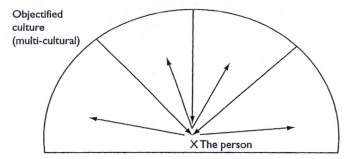

Objectified
culture
(multi-cultural)

X The person

Figure 1.5 The internalisation and externalisation of culture.

tremendous insights into human learning and points us beyond its own bound-aries. Both raise profound questions and both include the idea of the human being in relation to the social world which I try to depict in Figure 1.5.

The psychologist traces the arrows out from the person to the external, objectified culture, while the sociologist starts with the objectified culture and points inwards to the individual person. A person's learning must be seen from both perspectives! This leaves us with major problems about how we study learning. I would argue that we need to start with an understanding of the person – the learner – which is a philosophical perspective that has been sadly lacking from studies of learning, and, thereafter, begin to explore the psycho-logical and the sociological aspects of the learning process in tandem. But standing in the middle is the person – and analysis of the person calls for a philo-sophical anthropology. This also leads us to recognising the inter-subjectivity of social living and human learning – well captured by Buber's (1994) *I and Thou* – and I believe that this broader perspective will help us understand learning better, although it is impossible to have a theory that explains the learning process in every detail. Paradoxically, despite all that we know and all that we have learned, we will spend the remainder of our lives learning to be ourselves – people in society.

References

Arendt, H. (1978) *The Life of the Mind*. San Diego: Harvest Books, Harcourt.
Bauman, Z. (2000) *Liquid Modernity*. Cambridge, UK: Polity Press.
Bourdieu, P. (1992) The Purpose of Reflexive Sociology. In Bourdieu, P. and Wacquant, L. (eds). *An Invitation to Reflexive Sociology*. Cambridge, UK: Polity Press.
Buber, M. (1994 [1923]) *I and Thou*. Edinburgh: T&T Clark.
Erikson, E. (1963) *Childhood and Society*. New York: Norton.
Falzon, C. (1998) *Foucault and Social Dialogue: Beyond Fragmentation*. London: Routledge.
Fowler, J. (1981) *Stages of Faith: The Psychology of Human Development and the Quest for Meaning*. New York: Harper & Row.
Illeris, K. (2002) *The Three Dimensions of Learning: Contemporary Learning Theory in the Tension Field Between the Cognitive, the Emotional and the Social*. Leicester: NIACE.
Jarvis, P. (1987) *Adult Learning in the Social Context*. London: Croom Helm.
Jarvis, P. (1992) *Paradoxes of Learning: On Becoming an Individual in Society*. San Francisco: Jossey-Bass.

Jarvis, P. (2001) *Learning in Later Life: An Introduction for Educators and Carers.* London: Kogan Page.

Jarvis, P. (2006) *Towards a Comprehensive Theory of Human Learning.* London: Routledge. (Vol 1 of *Lifelong Learning and the Learning Society*).

Jarvis, P. (2007) *Globalisation, Lifelong Learning and the Learning Society: Sociological Perspectives.* London: Routledge. (Vol 2 of *Lifelong Learning and the Learning Society*).

Jarvis, P., Holford, J. and Griffin, C. (2003) *Theory and Practice of Learning (2nd edition).* London: Routledge.

Jarvis, P. and Hirji, N. (2006) Learning the Unlearnable: Experiencing the Unknowable. *Journal for Adult Theological Education*, 1, pp. 88–94.

Jarvis, P. and Parker, S. (eds) (2005) *Human Learning: An Holistic Approach.* London: Routledge.

Kohlberg, L. (1981) *The Philosophy of Moral Development: Moral Stages and the Idea of Justice.* San Francisco: Harper & Row.

Kolb, D. (1984) *Experiential Learning: Experience as the Source of Learning and Development.* Englewood Cliffs, NJ: Prentice Hall.

Loder, J. (1998) *The Logic of the Spirit: Human Development in Theological Perspective.* San Francisco: Jossey-Bass.

Maslin, K. T. (2001) *An Introduction to the Philosophy of Mind.* Cambridge, UK: Polity Press.

Piaget, J. (1929) *The Child's Conception of the World.* London: Routledge & Kegan Paul.

Schutz, A. and Luckmann, T. (1974) *The Structures of the Life-world.* London: Heinemann.

Strauss, A. (ed) (1964) *George Herbert Mead on Social Psychology.* Chicago: University of Chicago Press.

Wenger, E. (1998) *Communities of Practice: Learning, Meaning, and Identity.* Cambridge, UK: Cambridge University Press.

CHAPTER 2

IT IS THE PERSON WHO LEARNS

Originally published as 'It Is the Person who Learns' in D. Aspin, J. Chapman, K. Evans and R. Bagnall (eds) (forthcoming), *The International Handbook of Lifelong Learning*, second edition, Springer. Cross-references refer to the original publication.

In this chapter I want to begin to explore a fundamental problem about human learning – it stems from my recent writing and studies (see, for instance, Jarvis 1992; 2006) and is summed up by the title of the paper itself – 'It Is the Person who Learns' (Jarvis, 2009). Over the years I have tried to understand the learning processes and as a result I (Jarvis, 2009, p. 25) have defined learning in the following manner:

> the combination of processes throughout a lifetime whereby the whole person – body (genetic, physical and biological) and mind (knowledge, skills, attitudes, values, emotions, meaning, beliefs and senses) – experiences social situations, the content of which is then transformed cognitively, emotively or practically (or through any combination) and integrated into the individual person's biography resulting in a continually changing (or more experienced) person.

However, this definition only relates to human learning and not all animal learning and there is a fundamental assumption in it – that in some way we can distinguish body and mind and this is what I want to explore in this paper. Nevertheless, in order to explore this relationship I want to pose three very simple questions, give two examples and ask one question and reach a single tentative conclusion! Initially, then, there appear to be three possible types of relationship between body and mind and so this paper will have three parts, one dealing with each aspect of the relationship: dualism, monism and non-reductive monism. We will conclude that the learner is a complex person and that learning is a complex set of processes in which body and mind appear both separate and yet united.

My three questions are:

- When I learn knowledge – what part of me learns?
- When I learn a skill – what part of me learns?
- When I learn an emotion – what part of me learns?

Now we know from neuroscience that when our brain is activated, different experiences/skills, and so on, activate different parts of the brain (Gardner, 1983; Blakemore and Frith, 2005; OECD, 2007 *inter alia*). This led Gardner to postulate different forms of intelligence since we can locate the brain activity for each experience quite clearly in different parts of the brain – the follow-up question must be – might this mean that we are lots of different minds, as Kant might have suggested, or are we super-complex people? This is the question that I want to explore here.

Now, we move to two personal learning experiences:

Experience 1: As an international traveller I am often taken into restaurants which serve the indigenous foods: this is my preference in my travelling. I leave it to my hosts to choose from the menu and when my food arrives there is sometimes something on the plate that I do not recognise, and so I ask my hosts what the food is – they tell me. And so, firstly, I learn its name – a cognitive experience. Then I taste it and I decide whether I like it or not. Secondly, then I learn a taste – this is a non-cognitive experience. Thirdly I learn whether like it or not – an emotive and cognitive experience. Fourthly, then I am left with other questions afterwards – whether I will recognise the taste when I have the food again and will I be able to associate it with the food that I have eaten – I am less than confident that I can – and so I have learned something about my confidence which is emotive and something more, perhaps, about myself.

This is a common and almost trivial incident about everyday learning yet we rarely analyse it like this to see the learning processes.

Experience 2: A number of years ago I was teaching in Zambia and at the end of the period I was taken to see Victoria Falls. We arrived there at the end of the day, just as the sun was setting over the Zambezi. The sight was breath-taking – beyond anything that I had anticipated. Firstly, then, I had an emotive experience about what I considered to be beautiful and magnificent. But secondly, I felt small in the face of the majesty of that experience and so I learned something about myself. Thirdly I was forced to ask myself the question – is all of this mean-ingless? I reached the conclusion that somehow it would be illogical for this and the whole cosmos to be meaningless. In this case the learning began with an emotive experience and finished with a cognitive question and a belief answer.

I have deliberately chosen learning experiences from my life that relate to everyday learning but we often restrict learning to formal learning when we are undertaking analyses of learning, which tend to be depicted as individual cogni-tive experiences that are distilled from our life-world and then artificialised by their isolation. But in this case it is me who has learned these things and I am an individual whole person, and so now we need to answer the one question.

The question is – what is the nature of the person who learns?

Underlying this argument is another one that suggests that the validity of any theory of learning depends quite fundamentally on the validity of our understanding of the nature and structure of the person who learns. There are a number of theories about the nature of the person and this discussion goes back hundreds, even thousands of years when the ancient Greek philosophers and the early Christian theologians explored the nature of the soul and its rela-tion to the body – but this now finds its form in the brain/mind debate. However, we have to recognise that before the concept of mind existed, ancient philoso-phers used soul to describe it. We cannot explore the whole of this debate in this brief paper but we do need to recognise it in order to reach an initial answer to this question. These theories can be summed up as dualist, monist and non-reductive monist.

Dualism

This theory claims that the brain (mental substances) and the body (material substances) are entirely separate entities and in some ways this appears to make a great deal of sense. Indeed, it appears almost obvious to suggest that the identity of the person resides in the mind and that the body is additional to it – a link which may be severed at death. For instance, thought seems immaterial whereas the body is material and so there appears to be two separate entities in the human being – thought and action – one about the mind and the other about the body. Descartes' Meditations on this question have been among the most significant in the history of Western philosophy, although these questions were also discussed in great depth by Plato, Aristotle, Aquinas and many other thinkers before him. Descartes employed his famous method of doubt and questioning to explore this question – even to questioning whether he himself existed. He came to the conclusion that because he could think, he must exist – *Cogito ergo sum.* He went on to argue that he could always be sure of his existence when he was thinking – even if his body changed or even ceased to exist, so that he concluded that he was only a thinking thing when he was thinking! And so he separated the body and the mind although he admitted that there is a two-way interaction between body and brain through the pineal gland. Consequently, it has been easy for early learning theorists, amongst others, to follow this position and make the same separation – we learn cognitions in the mind and skills in the body – and even the learning of a skill, even though it activated the mind, is still a separate phenomenon. Indeed, it was taken for granted that learning was fundamentally cognitive and tremendous emphases was placed on the work of Piaget (1929) and cognitive development (see also Kohlberg 1981 and Fowler 1981) and that a lower form of learning was that which was related to skills – we also had the well known debate and distinction between education and training (Peters, 1972) – these were all assumed by educational theorists until fairly recently and were based on dualistic theories of the person.

At first sight this distinction may seem obvious and common-sense, but since Ryle's (1949) famous rejection of dualism in *The Concept of Mind* in recent years this has been open to question: Ryle talked about 'the ghost in the machine' and claimed that an action is one act not two – encapsulating many of the objections to dualism. Over the years there have been other criticisms of dualism such as: if all learning goes on in the mind then the brain seems to have little function and yet it is one of the largest and most complicated parts of the human body. But also what of the taste I learn in the restaurant – do I only learn taste through the mind or is this learning not also a bodily function? (This problem has given rise to the notion of qualia – private and subjective aspects that relate to what an individual feels.)

But, as Kant also asked, how do we know that there is only one soul/mind – if there is one mind separate from the body then there is no reason why there should not be others. Kant also offered other criticisms of this position and he argued that Descartes separated an external world, whose defining characteristic is extension, and an inner and immaterial world – the mind – which is extensionless and whose defining characteristic is thinking. Kant argues that there is just one world, the world we experience, and that we who experience it and think about it are just one of its ingredients – the familiar persons in experience rather than immaterial minds.

(Politis 1993, p. xxix)

As we noted at the outset, neuroscience has tended to support the position that we are one substance, and we can see that whether our learning is cognitive or active, we activate the brain – albeit different parts. We cannot separate the mind and the body in this manner since both cognitive and physical activity activate the same brain as electro-magnetic imaging shows. Dualism is not, therefore, a very convincing position and it can be questioned, so that *cognito ergo sum* appears to be an unproven claim. Consequently, the weakness of separating education from training becomes apparent, and the idea that learning knowledge is different and of a higher status than learning a skill is also seen to be questionable. In contrast, people live in their own life-world and because we are alive, we think and consequently we can reverse Descartes' claim and say that 'I am therefore I think', or within our present context, 'I am therefore I learn', although we do need to recognise that there is a complex process in early childhood between living, consciousness and thinking (see, for example, Tomasello, 1999, Gerhardt, 2004). But this may mean that the mind is not separate from the brain but a part of it, and this would appear to make sense if we accept the evidence from neuroscience – then we reach the monist position.

Monism

Monism is a theory that claims that there is only one substance so that mind and body are the same in substance, but, following Maslin (2001), it has taken three major forms in recent years: mind–brain identity, behaviourism and functionalism. It should be pointed out that the social science and philosophical use of the latter two terms differs considerably and this will become clearer as we examine them.

Mind–brain identity: This theory basically claims that mental states can be identified as physical states: they are all part of the activities of the brain: mental activity is brain activity and there is no separate mind. The strengths of this position are that the problems of the dualist mind–body interaction disappear, we can see how changes in the brains due to medical operations, drugs and so on affect mental functioning and we can see that theory reduction actually enables us to incorporate ideas of short-term memory within terms of brain states (Rose, 2006). But there are also problems with this theory as we can see from our two learning examples. Firstly, when I think, it might be possible to locate where in the brain that activity occurs but it is not possible to specify from a scan whether I like the taste of the food or whether I am in awe at the sight of the sun setting over the Zambezi and Victoria Falls. Secondly, it is not possible to decide what meaning I might want to give to the experience of awe even though we know the part of the brain where the thought activity is occurring. Neither is it possible to identify from the brain scan whether I can remember the taste of the food so that I would be able recognise the taste and relate it to the food on a future occurrence, indeed, these mental states *cannot* apparently be identified with or reduced to a physical state – there appears to be no identity between mind and brain and all the learning that occurs cannot be reduced to recordable data. And we can see learning experiences that we have described here cannot be explained by identity theory and so it is necessary now to examine the behaviourist one.

Behaviourism: As a theory this first came to the fore in the 1920s with the publication of Watson's (1925) book on the subject. In philosophical behaviourism it is claimed that, 'statements described as mental or psychological states can be translated, without loss of meaning, into statements describing possible or actual behaviour' (Maslin, 2001). This is analytical behaviourism but it also reflects methodological behaviourism which argues that the only way to study what goes on in the brain is through observable behaviour. Underlying this approach is a metaphysical position which maintains that consciousness does not exist but what does exist is living organisms and it is these that we can study. These are reductionist claims, something Bruner (1990) warned against, and we can see immediately that it is difficult to reduce the fact that I liked my food to a behavioural statement neither can the awe I experienced at Victoria Falls be reduced in the same way. If we could reduce these responses to behavioural statements we would effectively be denying the existence of inner states of mind which is precisely what behaviourism does – but I cannot deny my experiences and neither of the two learning experiences I have described can be translated into behavioural statements. That I might want to give meaning to the Victoria Falls experience is not a behavioural statement but one of intention and the meaning that I give may merely reflect my cultural biography but it is not a behavioural state.

It is also possible here to turn briefly from the philosophical to psychological behaviourism where learning might be defined as 'any more or less permanent change of behaviour which is the result of experience' (Borger and Seaborne, 1966, p. 14). There are many criticisms of the definition (see Jarvis, 2006, *inter alia*) but we can see that learning to like the taste of the food and being in awe at Victoria Falls are the learning outcomes of sense experiences but they do not inevitably result in behavioural change and they cannot be measured by behavioural change. Moreover, while behaviourism can test the outcome of some of my mental states by experimentation, such as whether I have learned to relate the taste of the food to the actual food substance, it cannot test the lack of confidence that I have that I could relate the two on a future occasion.

Behaviourism, then, both philosophical and psychological, demands that the existence of inner states of mind is unnecessary but both of the two learning experiences that we have looked at demand that we acknowledge the existence of mental states that do not demand or imply possible or actual behaviour – they demand some form of recognition that there are both mental and physical states which are a response to experience of the external world. If we accept this argument, learning theories founded upon behaviourist principles are problematic – but this does not mean that behaviouristic practices do not result in learning in many different situations.

Functionalism: In precisely the same way as we had to distinguish philosophical behaviourism from psychological behaviourism, we have to distinguish philosophical functionalism from sociological functionalism. Sociological functionalism starts from the 'wholeness' of an entity and seeks to examine the part played by individual elements of the identity in maintaining the whole: in other words, the function is the outcome of the existence of the phenomenon as it contributes to the unity of the whole entity. Philosophical functionalism, however, claims that the mind is a function of the brain; that is, that the mind is the outcome of the brain operating (functioning), and that if we can understand all the inputs and outputs to the brain and the state of the operating mechanism, then we can see how the brain operates without a separate mind. The first and most obvious difficulty with this position is that it is seeking to isolate all the inputs and outputs and understand fully how the brain operates – this is almost certainly impossible to achieve and so functionalism starts from a problematic premise. However, it may be seen from this description that the brain is conceptualised as some form of computer, or that it is many computers (or modules) (see Fodor, 1983): one of the exponents of this position is Carruthers (2004, p. 302) who argues that:

- the mind is computationally realized;
- modular, or holistic, processes are computationally intractable;
- and so the mind must consist wholly or largely of modular systems.

Carruthers goes on to demonstrate how he perceives the brain to function and how learning might occur, which demands that we examine what he meant by learning. Indeed, Carruthers (2004, p. 296) had to restrict learning to cognitive systems in order to make this analogy work, rather than regarding learning as the transformation of any experience which can then incorporated into the biography. But this does not deny that information processing does not work in some instances, and because it overcomes some of the weakness of the previous positions, it has gained considerable credibility. But there are still problems with it as Woodward and Cowie (2004) explain in a number of telling points: amongst their objections is one that reflects the complexity of the learning stories that we have looked at: they make the point that the idea of the complex computer 'is inconsistent with what is known about the role of experience-dependent learning and development in shaping the mature mind' (p. 313). Learning experiences, like the ones that I have used in this paper may be simply too complex to be reduced to material items that can be contained in modules in the computerised brain: the way that I learned the emotion of awe or even that I actually learned to like the food may be too complex for a theory of hard-wired computer-type modules. The impossibility of developing a hard-wired brain capable of coping with the complexity of human experience is also a point made by Donald (2001) when he argued that although a single event could be hard-wired into the brain a continuous sequence of human interaction is impossible to hard-wire since an extended interactive process cannot be programmed. Additionally, Rose (2005, p.102) makes the point most strongly:

> Modules or not, it is not adequate to reduce the mind/brain to nothing more than a cognitive, 'architectural information-processing machine . . . brains/minds do not just deal with information. They are concerned with living meaning.

As Maslin (2001, p. 146) says functionalism is unable to capture the subjectivity and privacy of mental states or the intentionality of propositional attitudes and we have shown that it cannot capture the complexity of everyday human learning. The analogy of the human being as being like a computer is not attractive and nor is it sustainable, but this does not deny than in some instances the computer may reflect some of the ways in which the human brain functions: indeed, the person is more than a computer and the person learns from the complexity of human experience.

Once we have questioned this approach to learning, then we have to question information processing as a universal theory of learning – it is only useful if we restrict information to the cognitive and omit all other aspects of experience from our understanding of learning.

Neither dualism nor any of the three monist theories that we have looked at can be sustained in the light of the two informal learning processes although they all offer explanations for some types of learning as we have seen and so, finally, it is necessary to examine the non-reductive monist position.

Non-reductive monism

This is a form of monism – there is one substance only, but it claims that mental properties are of a different kind to its physical ones and so we cannot reduce mental properties to physical ones. This allows us to accept the strengths of the dualist position without having to defend its weaknesses. In a sense, it is similar to Aquinas' idea that the soul was created at the end of the biological process of human creation and mind is the sum of the mental properties of the brain. Mental properties are supervenient (to be on top of, or dependent upon a subvenient base) on physical properties and cannot be reduced to them but can change with them. They are actually dependent on them – so that this position argues that while the brain and the mind are the same physical phenomenon, they differ in their properties. Consequently, this position seeks the middle way between monism and dualism, but we can see immediately that this type of relationship is very hard to understand and controversial: we are dealing with a form of super-complexity. It still leaves us with massive questions about the nature of mental properties and we still cannot understand how physical properties give rise to mental ones and, finally, we have to ask whether the mind is a mere spectator to what goes on in the world and is it the generator of these mental properties as a result of physical experiences (Maslin, 2001, pp. 177–185)? Each of these questions is in many ways unanswerable and in trying to answer them we are confronted with even more fundamental ones – for instance, once we begin to ask what mental properties are we are forced to discuss the whole notion of consciousness and we may never be able to solve the question of how consciousness emerges from brain activity (Maslin, 2001, p. 180), but this takes us a long way beyond the remit of this paper and so we will not pursue it here. But non-reductive monism seems to be able to account for both of my learning experiences while not opening itself to the criticisms of either dualism or monism. It appears to be the strongest, if not the only position upon which we can base a universal theory of learning. For instance, if we look at my two learning experiences the fact that the non-material elements of my learning – liking a taste, being in awe at the wonderful view – do not need to be reduced to physical ones but can be incorporated into the structure of my mind/brain in precisely the same way as the cognitive and behaviour aspects is a major strength. But the theory cannot be proven although it can account for the complexity of my learning experiences.

While non-reductive monism may explain something about my learning experiences, which is its strength since my mental experiences cannot be reduced to physical ones, the actual relationship between mind and brain remains unresolved and this remains a fundamental weakness. All that we can say is that some form of dualism/monism can be a base upon which we can build a universal theory of learning, but the mind–brain relationship continues to be an unresolved problem.

Conclusion

Theories of learning have been developed that relate to each of the different theories of body and mind and while we can show the apparent weaknesses of the theories of mind and body and, therefore, the apparent weaknesses of these theories of learning, we cannot prove or disprove the relationship between the brain and the mind incontrovertibly and so we cannot reach a universal theory of learning. But each theory of learning can only be regarded as acceptable within its specified theory of body/mind and with that limited validity, but we can question those learning theories that are based on what appear to be the weaker theories of the relationship between mind and brain. Despite all its problems, it does appear that non-reductive monism does explain the complexities of my learning and so it appears to be a most acceptable base upon which theories of learning might be constructed, although it might be dangerous to generalise from the particular without a more sustained argument. Above all, this theory does recognise that it is the whole person who learns and, to return to my original definition, learning is a life time phenomenon through which the person develops and becomes more experienced.

References

Blakemore S-J and Frith Y (2005) *The Learning Brain* Oxford: Blackwell

Borger R and Seaborne A (1966) *The Psychology of Learning* Harmondsworth: Penguin

Bruner J (1990) *Acts of Meaning* Cambridge, Mass.: Harvard University Press

Carruthers P (2004) The Mind is a System of Modules Shaped by Natural Selection in Hitchcock *op cit* pp. 293–311.

Crane T and Patterson S (eds) (2000) *History of the Mind–Body Problem* London: Routledge

Dearden D, Hirst P and Peters R (eds) (1972) *A Critique of Current Educational Aims* Vol 1 *Education and the Development of Reason* London: Routledge & Kegan Paul

Donald M (2001) *A Mind so Rare* New York: W.W. Norton & Co

Fodor J (1983) *Modularity of Mind: An Essay of Faculty Psychology* Cambridge, Mass.: MIT Press

Fowler J (1981) *Stages of Faith* New York: Harper & Row

Gardner H (1983) *Frames of Mind* New York: HarperCollins (Second edition, 1993)

Gerhardt S (2004) *Why Love Matters* London: Routledge

Hitchcock C (ed) (2004) *Contemporary Debates in the Philosophy of Science* Oxford: Blackwell

James S (2000) The Emergence of the Cartesian Mind in Crane and Patterson (eds.) *op cit* pp. 111–130

Jarvis P (1992) *The Paradoxes of Learning* San Francisco: Jossey-Bass

Jarvis P (2006) *Towards a Comprehensive Theory of Human Learning* London: Routledge

Jarvis P (2009) *Learning to Be a Person in Society* London: Routledge

Kant I (1781) *Critique of Pure Reason* London: Dent 1934 (republished 1993 in Everyman's Library series)

Kohlberg L (1981) *The Philosophy of Moral Development* Vol 1 *Essays in Moral Development* San Francisco: Harper & Row

Maslin K (2001) *An Introduction to the Philosophy of Mind* Cambridge: Polity Press

OECD (2007) *Understanding the Brain: the Birth of a Learning Science* Paris: OECD

Peters R S (1972) Education and the Educated Man in Dearden *et al.* (eds) *op cit*

Piaget J (1929) *The Child's Conception of the World* London: Routledge & Kegan Paul

Politis V (1993) Introduction to Kant's *Critique of Pure Reason*

Rose D (2006) *Consciousness: Philosophical, Psychological and Neural Theories* Oxford: Oxford University Press

Ryle G (1949) *The Concept of Mind* London: Hutchinson

Tomasello M (1999) *The Cultural Origins of Human Cognition* Cambridge, Mass.: Harvard University Press

Stone M (2000) The Soul's Relation to the Body in Crane and Patterson (eds) *op cit* pp. 34–69

Watson J (1925) *Behaviourism* New York: Norton

Woodward J and Cowie F (2004) The Mind is not (just) a System of Modules Shaped (just) by Natural Selection in Hitchcock *op cit* pp. 312–334

CHAPTER 3

▬▬▬

EXPERIENCE

Originally published as 'Experience' in P. Jarvis (2009), *Learning to Be a Person in Society*, London: Routledge, pp. 55–68. Cross-references refer to the original publication.

To say that we learn from experience is a truism – and so, why has the idea of experiential learning developed into such a popular area of learning theory? Perhaps the answer to this is that educationalists have taken for granted the idea that we learn cognitively and usually in formal settings, such as schools and in pedagogic processes. Once it was recognised that practice is more basic to learning than cognitive theorising, so the idea of experiential learning became more popular. Knowles' (1980) work on andragogy in the USA in the 1960s and 1970s led a great number of practitioners to utilise his thinking and his techniques – which were the traditional adult education ones to a great extent. Andragogy, therefore, led to a considerable growth in thinking about experiential learning. But it also came to reinforce the idea that vocational learners had to spend some time in a placement during their occupational preparation and, eventually, this even led to the rediscovery of apprenticeship models of vocational training. But an interesting paradox emerged – while experience became a common and taken-for-granted concept in the educational vocabulary philosophers have always claimed that the concept of experience is one of the most difficult in the philosophical vocabulary (Oakeshott, 1933, p. 9). Knowles (1980), however, referred to it in only one way – that of our personal biography – the experience we bring to learning which is very fundamental to adult learning and so anthologies of experiential learning (e.g. Weil and McGill, 1989) were more concerned with practice and early major studies were more concerned with reflection on practice – the cognitive (Boud *et al.*, 1983, Schon, 1983) than with theorising about this complex concept. For others, the term 'experience' was not only a focus (Marton *et al.*, 1984) rather a basis for dealing with the philosophical niceties of the concept and these points remained true even for some later studies that examined experiential learning (Fraser, 1995). But the foundations were being laid in education for a move towards a more philosophical approach (Jarvis, 1992, Marton and Booth, 1997). In my most recent book on learning I tackled this topic more fully (Jarvis, 2006, pp. 70–86) and this chapter is a development of the material that I put into that chapter: there is obviously some overlap with it, but there is also a lot of new material.

Fundamentally there are two forms of experience: primary and secondary. If I were to describe my recent teaching experience in different parts of the world, you would be having a secondary experience – you would be hearing my words but not experiencing either the place in the world about which I was talking or my teaching there. In precisely the same way if I were to teach you about my theory of globalisation (Jarvis, 2007), you would be having a secondary experience. But so would you if I were to discuss any theory with you because theory is secondary experience – it is information mediated to one person via another even though that information may be the other's own knowledge, although this does not have to be the case. In such experiences, we can learn *knowledge what* and even *knowledge how* but this is as far as we can go. It is generalised information and even if we learn it and make it our knowledge it is still insufficient. *Knowledge how* does not equip us to do anything – it is still knowledge. However, if I taught you how to play the card game 'Whist', you still cannot play it until you have the cards in your hands and the experience of playing the game: this is primary experience. Now we learn from that experience and we are *able to play*, but we also learn from that experience a different form of *knowledge how* and even *knowledge that* – now it is the subjective, personal knowledge learned from primary experience – it is our knowledge. There is no conceptual relationship between the *knowledge learned* in secondary experience and *being able to* – we can only learn that by doing and having done so we have learned our own knowledge – it has never been information or data and it only becomes data or information if we try to teach another person our knowledge. However, as we pointed out previously, once we do this, we are confronted with at least two insurmountable problems: firstly once we try to put our experience into words, we can only speak from memory – and however immediate the memory we cannot convey the sense of emotion contained in the experience or the learning that ensued; secondly, experts in card playing, for instance, may know all the rules of the game but a great deal of their expertise lies not in rule-knowing but in the tacit knowledge of reading persons, situations or even the strategic stage in the game. Tacit knowledge, as Polanyi (1967) showed us is also an intrinsic part of our knowing but it is one which we find difficult, if not impossible, to articulate. He gives the example of a face in a crowd – we can recognise it but we find it impossible to describe it accurately. But Freud also taught us about the significance of the unconscious and later in this chapter we will explore the pre-conscious, so that experience is broader than even awareness itself but not broader than experience as consciousness: perhaps 'conscious experience is not all there is to the mind' (Chalmers, 1996, p. 11).

At the heart of this is that all the forms of knowledge are learned – either from primary or secondary experience. It is from the experience that we learn, but as we are beginning to see, when we use the word experience in experiential learning and education we are usually referring to a practicum rather than this rather complex notion of experience *per se*.

Experience has many different meanings and we learn from each of these manifestations that we call experiences, and in this chapter we are going to explore just a few of these notions and seek to understand how each affects our understanding of learning. We will explore experience as consciousness, biography, episode/event and expertise (skill and wisdom), and we will conclude with two other conceptual difficulties about experience that point us to future deliberations. And so the question needs to be posed: precisely what do we mean by this profoundly difficult concept the meaning of which we tend to take for granted? *Collins English Dictionary* (1979) offers seven diverse interpretations:

- direct personal participation;
- a particular incident;
- accumulated knowledge;
- impact made on an individual by culture;
- totality of a person's thoughts, emotions, perceptions, encounters;
- to participate in;
- to be moved emotionally.

In contrast, a philosophical dictionary (Speake 1984) is more concerned with the distinction between philosophical empiricism and philosophical rationalism: the former is about a person's cognitive dealings with the external world and the latter more concerned with the subjectivity or privacy of our perceptions of the world and that we can claim little beyond these. It will have probably become obvious from our previous discussions that we are suggesting that learning is individual and totally private although it can occur in a public place: it is subjective since we learn from our own experience of external reality, even though individuals with similar backgrounds and in common situations may appear to have group experiences from which we learn together. Our individual learning, however, must find social outcomes to be meaningful – or even testable, although much learning is not testable in the crude way that education has often endeavoured to test it!

So then how do we define experience? To offer a simple definition in response to the question would, therefore, be unwise: rather we will examine the concept from a variety of perspectives that recognise this complexity and which relate to the processes of human learning. We will examine the idea of experience under the following – experience as consciousness, biography, episode/event and expertise (skill and wisdom), and I want to conclude with two other conceptual difficulties about experience.

Experience as consciousness

Understanding learning from experience means that we look at a wide range of disciplines across the whole lifespan and learning cannot be understood in any other way since this is a human activity of which cognition is but one part. Chalmers (1996, pp. 11–16) suggests that there are two forms of conscious experience:

- *phenomenological* – the mind as conscious experience and as a consciously experienced mental state in which we feel in certain ways;
- *psychological* – the mind as a causal basis of behaviour.

He regards these two approaches as close to each other since many kinds of psychological states can be associated with phenomenological states, and so on – but they do not coincide and in some ways this distinction relates to the I–Me situation discussed previously and to which we will return towards the end of this book.

Soon after birth we do have experiences and we learn to memorise from sensations; Donald (2001, p. 75) suggests that memorising sensation is the basis of consciousness itself and that we learn consciousness as we learn and remember. But the significant thing about consciousness is that we need to be conscious of something – we need to experience external reality in some way. Consciousness is a bridge between the bare life within human being (Agamben, 1995) – this is a concept that is even more basic than the idea that existentialists call Being – and external reality itself, but it needs external stimulation to generate awareness and also for it to remain stable. This latter fact was clearly demonstrated in that experiment at McGill University which we described previously when some students were paid a financial reward to do nothing – in fact to be denied sensory perception for as long as they could. None lasted longer than three days before they gave up and even then some were temporarily mentally harmed: consciousness requires external stimuli – or experiences – in order to be consciousness. In other words we need both people with whom to interact and the cultural experience that such interaction produces. We become ourselves in such a cultural environment: ultimately we are not individuals but individuals-in-groups and in social situations – and this relationship is something of an entity in itself – as we have already argued, following Buber (1959), that relationship is something with which we start life.

However, we may not be born with conscious awareness as we all recognise when we see a newborn baby but we learn it by experience and like its evolution, it grows and develops in each of us. Following Donald (2001, pp. 178–200), there appear to be three evolutionary dimensions of consciousness:

- *Selective binding*: Binding is the process whereby we link together phenomena to produce a perceptual unity and it is only through consciousness that we can be aware of the external world;
- *Short-term memory*: This dimension follows from the previous one in so much as any binding requires a short-term memory in order to hold the whole together and as the brain evolves the focus changes from the binding mechanism to give the brain power to be free from the immediate context. In this freedom lies the capacity to develop human learning;
- *Intermediate and long-term governance*: This builds on the previous two stages and expands the range of experience which forms the basis of our continued learning: it was during this stage of our evolution that the prefrontal cortex and other regions of the tertiary cortex expanded and this process occurred as a result of social interaction and the growth of culture.

It can thus be seen that consciousness itself has evolved through learning and remembering and this same process is evident in our human development: it is the expanding brain that provides us with the opportunity of broadened experience from which we can continue to learn. Indeed, we are freed from the immediate experience and able to memorise past experiences. The basis of our learning is awareness itself – the act of experiencing – although it is attention that focuses our learning in a conscious manner. However, such conscious awareness is perhaps best recognised in language itself – when we can speak about an experience we are fully conscious of it but once we actually speak about it we change its nature as Eliade (see Ricoeur 1995, pp. 48–55) explains, calling this phenomenon hierophantic when he writes about religious experience and we will return to this later in this chapter.

Bare life then is embodied and through the senses exposed to external stimuli, or qualia, which are processed through the brain. A more narrow use of this term *qualia* includes the idea of quality in sensory experience, such as colour, an approach that is favoured by some researchers (e.g., Rose 2006) whilst others employ it more broadly to refer to all sensory experiences. However, the McGill experiment showed that we, humans, need much more than just consciousness to survive as normal human beings – we need experiences that are based in an external context about which we can become aware, or to which we can pay attention. This latter distinction is important – we are no doubt more aware of a wider context when we focus our attention, so that we can say that at one level we have an experience of the phenomenon to which we attend but we are often conscious of a wider reality. Consequently, there are degrees of awareness – some at the heart of our concentration while others are at the periphery of our focus of attention, and in such skills as speed-reading we actually learn from our periphery as well as from the focus of our attention. From my own experience of getting people to write down their own learning experiences, it is clear that a great deal of learning in everyday life occurs at the periphery of our conscious awareness and even in our pre-consciousness. In these situations much of our knowledge is tacit. Our tacit knowledge is also reflected in a phenomenon that Marton and Booth (1997, pp. 99–100) call appresentation – that is, when we complete an incomplete experience by recalling knowledge that has been internalised without our full conscious awareness of it from an earlier experience.

Consciousness, however, spans all the levels of awareness but it is expanded by language and ultimately by all other means of storing knowledge. What Crawford (2005) called attentive experiencing is significant here since it concentrates the mind on a specific phenomenon. In a sense attentive experiencing is the type of awareness that occurs in in-depth thought, concentration or religious contemplation: in-depth learning that occurs as a result of our being more aware of the significance and content of that experience. The more that we attend to our experiences the more that we see in them and the more that we learn from them: 'paying attention' is important to our conscious experience and is one of the most significant factors in learning. Significantly, in this rapidly moving world where people seem to have little time for anything a new movement is beginning – the slow movement (Honore, 2004) which seeks to offer a challenge to the speed of the world and points us to the need for more attention to be given to the nature of experience. So that, at one end of the spectrum we can have experiences of which we are not conscious because they happen so speedily but which require a further conscious experience to bring them to our conscious awareness and at the other end of the spectrum we focus upon concentration from which we gain a greater insight into our experience since we are more conscious of it and learn more from it.

However, we are confronted at this stage with Freud's work who pointed us to the unconscious mind and Polanyi (1967) who highlighted tacit knowledge and to my own research into learning in which I discuss the significance of the pre-conscious in learning. Indeed, we can actually now see how the pre-conscious experience occurs: which is both important in our thinking about perception and about learning. Goleman (1995, pp. 17–20) reports on work by LeDoux (1996) who shows that:

> sensory signals from the ear and eye travel first in the brain to the thalamus and then – across a singe synapse – to the amygdala; a second signal is routed to the neo-cortex – the thinking brain. This branching allows the

amygdala to begin to respond *before* the neo-cortex which mulls information through several levels of brain circuits before it fully perceives and
finally initiates a more finely tailored response.

Consequently, those early information signals allow a pre-conscious response to
sensations and, therefore, we are enabled to have pre-conscious experiences that
also lead to pre-conscious learning.

Recently, as I noted earlier, I detected a conceptual anomaly in my own work:
in my definition of learning in the opening chapter, I included the phrase 'the
perceived content of which' which implies that what gets into my mind is something of which I am aware – but I have also written about pre-conscious learning
which suggests that things get into my mind about which I am not aware. There
is no doubt that we all have pre-conscious experiences which get imprinted, as
it were, in the brain – when the bodily sensations are transmitted to the brain
and the network of neurons reconfigured in some small or large way. But
conceptually does learning stop at the point when we are not aware of the initial
stimulus? From my own observations and experience it seems that pre-conscious
learning happens in two stages: we can experience events although we are not
aware of every facet of what we have internalised but the whole event has been
experienced and stored in the brain pre-consciously. A subsequent experience
acts as a stimulus, the response to which is to call to conscious awareness an
aspect of a previous experience of which we had not been conscious before and
from which we can now learn. This is the fuzzy boundary of experience and,
therefore, the fuzzy boundary of learning but the actual learning still requires
conscious awareness although the experience from which we learn need not be
conscious at the time when we experience it.

Experience, then, is wider than conscious awareness but it cannot be wider
that being itself– but the pre-conscious is clearly a significant aspect of our
biography.

Experience as biography

In my own definition of learning which was discussed in the opening chapter I
suggest that the outcome of every learning event is built into our biographies,
although these need not only be our cognitions (see OECD, 2007a) as our definition makes clear, and in this sense we are learned persons but we see from the
discussion in the first part of this chapter that memory itself has evolved and
that memory itself frees us from the immediate experience and yet in a complex
manner it is a working memory that enables us to recall past experiences as and
when they become relevant. Consequently, when we exclaim: 'In all my experience . . .' we are really talking of all the learning events that have made us what
we are at that moment in time. Biography is the sum of those experiences from
which we have learned and we are the product of those experiences. It is no
accident that the influential *Faure Report* (1972) was called *Learning to Be*.

Our biographies are our understanding about ourselves as we pass through
time. Time, however, forms a major problem when we consider experience and
Rose (2006, p. 394) remarks that more 'needs to be done on this baffling
problem' and we will look briefly at one aspect of this in the next section of this
chapter. Relating time to consciousness he (p. 394) says that all higher levels of
consciousness are formed by binding between:

(1) current input representations, short-term records and current motor effer-
    ence (something that conducts outwards from the centre-author's defini-
    tion) to give retention or protention of the phenomenologists' 'thickness' of
    experience;
(2) various durations of long-term memory . . . to generate conscious aware-
    ness of identity and meaning of a stimulus; and
(3) long-term autobiographical memory and long-term plans, desires and life
    goals . . . our memories of the most significant events so far, and imagined
    goals of what we want to reach in the future – to give us a sense of who we
    are and our sense of self.

Consequently, we can see that for as long as we are alive we are compiling our
autobiography through experience and learning, and that we are always
becoming (see Chapter 17) as we move from experience to experience or even
from social status to social status. Phenomenology can be placed within this
context since it is a process of 'binding across time to form systematic structures
connecting memory, current inflow and plans for the future' (Rose, 2006,
p. 395).

This process is clearly shown in the anthropological studies of Van Gennap
(1960[1908]) and Turner (1969). More recently, and from a specifically learning
perspective, Camilleri (2009) demonstrated this when she traced ten nursing
students through the period from their final year in university and their first
eighteen months of practice. She showed quite convincingly that it was the experiences in the work place, above all, that provided the basis for the incidental
and often pre-conscious learning that led to the students going through the
process of playing the role of nurse and being identified as nurses by patients
and others to actually identifying with the role, feeling that they were nurses and
so eventually they actually became nurses in their own minds. At some stage in
their careers they become a nurse – they gain a self-identity as a result of their
experiences – in which they identify themselves with the social identity that
wearing the uniform generated.

It is not surprising, therefore, that there has grown up in research into human
learning the whole field of life-history: individuals tracing their life histories and
engaging in a process of learning from the experiences of life that they can
remember (see, for instance Alheit and Dausien 2007: West, 1996, 2001, 2007).
Noonan (2003, p. 9) refers to this as 'experience-memory' in order to separate
it from the process of memorising; memory of past experiences is quite fundamental to the process of identity building, which is at the heart of our
biography.

It is through the process of living and learning that we gain wisdom, as
Aristotle (VI.8, p. 148) noted. Wisdom is the result of experience rather than its
being a science, like mathematics, that the young can master. Wisdom comes
from the practical rather than the theoretical. Ageing also is clearly related to
experience as biography and as we live in an ageing society it is not surprising
that educational gerontology is emerging as a very significant area of study: how
older people learn, utilise their learning and also how they feel isolated in a very
rapidly changing society since it is hard to keep abreast with everything that
is changing. Significantly, however, wisdom is one of the concepts that appears
to play a less significant role as our work-orientated society concentrates on
technical rationality and competence – knowledge of the present. Wisdom,

however, is gained pre-consciously and incidentally in the process of living and learning from experience: it is tacit. Like wisdom, another concept that has not been fully studied in recent year has been the one with which it may be coupled – expertise – and we will turn to this shortly. However, we have to recognise that not all become wise as a result of living because there are many times when we fail to learn from our experiences – we presume upon them and take them for granted. Non-learning from experience is something quite vital to our understanding of learning (Jarvis, 1987), although there may be tacit changes in our understanding of ourselves as a result of this process.

Experience as episode/event

In my previous work I did not separate these two terms but following Donald (2001) I now think that this was a serious mistake, and much of my work has been based on events, which I called episodes, although episodes are actually series of events bound together in conscious awareness of their unity. It is, however, a major flaw in those evolutionary psychologists who consider that the brain is hard-wired as a result of our evolution and that we are programmed by our past to respond to stimuli in specific ways and at specific times. Donald argues that this flaw occurs with some of those scholars who believe that they are constructing a science of learning (OECD, 2007b, p. 11) and consider that our brains are fully wired at birth: scientists can claim that our brains are hard-wired based upon experiments that are no longer than a single event but not for those which span a whole episode or sequence of events. Laboratory experiments can be carefully designed to record the here and now – they study sensations and very short-term memory but these are not the limits of consciousness: this has 'a much larger window of experience than short-term memory' (Donald, 2001, p. 47). We can have an experience of a whole class or even a whole course – experience is an episode in our lives. The capacity of our brains is much larger than that required for the consciousness of a single sensation. We continue to be aware of the situation for a much longer period of time than the immediate and we hold it in our working memory for as long as necessary and no brain can be programmed to respond to a whole episode and this undermines a great deal of the theory of the hard-wired brain. It is what Schutz and Luckmann (1974, p. 51) called 'a stream of consciousness': experience is a sequence of events that overlap and form a continuous whole and yet, like biography, it is a single episode in our lives.

We sometimes live in the flow of time, an episode in which we seem to have heightened awareness all the time – what Csikszentmihalyi (1990) calls optimal experience – our awareness enables us to learn rapidly and effortlessly without interruption. He (1990, p. 39) describes this as when 'information that keeps coming into awareness is congruent with goals' that leads to psychic energy flowing effortlessly. An interruption to this flow can occur – a disruptive disjuncture – which can re-focus our attention on a different event. When I started my own research into learning I was interested in a sense of 'feeling at home' in our own life world upon which we can presume in an almost unthinking manner – a process which Bergson (1999[1965]) called *durée*. We take the world for granted and as it were act in an 'almost mindless manner' but suddenly something occurs which we can no longer take for granted and we experience a degree of disjuncture; we have a heightened consciousness or awareness and we are forced to question our expectations of the situation – we ask: Why? What for? How do I do it? And so on. These events occur more frequently than optimal experiences; they are common to everyday living whereas flow happens from time to time. A moment in time constitutes the time of an event and it is in this that we experience the situation.

My own model of learning is based on this idea that we learn from events such as this and that episodes are series of events bound together in a continuing awareness, hence in my diagram of learning I show the start of the next learning cycle in each diagram. It is important to recognise that awareness spans time and that we learn to live within the flow of time but learning occurs as joined up series of events upon which we concentrate.

Understanding the disjuncture created by the event is important in seeking to grasp the beginning of learning processes: we become aware that we do not know and that we need to know if we are to continue in either doing what we were doing or thinking what we were thinking. We have to re-establish that harmony through learning. Children go through this period early in their lives when they are continually confronted with phenomena that they do not understand: Why this? And, why that? All parents are aware of this stage of cognitive development – children need answers so that they can feel at home in their world and parents and significant others provide those answers and we all become part of our culture, or sub-culture. We all experience this disjuncture when we enter different cultures and sub-cultures.

As Donald (2001) shows, it is the single event that is much easier to capture in laboratory experiments which has formed the basis of certain forms of research and which is even the basis of the conjectures of those scholars who think that most of our learning is hard-wired into our brains. However, an episode is much harder to capture in a laboratory experiment and so the longer time frame actually casts doubt upon the idea that we are hard-wired before birth and places much more focus on learning from continuing conscious experiences through which we construct our biography. Experiences are both single events and elongated episodes and we learn from both.

Experience as expertise

An expert is one who 'has extensive skill or knowledge in a particular field' or someone who is 'skilful or knowledgeable' (*Collins English Dictionary*). Perhaps the dictionary should also have offered the possibility that an expert is both skilful and knowledgeable. More recently Gardner (2007, p. 82), writing about the creating mind, suggests that:

> For every talented writer or composer who breaks new ground, however, hundreds are content – or resigned – to be 'mere' experts. An expert is an individual who, after a decade or more of training, has reached the pinnacle of practice in her chosen domain. The world depends on experts.

While the world depends on experts this is still a restricted definition, but nearly everybody is an expert in the art of living in society. Nevertheless, it would be true to say that for a number of years the word 'expert' has fallen into something like disrepute in some parts of the world as terms like 'competency' have dominated the vocabulary of political correctness in both work and education.

But we should not expect people to stop learning just because they have achieved the state of competence – it is a low expectation of achievement in social living and this should not be an aim in education. We have all been witnesses to this growth of political correctness in UK that downplays the expert who is better than others and yet the sum total of every individual's practice is their experience – their expertise – in this or that area of behaviour. We learn our expertise through experiencing and learning from the experience.

> One becomes an expert not simply by absorbing explicit knowledge of the type found in text-books, but through experience, that is, through repeated trials, 'failing, succeeding, wasting time and effort . . . getting a feel for the problem, learning when to go by the book and when to break the rules'. Human experts gradually absorb 'a repertory of working rules of thumb, or "heuristics", that combined with book knowledge, make them expert practitioners. This practical, heuristic knowledge, as attempts to simulate it on the machine have shown, is 'hardest to get at because experts – or anyone else – rarely have the self-awareness to recognize what it is. So it must be mined out of their heads painstakingly, one jewel at a time.
> (All quotations from Feigenbaum and McCorduck, 1984)
> (Nyiri, 1988, pp. 20–21)

The whole point here is that we just cannot apply theory to practice: the practice situation is a new learning situation and in it we have to find out if the theory can be utilised in any way but primarily we have to learn from the situation itself. There is no logical connection between *knowing how* and *being able to*. We have to generate our own practical skill and the ensuing knowledge and ultimately our own practical theories (Jarvis, 1999) that may be a combination of book knowledge with what we have learned from the years in practice, often repeating similar manoeuvres and procedures many times but in each learning and reinforcing our learning. It is those years of experience that constitute the basis of expertise and expertise is specific to the situation – in many cases it may be a generalisable technique that can be replaced by a machine but in others it is specific to the type of situation in which the actor performs.

As the years go by the experts not only gain knowledge and skills, they might also gain wisdom but we learn this pre-consciously – and this is one of the fundamental problems in seeking to understand experiential learning. But expertise may not be associated with time in this simple manner because we can repeat behaviours and not learn from them because we do not pay attention to them or to the small differences similar situations have or the slightly different problems each situation poses – only if we treat every experience as an individual learning experience can we gain expertise. Consequently, when we praise someone for their experience we are basically praising them for having continually gained expertise, learned from their experience.

Concluding discussion

From the above discussion, it can be seen that learning is not just a psychological problem, it is a human one and the study of learning is an existential one, but we have not started with Descartes' assertion that I think, therefore I am

– but rather we have reversed it and started with being and claim that I am, therefore I think – or rather and more accurately – I am therefore I experience – and in the light of pre-conscious experience this is the more correct claim. Experience then, is mostly about consciousness and awareness; about being and becoming; about episode and event, about wisdom and expertise: it is also either direct or mediated and it is about the actual process of doing things. We can relate learning to each of them and see how we learn from experience throughout the whole of our lives, but there are many other major conceptual problems that surround learning from experience, such as the mind–brain relationship, but in conclusion I want to turn to turn to one major question:

- Can I have an experience from which I learn without the end-product of the learning being knowledge?

It is a topic that demands a full paper rather than one or two concluding paragraphs, but it is included here in order to complete the discussion about experience and we will refer to it again later in this book.

In 1999, Jossey-Bass published a book of mine *The Practitioner-Researcher* and two of my then MSc students (both nuns working in Zambia) asked me if I would go out to Zambia and conduct workshops on this study with community doctors and community, which I did. Towards the end of the week, they asked me what they could do to repay me and I, not knowing the geography of Zambia very well, said 'I would love to see Victoria Falls'. Well on my next to final day – my first free one, they packed me into a small car and drove hundreds of kilometres across Zambia to Victoria Falls – and we stood there as the sun set and watched the wondrous scene of the sun through the haze of the Falls and over the beauty of the Zambezi river. Again, early the following morning, I, amongst only about six people, stood there and watched the sun rise over the river and the Falls. What experiences – words could not describe my feelings – and as we travelled back to the airport, I said to them that no fee could have paid for those experiences.

What I experienced was awe-inspiring – a religious experience (?) – it was a feeling of creature-consciousness that Otto (1959 [1917]) called the numinous. Otto (1959 [1917], p. 24) describes this as 'the emotion of a creature, submerged, and overwhelmed by its own nothingness in contrast to that which is supreme above all creatures'. But, significantly, once I describe this non-rational, emotional experience it ceases to be that experience and my description can only be transmitted in words that are non-emotional and rational. Any explication does this to sense experience and in order to understand it we need to understand something of the nature of experience. In a sense, explaining my feelings is a stage in understanding the situation but it is a stage removed from the experience itself and once I try to interpret it I may do so in the language of a community of which I am a member and have generalised a particular. Then, telling you about it creates a secondary experience for you. But, the experience had no meaning and I only learned in awe about the beauty of the world – cognitive learning was a stage removed from the actual experience. It is this that Ricoeur (1995, pp. 48–55) accurately describes, in which he both captures the process that I went through and also illustrates the way in which we learn from the senses in general. He makes five points and these are similar to the process I have described here:

- The 'numinous' element of the sacred is not first of all something to do with language.
- Following Eliade, this is hierophantic – that is, while we cannot describe the numinous element as such, we can at least describe how it manifests itself. This I have already done.
- The sacred may also reveal itself in significant behaviour – although this is only one modality of the numinous and it may have been my intense concentration, my contemplative nature, and so on that could be described as behavioural.
- The sacred is dramatic.
- Each of these elements point to a logic of meaning – to signify something other than itself.

But the point is that there was no intrinsic meaning to that experience and I learn that not every experience has meaning – the logic of meaning is not necessarily the meaning of the experience, if there is one: the outcome of the learning was awe, wonder – an experience of a life-time if you like – but then every learning experience is an experience in a lifetime.

There is also another way of responding to this question – the body can learn almost independently of the mind. Pianists, for instance, can practise a very complicated piece of music so thoroughly that their fingers learn the sequence of notes almost independently of the body: when this has been very thoroughly accomplished then pianists can listen and reflect on the product of their playing and just feel that the fingers played the right notes at the right time, or vice versa.

Before we examine the processes of learning, however, one more concept needs exploration – meaning. We have already met this term in the third chapter but it is a concept that underlies our personhood and relates to every aspect of our learning.

References

Agamben G (1995) *Homer Sacer* Stanford: Stanford University Press

Aristotle (1925) *Nichomachean Ethics* (trans Davis Ross) Oxford: Oxford University Press

Bergson H (1999 [1965]) *Duration and Simultaneity* Manchester: Clinamen Press

Boud D, Keogh R and Walker D (eds) (1983) *Reflection: Turning Experience into Learning* London: Kogan Page

Buber M (1957) *I and Thou* London: Continuum

Camilleri M (2009) *Becoming a Nurse* Guildford: University of Surrey Unpublished PhD research

Chalmers D (1996) *The Conscious Mind* Oxford: Oxford University Press

Collins English Dictionary (1979) London: Collins

Crawford J (2005) *Spiritually Engaged Knowledge* Aldershot: Ashgate

Csikszentmihalyi M (1990) *Flow: The Psychology of Optimal Experience* New York: Harper & Row

Donald M (2001) *A Mind So Rare* New York: W.W. Norton

Faure E (chair) (1972) *Learning to Be* Paris: UNESCO

Feigenbaum E and McCorduck P, (1984) *The Fifth Generation* New York: Signet

Fraser W (1995) *Learning from Experience* Leicester: NIACE

Gardner H (2007) *Five Minds for the Future* Boston, Mass.: Harvard Business School Press

Goleman D (1995) *Emotional Intelligence* London: Bloomsbury

Honore C (2004) *In Praise of Slow* London: Orion

Jarvis P (1987) *Adult Learning in the Social Context* London: Croom Helm

Jarvis P (1992) *Paradoxes of Learning* San Francisco: Jossey-Bass

Jarvis P (1999) *The Practitioner-Researcher* San Francisco: Jossey-Bass

Jarvis P (2006) *Human Learning: Towards a Comprehensive Theory* London: Routledge

Jarvis P (2007a) *Globalisation, Lifelong Learning and the Learning Society: Sociological Perspectives* London: Routledge

Knowles M S (1980) *The Modern Practice of Adult Education: From Pedagogy to Andragogy* Chicago: Association Press (Revised and Updated)

LeDoux J (1996) *The Emotional Brain* New York: Simon & Schuster

Marton F and Booth S (1997) *Learning and Awareness* Mahwah, NJ: Lawrence Erlbaum Associates

Marton F, Hounsell D and Entwistle N (1984) (eds) *The Experience of Learning* Edinburgh: Scottish Academic Press

Noonan H (2003) *Personal Identity* London: Routledge (2nd edition)

Nyiri J (1984) Tradition and Practical Knowledge in Nyiri J and Smith B (eds) (1984) *op cit*

Nyiri J and Smith B (eds) (1984) *Practical Knowledge: Outlines of a Theory of Traditions and Skills* London: Croom Helm

Oakeshott M (1933) *Experience and its Modes* Cambridge: Cambridge University Press

OECD (2007a) *Understanding the Social Outcomes of Learning* Paris: Organisation for Economic Cooperation and Development

OECD (2007b) *Understanding the Brain: The Birth of a Learning Science* Paris: Organisation for Economic Cooperation and Development

Otto R (1917[1959]) *The Idea of the Holy* Harmondsworth: Penguin

Polyani, M. (1967) *The Tacit Dimension* London: Routledge & Kegan Paul

Ricoeur P (1995) *Figuring the Sacred* Minneapolis: Fortress Press

Rose D (2006) *Consciousness: Philosophical, Psychological and Neural Theories* Oxford: Oxford University Press

Schon, D.A. (1983) *The Reflective Practitioner* New York: Basic Books

Schutz A and Luckmann T (1974) The *Structures of the Lifeworld* London: Heinemann

Speake J (1984) *A Dictionary of Philosophy* London: Pan Books

Turner V (1969) *The Ritual Process* Harmondsworth: Penguin

van Gennap A (1960) *The Rites of Passage* London: Routledge & Kegan Paul

Weil, S. and Mcgill, I. (eds) (1989) *Making Sense of Experiential Learning*, Buckingham: Open University Press in association with SRHE

West L (2001) *Doctors at the Edge: General Practitioners, Health and Learning in the Inner City* London: FA Books

West L (2007) An auto/biographical imagination and the radiacal challenge of families and their learning in West L, Alheit P, Anderson A and Merrill B (eds) *The Uses of Biographical and Life History Methods in the Study of Adult and Lifelong Learning: European Perspectives* Munich: Peter Lang

CHAPTER 4

████

MEANING

Originally published as 'Meaning' in P. Jarvis (2009), *Learning to Be a Person in Society*, London: Routledge, pp. 69–78. Cross-references refer to the original publication.

We have already been faced with the ideas of both meaning and intention in early childhood. Meaning, however, is a very complex phenomenon and making meaning is certainly crucial to our understanding of both learning and personhood and so we intend to explore some of this complexity in this chapter.

Meaning *per se* has a wide variety of meanings, as *Collins English Dictionary* shows:

- sense of significance;
- the sense underlying or intended by speech;
- the inner, symbolic or true interpretation, value or message;
- valid content, efficacy;
- expressive of some sense, intention, criticism.

When I (Jarvis, 1992, pp. 155–176) discussed meaning previously, I covered the following topics:

- existence and knowledge;
- metaphysical meaning;
- socio-cultural meaning;
- meaning as intention;
- meaning and learning;
- meaning and understanding;
- meaning, truth and knowledge;
- meaning, truth and non-learning;
- meaning and legitimation crises.

From these two very similar lists we can see that the concept is not easy to capture. Fundamental to the development of meaning is language which can be both symbolic and narrative – both meaning and language are acquired during socialisation. Nevertheless, there is an underlying assumption that meaning is created as a result of rational thought but Kingwell (2000, p. 194) reminds us that there is a 'habitual error of the overweening theorist, of thinking that human meaning can be made entirely transparent by consistent application of human reason'. We are not all reasonable all the time, and neither are our meanings or our intentions. However, we have already touched upon some of these interpretations and others we will meet in the second part of this book. The aim of this chapter, however, is to provide an overview of the various meanings of the word *meaning* and even more to see how we acquire meaning in order to lay the foundation for the second part of this book. We will, therefore, look at the metaphysical and socio-cultural interpretations of the term, including its relation to knowledge, truth and belief, in the first part of the chapter – a cultural concept; in the second part we will deal with the subjective aspects of intention and significance – a more subjective and personal concept; in the third, we will look at meaning and learning – a process of acquisition. In this way we will cover the variety of meanings suggested by the above lists.

Cultural meaning

As a result of our evolution, human beings are born with a propensity to seek meaning: this is some thing that as a result of our existence, we reflect about ourselves and about the world in which we live, we question existence and seek to devise answers to those questions. It is as if curiosity has been built into us as a result of our evolution but it is not just a biological phenomenon. In Bruner's (1990, p. 34) concerns about the way that psychology was developing, he wrote that '. . . it is culture not biology, that shapes human life and the human mind, that gives meaning to action by situating its underlying intentional states in an interpretative system'. This we have already argued in the opening chapters of this book and we have also seen that in early childhood intentional states occur at very young ages. Existentially, Macquarrie (1973, p. 125) indicates this when he reverses the Cartesian dictum and claims that 'I am, therefore I think'. Once we do this, we question our experiences and seek to give them meaning – for experience itself has no meaning as we will argue below but our meanings stem from our relationships with other people in our life-world, from our own interpretations of our experiences, from questions about the cosmos or any combination of these. There are metaphysical and socio-cultural perspectives on this.

Metaphysical: One of the interesting paradoxes about the concept of meaning is that while we are born with this propensity to seek meaning as a result of our evolution we know that there is no intrinsic meaning in the universe. Fromm (1949, pp. 44–45) summarises this paradox thus:

> Man can react to historical contradictions by annulling them through his own actions: but he cannot annul existential dichotomies, although he can react to them in different ways. He can appease his mind by soothing and harmonizing ideologies. He can try to escape from his inner restlessness by ceaseless activity in pleasure or business. He can try to abrogate his freedom and to turn himself into an instrument of powers outside himself, submerging himself in them. But he remains dissatisfied, anxious and restless. There is only one solution to his problem: to face the truth, to acknowledge his fundamental aloneness and solitude in a universe indifferent to his fate, to recognize that there is no power transcending him which can solve his problem for him. Man must accept responsibility for himself and the fact that only by using his own powers can he give meaning to life. But meaning does not imply certainty. Uncertainty is the very condition to impel man to

unfold his powers. If he faces the truth without panic he will recognize that *there is no meaning to life except the meaning that man gives his life by the unfolding of his powers, by living productively;* and that only constant vigilance, activity and effort can keep us from failing in the one task that matters – the full development of our powers within the limitations set by our own existence. Man will never cease to be perplexed, to wonder, to raise new questions.

(italics in original)

Whilst some may not be happy with his conclusions, it is clear since there is no intrinsic meaning in matter itself, then there can be no intrinsic meaning nor obvious explanation to the cosmos and that all interpretations – whether theist, agnostic, non-theist, or atheist are meanings given by individuals, peoples and cultures in their quest to understand existence. Metaphysical explanations are responses to our human quest to make sense of our existence and to ask if there is an ultimate meaning to it all: they are belief systems and we will look more closely at this when we examine knowledge and beliefs later in this study. Throughout the ages there have been teachers and preachers who have expounded meanings and some of these have in different ways become embodied within the cultures of different societies and, in this sense, meaning is 'ultimate meaning' for the cultural group who have accepted it. But one of the fundamental paradoxes of meaning – in fact a paradox of human living – is that we think that we have arrived at the ultimate, only to find more questions and more endeavours: meaning can never be ultimate – it is always relative and to be discovered within the socio-cultural world.

Socio-cultural: Some of these teachers and preachers have been very successful within their own or other's cultures and so, in different ways, their interpretations have been accepted and become embedded within cultures as symbolic universes of meaning. These are then learned through the socialisation process and transmitted to children through interaction with significant others. Luckmann (1967, p. 44) writes of the universes of meaning into which individuals are born:

> Symbolic universes are objectivated meaning systems that relate the experiences of everyday life to a 'transcendental' layer of reality. Other systems of meaning do not point beyond the world of everyday life; that is, they do not contain a 'transcendental' reference.

We can see that such systems are slow to change because they are built into national and ethnic cultures and learned in childhood – imprinted, as it were, in newly emerging minds. Children learn to believe them and it is hard to eradicate these early impressions since they are the institutionalised meanings of society and they are also the meanings that are most significant to the family within which we are born and raised.

However, sociologists have long been pre-occupied with the structures of society and so it would be over-simplistic to talk about meaning as if it were a single entity. Since we also live within our life-worlds we may find a greater sense of conformity and agreement by those significant others within them than between them. Nevertheless, we are exposed to both the pressures of society as a whole and also to those of our life-worlds: we are going to be exposed to a unique combination of meanings that we learn and which we will in some way combine and reflect. Society's structures have undergone considerable change over the past century or two and with it a sense of shared meaning has probably become less strong, although there are still shared meanings in such ideas as the imagined community, nationalism, and so on. As early as 1893, however, Durkheim was aware of the significance of the changing social structures on people's lives and even on their consciences or even their consciousness (see Durkheim, 1933, p. ix in which the translator debates the meaning of the French word *conscience*) are related to their social position. Durkheim traced society through three phases: mechanical, organic and contractual solidarity. Even in his *Introduction* Durkheim shows his awareness of the way that people view the world is changing with the changing social structures. In this sense, meaning is not only social but relative: this relativity could be traced historically across time or socially and hierarchically through a cultural group. Durkheim (1933, p. 43) wrote of education, for instance, that:

> Education is growing more and more specialized. We deem it more and more necessary not to submit children to a uniform culture, as if they were all to lead the same life; but to train them differently in the light of the different functions that they will be called on to fill.

But now in a society having contractual solidarity there is no uniform socio-cultural meaning to life. The changing nature of contemporary society has led to our developing changing meanings to social life and even to life itself. We, in the West, now live in a global consumer society (Jarvis, 2008) in which our children learn that one meaning of life is to be happy and in order to achieve this we have to work in order to acquire goods and finance and spend and consume. It is this consumer culture which we suggested is the basis of an alternative learning society – but for many, this meaning of life is not satisfying. Bellah *et al.* (1985, p. 290), in their study of individualism and the American way of life record the fact that 'few have found a life devoted to "personal ambition and consumerism" satisfactory and most are seeking in one way or another to transcend the limitations of a self-centred life'. Hence, the quest for meaning is not socially determined, although the dominant meanings are propounded by those who have the power to perpetuate an interpretation of life that they wish to see others adopt.

Underlying a great deal of advertising are ideologies of life that those who are 'other directed' (Riesman, 1950) may become dependent upon, while those who are 'tradition directed' may prefer to accept, those dominant meaning systems that have been built into the culture over the ages; those who are 'inner directed' may be the ones who seek to step outside of the dominant self-centred ideologies of global capitalism and discover a system of meaning that transcends their social situation. This is an element of the learning process that certainly requires further research.

Clearly the organisations, groups, social classes, and so on, that individuals occupy in society are going to affect, or reinforce, the meanings that they place upon their lives and even upon the meaning that they give to all other aspects of social life. Meaning is, in this sense, a social construct and even a personal one in the light of our understanding of the nature of society. Meaning is not just a metaphysical quest; it is a social and personal quest to understand the experiences of everyday living. Experiential learning, therefore, must always be seen within the social context within which the learner is living. While much of the remainder of this chapter assumes psychological overtones, it would be false to view the psychological processes as being divorced from the sociological context within which they occur.

Many of these universes of meaning that assume a significant place in a culture claim that they contain 'the truth' – indeed, what is the truth? This is a question that has haunted humanity almost since the beginning of time. Can there be an ultimate truth or is Fromm right when he claims that the universe has no meaning? Certainly, there is no obviously ultimate truth but this does not negate the idea of holding a reasoned belief position about meaning – whether it is religious or not. But this is a matter of belief, faith and commitment to a cultural or a personal position – but not truth. Meaning does not reside in phenomena at all but only in those who construct meaning and use it to interpret their experiences of the world.

Individuals, however, carry many of the personally and socio-culturally accepted meanings, as well as their individuality, within their own memories and they transmit them through their actions and interactions. This is how we are all socialised into the dominant culture of our society and into our own life-worlds – but this is itself a complex process that has received much greater attention in the past few years.

Personal and subjective meaning

Children are born into a cultural milieu and they learn the cultural symbols – the language, gestures, artefacts that carry the institutionalised meaning: these are the symbols of meaning. They are learned – in the first instance through imitation and trial-and-error – but this is not really a mindless act and at about nine months children realise that the significant others with whom they interact are intentional agents, like themselves. Once more we see the significance of relationship; as Tomasello (1999, p. 89) writes:

> As infants begin to follow into and direct the attention of others to outside entities at nine to twelve months of age, it happens on occasion that the other person whose attention the infant is monitoring focuses on the infant herself. The infant then monitors that person's attention to *her* in a way that was not possible previously . . . She now knows that she is interacting with an intentional agent who perceives her and intends things towards her. When the infant did not understand that others perceive and intend things toward the outside world, there could be no question of how they perceived and intended things toward *me*.
>
> (italics in original)

This is the birth of the 'self – the Me', as George Herbert Mead claimed (see Jarvis, 1987 for a full discussion of Mead's work in relation to learning) the emergence of which happens in the second year – and it can only occur in joint attentional situations. Children begin to learn the socio-cultural meanings that others attach to words, symbols and gestures and this forms and then transforms the way that they view the world – they do this through imitation and trial-and-error: they seek to imitate the significant others and they experiment with words and their meanings to discover how they fit into their position in the social structures. They are already beginning to learn to reflect their social position through the significant others with whom they share meaningful situations. They have a shared sense of meaning, and Nelson (2007, p. 106) points out that this sense of shared meaning means that 'everybody can see me (and perhaps know what I am thinking)'. And so children become capable of reflecting both on what others think of their behaviour and even beginning to reflect on their own knowledge.

What can be seen here is that meaning is learned: it is both learned from experience and constructed through the combination of experiences and memories of previous significant events. Nelson (2007, p. 110) suggests that 'these on-going dynamic processes organize memory in terms of meaning structures'. She (p. 111) goes on the suggest that:

> Over time events (the basic unit of experience) may be combined to form generalized, meaningful wholes that are termed schemas or scripts, concept and categories, and they may be broken down into parts that are then made available for organizing into other concepts and categories.

Every event that we experience consciously enters into the memory: it has some degree of significance although some have much more significance than others. In other words, it is meaningful to us and in this sense 'memory is meaning' (Nelson, 2007, p. 111) – our memories of events are the building blocks of the meanings that we place on our lives but our biographies are not unaffected by these meanings. With the development of language, children learn the meaning of words through shared attentional situations and imitating the sounds: these joint situations mean that children will learn words and their meanings that reflect their socio-economic position in society, their education, and so on. In this sense, it would be hard to accept the idea propounded by Chomsky that locates language in the brain since there are few, if any, universal meanings to words that do not have an empirical referent. Shared meanings in joint attentional situations enable children and their significant others to communicate and the same sense of shared meanings exist in linguistic communication throughout life – however, the process of learning meaning begins with primary experiences in early childhood but in later life many of the experiences that relate to individual's meaning systems are learned from secondary or mediated experiences reflecting Durkheim's contractual solidarity.

Having learned word meanings and speech, children have to articulate their meaning and Bruner (1990, p. 97) summarises this process thus:

> . . . our capacity to render experience in terms of narrative is not just child's play, but an instrument for making meaning that dominates much of the life of culture – from soliloquies at bed-time to the weighing of testimony in our legal system.

We tell our stories and embody our sense of meaning – indeed, in and through the process of articulation we actually refine our meaning system as we organise our memories of events to expound our meaning system – or our world-view. Indeed, Bruner goes on to suggest that the stories we tell and the sense of self that we construct are a result of this process of meaning making. The self,

Bruner (1990, p. 138) declares 'does not arise rootlessly only in response to the present; (it) . . . takes meaning as well from the historical circumstances that give shape to the culture of which they are an expression'. Whether we are anything more than our memories and narratives is another question but once we can see the development of the 'self' in this way, we can see that the mind is more than just the brain with which we are born.

Meaning and learning

In the previous two parts of this chapter we have seen how meaning forms a crucial element in lifelong learning: from the earliest years until late in our lives we seek to understand, to give meaning, to our experiences – to the events that occur in our lives. We can see how children from the earliest age have experiences and that from before they are one year old their experiences tend to be meaningful and intentional. New experiences will reinforce or transform these meanings, as will new knowledge, new skills, and so on, and so they continue to grow and develop. Learning, then, is at the heart of growth and development and a major aspect of that learning is the way that we seek to give experiences meaning and that meaning will change and deepen as our experiences of the world and of the people with whom we interact. This is a process that begins early in life and continues until late in life – but as we do grow and develop so we become aware that some of our meanings do not fit our experiences and so they need to be changed. We learn to reflect on our experiences and this element of reflection is what Mezirow (2000, p. 26) regards as the mark of adult learning. Indeed, he (1991, p. 7) wrote that, 'Adult development is seen as an adult's enhanced capacity to validate prior learning through reflective discourse and to act upon the resulting insights'. However, children from much earlier in life become critical of their meaning systems – for instance, it is well known in sociological studies of religion that adolescence is a time when young people are prepared to reject some of their meaning systems and adopt others. Consequently, we feel that Mezirow makes too great a distinction between adult learning and young people learning while we prefer to see the distinction between early childhood learning and learning throughout the life being drawn more clearly. Indeed, this is always a problem when we start a study of something which is a lifelong process in adulthood, whereas starting with the early years shows how even critical reflectivity develops and that there is not really a sharp distinction to be made between the age groups in the way that some adult educators do – and which in many ways Mezirow acknowledges.

However, for Mezirow (1991, p. 12), 'Learning may be understood as using a prior interpretation to construe a new or a revised interpretation of the meaning of one's experience in order to guide future action' but a weakness in this definition lies in the fact that he does not explain where the prior interpretation comes from if it was not learned – we get an infinite regress unless we build culture into the equation. Learning involves learning new things as well as reconstructing our own meaning schemes. However, Mezirow regards this process of changing one's perspective as transformative and it is this which lies at the heart of his understanding of adult learning. His study is extremely comprehensive and is well grounded in research evidence but the failure to relate it to lifelong learning as a whole is one of the points of criticism and another is that it is not the meaning system that is necessarily transformed (although it may be) but in human learning it is the experience itself that may be transformed. There are others, such as his concentration on meaning rather than looking at the other elements in the content of learning such as knowledge or skills. Nevertheless, Mezirow's work has made a considerable impression in the field of adult learning and he has been a major force in relating learning and meaning.

The idea of transformation underlies two other learning phenomena: 'changing one's mind' and 'conversion'. As we grow and develop we all become aware from time to time that we have made a mistake in our understanding and this might result in our changing our minds but in religious belief there is also the idea of conversion (Robertson, 1978), which is itself a complex process because it usually involves not only meaning change but emotional changes as well. It is beyond the scope of this study to explore this further here (see Robertson 1978, pp. 186–222).

But Mezirow's approach to learning and meaning is not the only one: Marton and Saljo (1984, p. 40) suggested that there are two types of approach to understanding meaning in texts: in the first the students sought to memorise the text, seeing themselves as it were, as empty vessels that had to be filled, whereas, in the second, the learners saw themselves a creators of knowledge by examining the text in relation to the world, and so on. The first approach is a 'surface approach' to meaning whereas the second is a 'deep' approach. We will return to this discussion when we examine reading and writing later in the book.

Conclusion

Meaning can also be understood in terms of 'I meant' – or 'I intended' – and as such it relates quite closely to intention and even motivation, subjects upon which we will focus in the sixteenth chapter of this book.

Meaning is, however, the final concept that we look at in the first part of this book: in common with all the other concepts it is basic to learning to be a person in society and, as we have seen, it is itself a learned phenomenon. In the second part of the book we are going to look at what the people do or have done to them in the learning processes.

References

Bellah R, Madsen R, Sullivan W, Swidle A and Tipton S (1985) *Habits of the Heart* Berkeley: University of California Press
Bruner J (1990) *Acts of Meaning* Cambridge, Mass.: Harvard University Press
Collins English Dictionary (1979) London: Collins
Durkheim E (1933[1893]) *The Division of Labor in Society* New York: Free Press
Fromm E (1949) *Man for Himself* London: Routledge
Jarvis P (1987) *Adult Learning in the Social Context* London: Croom Helm
Jarvis P (1992) *Paradoxes of Learning* San Francisco: Jossey-Bass
Jarvis P (2008) *Democracy, Lifelong Learning and the Learning Society: active citizenship in a late modern age* London: Routledge
Kingwell M (2000) *The World We Want* Toronto: Penguin, Canada
Luckmann, T (1967) *The Invisible Religion*, London: Collier-Macmillan
Macquarrie J (1973) *Existentialism* Harmondsworth: Penguin
Marton F and Saljo R (1984) Approaches to Learning in Marton *et al.* (eds) *op cit* pp. 36–55

Marton F, Hounsell D and Entwistle N (1984) (eds) *The Experience of Learning* Edinburgh: Scottish Academic Press

Mezirow J (1991) *Transformative Dimensions of Adult Learning* San Francisco: Jossey-Bass

Mezirow J (2000) Learning to Think Like an Adult in Mezirow *et al. op cit*

Mezirow J and Associates (2000) *Learning as Transformation* San Francisco: Jossey-Bass

Nelson K (2007) *Young Minds in Social Worlds* Cambridge, Mass.: Harvard University Press

Riesman D (1950) *The Lonely Crowd* New Haven: Yale University Press

Robertson R (1978) *Meaning and Change* Oxford: Basil Blackwell

Tomasello M (1999) *The Cultural Origins of Human Cognition* Cambridge, Mass.: Harvard University Press

CHAPTER 5

BEING AND HAVING

Originally published as 'Being and Having' in P. Jarvis (1992),
Paradoxes of Learning, San Francisco: Jossey-Bass, pp. 143–54.
Cross-references refer to the original publication.

The fact that human beings have both essence and existence, or mind/self within the body, has a major implication: they have the need both to be and to have. This chapter focuses on learning as a specific and basic example of this dichotomy. The first section explores the distinction between being and having, the second concentrates on being, having, and learning, and the third illustrates the discussion with special reference to education.

The distinction between being and having

The body is born into the world as a physical phenomenon, a biological mechanism, and as such has its own needs. As infants begin to develop, they reach out for things, and these attempts to possess actually occur before they have a self. Maslow (1968) places these needs in the lower strata of his hierarchy. Once the distinction between body and mind is drawn in this way, though, it is difficult to sustain the idea that a hierarchy exists at all, since his five levels of need fall into two distinct categories. The lower ones are *having* needs, whereas the needs for self-esteem and self-actualization might be conceived of as *being* needs. However, the having needs are biological ones, and unless they are initially satisfied there could be no body within which the mind and self emerge and through which they are sustained. Thus certain having needs are essential to human existence. In later life, unless these needs continue to be satisfied, the human being could become dehumanized.

It is important, therefore, to differentiate between being and having. Perhaps the clearest way to do this is to cite Fromm's (1981, p. 12) summary:

> In the having mode of existence my relationship to the world is one of possessing and owning, one in which I want to make everybody and everything, including myself, my property. . . .
>
> In the being mode of existence, we must identify two forms of being. One is in contrast to *having* . . . and means aliveness and authentic relatedness to the world. The other form of being is in contrast to *appearing* and refers to the true nature, the true reality of a person or a thing in contrast to deceptive appearances.

Not surprisingly, throughout history the being mode has been regarded as of a higher order than having. Since human beings are situated in a body that has physical needs, the satisfaction of which are necessary in order to exist, though, the being and having modes are not totally opposed to each other. There is a complex interdependency between them. But during most of the following discussion, we will treat the two modes as antithetical to illustrate their differences.

The having mode is self-explanatory in many ways, but a number of important points need to be made about it. We consider four briefly.

First, for the mind and the self to begin to emerge from the body, communicative relationships must exist between the young child and other human beings. The relationships themselves and the secondary experiences of communicative interaction are of crucial importance to the growth and development of the human essence. The significance of human relationship has already been discussed in relation to socialization and to human being and becoming. People are more important to people than are things. Objects possessed, such as beautiful works of art, can become the focus for contemplation and reflective learning can occur as a result, but the learning occurs as a result of the meditative response of the learner rather than through the possession as such; a live, dynamic relationship is never possible with things.

Second, the having mode attaches significance to things that have existence but not being, or if the phenomena actually have being, they are treated as if they are objects. Hence, to treat persons as slaves or as other kinds of possessions is to dehumanize them and treat them as if they merely have existence, which destroys the potential of the dynamic relationship. The same is true when people in the labor force are treated as cogs in a machine or as implements in the process of production. The possibility of relationship is eliminated, and the potential rewards from human interaction are lost.

Third, as Marcel (1976) points out, having always implies some act that was already over when the thing came into the possession of the person who possesses it, but being is an ever-present phenomenon.

Fourth, possession lies at the heart of contemporary Western civilization and is a fundamental assumption of capitalist economics. A person who possesses many things is often given high status. Advertising encourages people to purchase commodities they do not need, and conspicuous consumption has become a major feature of the system. This way of life has become deeply ingrained. Any other set of values has come to be regarded as deviant, if not wrong. There is a certain irony in the fact that capitalism will not function unless there is a flow of money and a continual purchasing of new commodities, since its whole philosophy is grounded in the having mode.

One of the social and political ideologies of contemporary society that has apparently not encouraged possession has been communism; in such countries private property was disallowed and public ownership lauded. (See Ryan, 1987, for a clear discussion of some of the recent thought on this topic.) However, that system still rewarded social position with the control, if not the ownership, of property – with successful party officials having their villas in the countryside and so forth – and thus it still encouraged possession. It was neither true to its own communist ideology nor did it actually embrace a system of property rights, so that it gained the advantages of neither system. It clearly failed to achieve the egalitarian outcome it espoused and also failed to gain the type of respect that the great religious thinkers and practitioners have gained through their own condemnation of possession.

Possession inevitably affects the possessor in some ways. Macquarrie (1973, pp. 87–88), summarizing Marcel's work, writes:

> To have something is not just to stand in an external relationship to it. The very having of something affects the person who has it. He becomes anxious about it and instead of having it, it begins, so to speak, to have him. There is a real danger to our humanity as the world becomes increasingly indus-trialized, computerized, automated. . . . Rising affluence brings new dangers. It leads to the acquisitive society, the rat race, the infinite desire to possess. In its relation to the world, as in so many other aspects, human existence finds itself at the centre of a tension and must survive in the face of opposing pressures.

The body does have needs, and these must be satisfied. The having mode is important for human existence, but contemporary Western society has overemphasized its importance. The tension underlined in the preceding quotation between the human being and the values of the contemporary world perhaps indicates that there should be a critical relationship between the two and that the taken-for-granted, presumptive response to the world may not always be in the best interest of humanity. It will be recalled that the culture into which individuals are socialized is biased in favor of those who exercise power and consequently toward those who support the current system. Hence, reflective, critical learning is necessary in people's relationship with the world, though the paradox is that people seek to exist in harmony with their world.

Having or possessing can therefore be detrimental to being in some respects. But, by contrast, being refers to experience – something that cannot be possessed and retained since it occurs in a particular period of time and then survives as a memory. Though people sometimes try to capture an experience, they inevitably fail since they are attempting to ensnare being within having. All experiences offer the possibility of learning and growing, and it is through these experiences that the mind and the self emerge in the first place. Being, then, is about active involvement in experience through which the human essence emerges and is nourished. In this sense, Maslow's higher-order needs reflect reality – for they are about being involved in a loving relationship, about being self-confident without being arrogant, and about self-actualization. However, the way Maslow uses these terms seems to suggest that everything revolves around the self, rather than being oriented toward active relationships that encourage mutual growth. Being is about being alive, and in that sense being is always becoming. There is always more potential to be realized, since growth need not end as long as being remains.

Being and having are, in sum, two very different approaches to life, and their emphases diverge in many ways. Because of the nature of contemporary society, having often seems to predominate. This is true even with respect to language, as will become apparent in the following section. Since the learning process is at the heart of being, it will be useful to examine it within a society that emphasizes having.

Being, having, and learning

Mind and self are learned phenomena, and so learning is at the center of the process of growth. As was pointed out above, the learning that is involved in being is active, participative, and reflective. Gadamer (1976, p. 50) suggests that "understanding . . . cannot be grasped as a simple activity of the consciousness that understands, but is itself a mode of the event of being." Learners engage in relationships with the world and with their teachers in both primary and secondary experiences and in informal, nonformal, and formal situations. They bring their own biographies to the teaching and learning situation and enter a participative dialogue; in the learning process, the learners' knowledge, skills, and attitudes become fused with the knowledge, skills, and attitudes of the teacher. The same considerations apply outside the formal classroom situation. In seeking knowledge from books, people are actively engaged in the learning process and thus are gaining insight and growing. In discussions with others, they are trying to establish an active constructive relationship in which everyone participates and from which everyone benefits. If they specialize in specific areas of knowledge, that knowledge becomes part of their being and their experience, and others will acknowledge that they are authorities, giving them credit where it is due. Authorities do not need to demonstrate their expertise to impress others; the goal is to engage in a reflective, collaborative learning process so as to enrich oneself and other people.

There is a profound difference between knowing and having knowledge. It is the difference between actively participating in the process of creating knowledge, on the one hand, and on the other hand digesting whatever others transmit. In simplest terms, it is the difference between being and having. Having knowledge can mean having a certificate in such and such a field. Or students take notes in lecture sessions instead of engaging in active participation; they have books and seek confirmation from authorities that they are correct, not different or wrong; they demonstrate that they have attended certain classes. If they are then going to learn, they often do so through memorizing, internalizing the course material in a non-reflective manner. *Knowing* can also be used in another sense – that of having knowledge as if it were a commodity. It is this that Marcel (1976, p. 83) condemns when he suggests that having is always about assimilation. He notes (1976, p. 145) that "knowing is a mode of having. The possession of a secret. Keeping it, disposing of it – and here we get back to . . . the 'shewable.' The absolute possession of a secret or a mystery – mystery being that which by its very essence I cannot dispose of. Knowledge as a mode of having is essentially communicable." Students expect to take possession of what the teacher expounds or the author has written and communicate it back on an examination. Teachers often encourage this approach; they see themselves as the fount of wisdom and demand that the learners listen and memorize. But in exercising the authority of their position, they *have* authority rather than *are* the authority.

Adult educators are frequently confronted with the results of this process. Students want handouts and other supplements so that they can go away happy because they have something tangible from the learning experience. They can then inwardly digest it – that is, learn it in a nonreflective manner. This is not to suggest that teachers should not produce handouts. Handouts can be usefully employed to get the students away from the fear of not gaining knowledge as a result of a teaching and learning session, by telling them that there will be a handout at the end and so they should feel free to engage in the debate with the teacher and not worry about trying to capture the knowledge.

Education as having or being?

Since education is a social institution, we would expect it to reflect the values of the society of which it is a part. But education involves the institutionalization of learning; from this standpoint, we might expect it to encourage the being mode. It is, in short, trapped in a dilemma: will it emphasize the having or the being mode? It is argued here that it tends to adopt the rhetoric of being but the practices of having, and that this is inevitable because of its institutional status.

Some writers clearly distinguish between two types of education – one oriented toward being and the other toward having (Jarvis, 1985). With respect to the latter approach, Freire (1972b, pp. 45–46) offers these disparaging remarks:

> Narration (with the teacher as narrator) leads the students to memorize mechanically the narrated content. Worse still, it turns them into "containers," into receptacles to be filled by the teacher. The more completely he fills the receptacles, the better a teacher he is. The more meekly the receptacles permit themselves to be filled, the better students they are.
>
> Education thus becomes an act of depositing, in which the students are the depositories and the teacher the depositor. Instead of communicating, the teacher issues communiqués and "makes deposits" which the students patiently receive, memorize, and repeat.

As "depositories," the students are then assessed to discover if they have actually retained the material. If they can repeat it nonreflectively but correctly, they are judged successful.

The final step is the awarding of credit and certificates. Modern society demands that courses culminate in credentials that demonstrate to the world that the learners have acquired specific knowledge or skills. Without the proper certificates, students cannot continue to the next level of education – becoming imprisoned in a global classroom (Illich and Verne, 1976) – and cannot obtain certain jobs. Because of the enormous importance of certification, a market has grown up around it, and education sells its wares (certificated courses) in the marketplace. Fake institutions are also cashing in; there is a market for bogus certificates and fake qualifications, often purchased at exorbitant prices from pseudoeducational institutions. Even respectable universities have to award certificates for the shortest of courses so that, through the mechanism of credit transfer, students can construct a portfolio of awards to demonstrate to a skeptical world the amount of knowledge they have. Even if they no longer possess the knowledge because they might have forgotten it or have rarely used it, it does not matter – all that counts is that they have the certificate.

The one form of education that has traditionally avoided the certification process is liberal adult education, whose goal has been to help adults pursue an enjoyable pastime, learning what they wished without examination or certification. Over the past few years, however, a growing consensus has emerged that even liberal adult education should be like the other forms of education. Institutions are increasingly offering modules for credit, and liberal adult education is being threatened by the values of a having society. The danger is that it will end up emphasizing the certificates to the detriment of the teaching and learning experience. The problem for education is that it is expected to conform to the having ethos of contemporary society, even though its philosophy might be closer to the being mode.

This is not a diatribe against certification; it is a criticism of the abuse of what is a necessary system in education. Learning occurs in the private sphere, and society is anonymous and to some extent depersonalized. People move between locations and occupations. How can applicants for a place in a course or for a job be assessed when they are not known? References can be written about the person, but they may not tell the whole story. How can potential students determine the value of courses they want to take, unless there is a reputable certificate at the end? Public certification is a guarantee of something – even if only that the learners attended a reputable educational institution, or that they once possessed the knowledge or the skills, or that they were given the opportunity to gain them by taking specific courses. Certification, then, might be important for education in the being mode as well, because the privatization of learning and the anonymity of the public world provide almost no other way of recording and communicating experience.

Freire (1972b, pp. 56–57) has this to say about education in the being mode: "Problem-posing education affirms men as beings in the process of *becoming* – as unfinished, uncompleted beings in and with a likewise unfinished reality. Indeed, in contrast to other animals who are unfinished but not historical, men know themselves to be unfinished; they are aware of their incompleteness. In this incompleteness and this awareness lie the very roots of education as an exclusively human manifestation. The unfinished character of men and the transformational character of reality necessitate that education be an on-going reality."

Education involves a dialogical relationship in which human beings communicate and share experiences, so that their human essence might stand out more fully through their learning. This is to be found in many, but by no means all, forms of adult education. In some cases, this sharing occurs between the learners working in groups, where all the participants are regarded as equal members. This equal relationship is extended to the teacher, when one is present. It is not necessary for anyone to claim special authority; people's expertise is recognized in the ordinary course of things. In groups of this kind, all the participants are encouraged to give of themselves in communicative interrelationship. Here there is no nonreflective acquisition of facts, no perennial endeavor to hold onto a body of knowledge, but a consistent attempt to become more conscious of people and the world and of their richness.

In a well-known passage, Peters (1965, p. 110) offers a similar view of education: "Education . . . can have no ends beyond itself. Its value derives from principles and standards implicit in it. To be educated is not to have arrived at a destination; it is to travel with a different view. What is required is not feverish preparation for something that lies ahead, but to work with precision, passion, and taste at worthwhile things that lie to hand." Peters goes on to relate this to the quality of life. For him, this is about being rather than having – about education providing "that touch of eternity under which endurance can pass into dignified, wry acceptance, and animal enjoyment into a quality of living" (p. 110).

These approaches are much closer to the frequently expressed humanistic philosophy of adult education than to the practices involved in educating children (although Peters's philosophy of education concentrates on early education). There are reasons for this: for instance, the system of schooling through which children pass emphasizes the having mode rather than the being one; society expects the having mode to be emphasized; adult teachers find it harder to enter a communicative relationship with a class of children than with a small group of adults, and they also find it easier and sometimes very necessary to be in authority rather than to be recognized by the class as an authority and a person. (See Kohl, 1971, for a superb example of what happens when a teacher succeeds in the being mode with thirty-six children.) Does this mean that adult education actually has a different philosophy from school education, or that andragogy is different from pedagogy?

Certainly teaching and learning in the being mode are entirely different from teaching and learning in the having one. But this does not mean that the two modes occur in different forms of education, with school education occurring in the having mode and adult education in the being mode. Education as a whole – that is, lifelong education – can take both forms; the being mode often occurs in the creation of the relationships between teacher and learners and among the learners, and the having mode when education is regarded merely as a means to an end. Hence, Knowles's (1970) original approach was clearly wrong when he separated andragogy from pedagogy on the grounds of the age of the learners, as he recognized in later situations of his books (for example, Knowles, 1980). Whether the learning occurs in the being or the having mode is not intrinsically related to the age of the learner but is determined by the situation in which it occurs. The differences between the modes tend to stem from the nature of the educational activity and from the types of relationships that are forged between teacher and learners and learners and learners and also from the forms of learning and teaching that are emphasized. If the learners are encouraged to be active participants in an exciting relationship with the teacher, the being mode comes to the fore, but if the teacher presents the material for mechanical consumption by the students, the having mode takes precedence. Obviously, this form of relationship is more feasible with small groups of adult students, which helps explain why the distinction between adult and children's education has been drawn. But, as noted, this is an artificial distinction.

Conclusion

Education is, therefore, faced with an unresolvable dilemma, and this is especially true for adult education. Education is frequently regarded as a humanistic process (Jarvis, 1983c) in which individual students learn and grow and develop. It is regarded as a major element of being – as a process through which the human essence emerges from existence in active participative relationship with others, some of whom might be experts. Yet the very nature of the society in which education occurs emphasizes the having mode and expects repetitive action and nonreflective learning so that it can produce people who can rehearse what they have acquired. As a result, education has been forced to adopt the characteristics of contemporary society. In many ways, this market approach to education is acclaimed as the most efficient and beneficial to the society as a whole. But the paradox is that it seeks to implement the lower levels of learning and to reward the having of knowledge rather than being and the higher levels of learning and human development. The higher ones remain and people still manage to grow, even though the forms of learning that influence this process most sometimes lie outside the educational institution.

The paradoxes of learning in society are quite profound, as this chapter demonstrates. The following chapter pursues this by relating learning to meaning and truth.

References

Freire P (1972) *Pedagogy of the Oppressed* (trans. M B Ramer) Harmondsworth: Penguin

Fromm E (1981) *To Have or to Be* New York: HarperCollins

Gadamer H-G (1976) *Philosophical Hermeneutics* Berkeley: University of California Press

Illich I and Verne E (1976) *Imprisoned in a Global Classroom* London: Writers and Readers Publishing Cooperative

Jarvis P (1983) *Professional Education* London: Croom Helm

Jarvis P (1985) *The Sociology of Adult and Continuing Education* London: Croom Helm

Knowles M (1980) *The Modern Practice of Adult Education* Chicago: Association Press

Kohl H (1971) *36 Children* Harmondsworth: Penguin

Macquarrie J (1973) *Existentialism* Harmondsworth: Penguin

Marcel G (1976) *Being and Having* Gloucester, Mass.: Peter Smith

Maslow A H (1968) *Towards a Psychology of Being* New York: D. Van Nostrand Company (2nd edn)

Peters R (1965) Education as Initiation in Archambault R M (ed) *Philosophical Analysis and Education* London: Routledge

Ryan A (1987) *Property* Milton Keynes: Open University Press

PART 2

LEARNING AND RELIGION/ SPIRITUALITY

CHAPTER 6

LEARNING AS A RELIGIOUS PHENOMENON?

The paradox of the question – why?

Originally published as 'Learning as a Religious Phenomenon?' in
P. Jarvis and N. Walters (eds) (1993), *Adult Education and
Theological Interpretations*, Malabar, FL: Krieger, pp. 3–16.
Cross-references refer to the original publication.

Learning has been defined by many as "a relatively permanent change in behavior that occurs as a result of practice" (Hilgard and Atkinson, 1967, ed., p. 270) and definitions, such as this one, have reflected the behaviorist practices in education whereby the teacher sets the learning objectives, operationalizes the teaching plan and expects the learner to have acquired precisely what the teacher determines by the end of the session. In precisely the same way, in the work situation, there has grown up a "scientific management" school which assumes that the actual role demands can be determined precisely and that the worker merely acquires those techniques through practice which produce the most efficient and effective performance outcomes. For many, this is their conception of learning. This is the way they perceive that their employees or their students should learn. But there are other implications to this approach, one of which provides a focus for this paper. Examine the conception of the human being implicit in it—malleable and mindless! Is this the human being that the psalmist could wax lyrical about, when he wrote:

> What is man that thou art mindful of him,
> and the son of man that thou dost care for him?
> Yet thou hast made him little less than God,
> and crowned him with glory and honour.
> Thou has given him dominion over the works of thy hands:
> thou has put all things under his feet.
>
> (Ps. 8:4–7)

However, the question posed by this paper is: which perspective seems nearer to reality about the human being? Are the majority of humankind merely cogs in a large machine or is there more to human beings than this? Is learning merely the acquisition of pre-determined knowledge and skills or is there more than this to learning?

In order to explore these questions it is necessary to examine the human condition, and thereafter to apply that analysis to the questions that have been posed.

The human condition

Human existence might be characterized as being in time (Heidegger, 1962), space, society and culture, but one of the crucial factors of human being for human beings is that being is itself an issue. Human beings cannot and do not take themselves for granted and yet their quest to understand themselves is always ultimately doomed to some form of disappointment, for however hard they search, existence seems to be full of contradictions.

> Man can only react to contradictions by annulling them through his own action; but he cannot annul existential dichotomies, although he can react to them in different ways. He can appease his mind by soothing and harmonizing ideologies. He can try to escape from his inner restlessness by ceaseless activity in pleasure or business. He can try to abrogate his freedom and turn himself into an instrument of powers outside himself, submerging his self in them. But he remains dissatisfied, anxious and restless. There is only one solution to his problem: to face the truth, to acknowledge his fundamental aloneless and solitude in a universe indifferent to his fate, to recognise that there is no power transcending him which can solve his problem for him. Man must accept the responsibility for himself and the fact that only by using his powers can he give meaning to life. But meaning does not imply certainty; indeed, the quest for certainty blocks the search for meaning. Uncertainty is the very condition to impel man to unfold his powers. If he faces the truth without panic he will recognize that there is no meaning to life except the meaning man gives his life by unfolding his powers, by living productively; and that only by constant vigilance, activity, and effort can keep us from failing in the one task that matters—the full development of our powers within the limitations set by the laws of our existence. Man will never cease to be perplexed, to wonder, and to raise new questions.
>
> (Fromm, 1949, pp. 44–45)

Here in this full passage, Fromm depicts the heart of the human condition; humankind is a restless wanderer (Fromm, 1949, p. 41), always seeking meaning for existence and knowing that every experience is meaningless, unless it has meaning given to it. Naturally this is a debatable conclusion and one which those with a deep faith might wish to dispute, but it is not one upon which this chapter dwells—for the significance of this passage in this chapter is the endless quest to discover meaning.

Throughout history every tribe and people of the world have trodden this path and sought meaning for their existence. There have grown up profound stories, beautiful myths and complex theologies, all of which have become embedded in the cultures of the peoples of the world. Yet all have started from the same point, all have posed questions about existence. At the start and the heart of every complex theology and profound myth lies a simple word—why?

Individual human beings, therefore, are not alone—"no man is an island"—and every person is a member of a society and since every society has evolved its own answers to those questions about the unknowns of human existence, these systems of meaning have become part of the cultures of the people. As children are born into a society so they go through this same human process of asking questions and gaining answers from their sociocultural environment. Every parent is aware of those perpetual "why" questions and every adolescent has been plagued by that same question. At the heart of human existence lies that question—why? Whenever this question is posed a variety of answers may be produced, many of which relate to the cultural milieu into which the questioner is born, some of which may be regarded as religious and others as nonreligious.

Thus it may be seen that much human learning starts from this question. Perhaps it is the genesis of all knowledge and belief, and that all religious systems also start here. The chapter seeks to map a theory of learning that parallels it to the religious quest of humankind and it has seven parts: the birth of the self; why?; creation of order; conversion; growth and development; utopia; molding the human mind. Finally, there is a brief concluding discussion in which it is pointed out that this chapter seeks only to relate human learning to some profound questions of human existence rather than to produce definitive answers. Before embarking upon these issues it is necessary to clarify one major point. Religion, as a concept and as used in this chapter, refers to religious systems in general rather than Christianity in particular, although many of the references here are to Christian thought, and religiosity is the individual belief system that has emerged as a result of trying to answer some of these questions of human existence. Indeed, religiosity was defined elsewhere as a system of meaning about existence which relates it to a perceived general order of the cosmos (Jarvis, 1983).

The birth of the self

The human being is not born with a self. Peter Berger (1966, p. 117) makes the point that "identity is not something 'given,'" while Mead (Strauss, 1964) highlights the fact that the self emerges through social interaction. It might be clearer to suggest that children are born with brains but not fully developed minds. It is through interaction and the use of language and gesture that the mind is formed and only then can the self begin to emerge. This has been more fully discussed elsewhere (Jarvis, 1987), but note the significance of the idea of word. It is through social interaction that questions of meaning are posed and answers provided, so that individuals gradually acquire their own system of meaning, or as Luckmann (1967, p. 50) suggests:

> . . . human organisms do not construct "objective" and moral universes of meaning from scratch—they are born into them. This means that human organisms normally transcend their biological nature by internalizing a historically given universe of meaning, rather than constructing universes of meaning.

He argues that human beings become selves by constructing with others an "objective" and moral universe of meaning and in so doing transcend their biological nature. The significance of this is that with the birth of the mind and the emergence of the self, the human being is no longer merely a biological organism. This is the wonder of life and birth; it is the birth of something that is not only biological but intangible—almost spiritual. Luckmann develops this point in a very significant manner by arguing that this process of transcending the human being's own biological nature and becoming a self is fundamentally a religious process, but it is also a learned process. Hence at the heart of one of the most fundamental elements in the birth of every human being there lies a process of learning which might also be regarded as religious in itself.

According to the interactionist school of thought the self is a product of social interaction and the birth of the self is related to the beginnings of the acquisition of a system of meaning. The earliest belief system is a learning process and is itself involved in the formation of the mind from whence develops the self—which, for Luckmann, is a religious process.

Why?

Human beings do not go through the whole of life asking questions, rather the opposite. Schutz and Luckmann (1974, p. 7) write:

> Every implication within the life-world goes on within the milieu of affairs which have already been explicated, within a reality that is fundamentally and typically familiar. I trust the world as it has been known by me up until now will continue further and that consequently the stock of knowledge obtained from my fellow-men and formed from my own experiences will continue to preserve its fundamental validity. . . . From this assumption follows the further and fundamental one: that I can repeat my past successful acts. So long as the structure of the world can be taken to be constant, as long as my previous experience is valid, my ability to operate upon the world in this and that manner remains in principle preserved.

From the above it may be seen that many experiences of life do not result in any form of learning. Indeed, nonlearning is an important feature of human living and without it there could be no social stability (Jarvis, 1987, pp. 133–146). However, time and tide await no man and human beings change as they grow— they have different questions of meaning; society and culture change and their questions change with those changes; experiences change and the questions emerge yet again, why?

Many scholars, for example, Mezirow (1981), Jarvis (1987) *inter alia*, regard this process of questioning as the beginning of all learning, for if the meaning is taken for granted rarely does the experience evoke a question. For Mezirow it is a disorientating dilemma and for Jarvis it is disjuncture. Individuals enter every experience with their own biography, that is with a stock of knowledge, beliefs, attitudes and values gained as a result of previous experiences, and if that stock of knowledge and belief is sufficient then they enter a meaningful situation and are able to operate on the world in a nonlearning manner. But when that reservoir is insufficient then there is a disjuncture between the biography and the experience. It is the experience of disjuncture which stimulates the question— why? The question constitutes the start of the learning process—for once asked it demands an answer. Sometimes the question can be answered from the perspective of one of the disciplines of knowledge, sometimes there is an ideological response and sometimes the answer comes from another form of belief or religious system.

The significance of the question cannot be lost in any consideration of religion, since it is that question that occurs throughout life in this quest for ultimate meaning. While humankind longs for stability and even seems to assume that the static is the normal, in fact the world is dynamic and change is endemic and the human being is a restless wanderer within it for about three score years and ten, or a little longer. For most people, seeking to understand their existence is an intermittent, but lifelong, quest—at times they take it for granted but at other times that question emerges again—why? why? Questions are asked about the past and metahistorical past, about the future and the metahistorical future, about the present, about the self, people and the cosmos (Jarvis, 1983). All are questions about the meaning of human experience. But the ability to ask questions about these "unknowns" neither makes an individual religious nor describes the phenomenon of religion. It simply depicts the human condition. To have answers, however, is the expression of people's religiosity.

Human beings have to make sense of their experiences—for human beings are meaning seeking animals, so that not only is the self formed through this meaning-seeking process, people sustain their humanity through it. It is at the root of all knowledge and all belief. Being able to provide an answer to those questions of meaning indicates both a belief system and that the thinker has at least tried to respond to those questions. It is not knowledge, it is belief—but in order to be meaningful it has to be learned. If there were no genuine questioning there could be no authentic human being. It was William Temple who wrote somewhere that if eating of the forbidden fruit from the tree of knowledge led to a fall—then it was a fall upwards!

The creation of order

Religious systems of the world have all tried to impose order on the apparent chaos of creation. The Genesis story is not alone in the Old Testament that seeks to do that, the abominations of Leviticus are also a system of order imposed by early thinkers upon an apparently unstructured world (Douglas, 1966). Trying to impose meaning upon an apparently meaningless world is part of that human condition described so cogently by Fromm and cited above. But what happens when the meaninglessness of a situation becomes apparent and oppressive? What happens when events seem disordered and the problems of life become apparent? That question is posed again—why?

The question leads to the start of the learning process but in a great deal of recent writing about human learning the process of reflection has become a central concern (Mezirow, 1981, Boud *et al.*, 1985, Jarvis, 1987). However, it is perhaps significant that many years ago Dewey (1958 ed., p. 66) wrote:

> When thinking is successful, its career closes in transforming the disordered into the orderly, the mixed-up into the distinguished or placed, the unclear and ambiguous into the defined and unequivocal, the disconnected into the systematized. . . .
>
> Reflective inquiry moves in each particular case from differences to unity; from indeterminate and ambiguous position to clear determination, from confusion and disorder to system. When thought in a given case has reached its goal of organized totality, of definite relations of distinctly placed elements . . .

Here, then, Dewey is suggesting that as a result of reflection order is created out of chaos. Like the early thinkers who suggested theologies that related the imposition of ordered meaning upon a disordered physical cosmos, so the reflective learning process does the same on a disordered subjective experience of the world. The question is answered and a system of meaning is created out of disorder and the parallel between the biblical and the learning process is complete. Reflection—meditation—is at the heart of the process of religious growth and further reference is made to this below.

Conversion

Over recent years the work of Mezirow has been significant in adult learning theory and it is to one of his earlier papers on this topic that attention is focused here. In it he (1978) first discussed the idea of perspective transform which he (1978, p. 101) describes in the following manner:

> A meaning perspective refers to the structure of cultural assumptions within which new experience is assimilated to—and transformed by—one's past experience.

Mezirow's position and the thesis of this paper are close in as much as the personal meaning perspective is cultural and assimilated by the individual within the process of socialization. It is by using the biographical store of culture that enables the person to give meaning to an experience but also when a major life change is experienced it enables the learner to see experiences differently, that is, to derive a different sense of meaning from them or impose a different sense of meaning upon them. However, through the process of maturation human beings have a variety of experiences some of which might intergrate creatively with the previous biography but sometimes a process of restructuring occurs. Mezirow suggests that it occurs in three stages: alienation from previous perspectives, reframing and reconceptualizing and, finally, re-integration.

Mezirow admits that he was greatly influenced by the work of Paulo Freire who also regarded learning as transformation, but he used the term *conscientization*, which refers to "the process in which men, not as recipients but as knowing subjects, achieve a deepening awareness both of the sociocultural reality which shapes their lives and of their capacity to transform that reality" (Freire, 1972b, 51n). But Freire's work arose within the context of liberation theology (Gutierrez, 1974) with its exciting synthesis of Christian thought and Marxism.

Indeed it was Karl Marx who considered that because of the structures of society, the socialization process resulted in a false class consciousness. This has led critical theorists, such as Habermas (1972), to postulate that people acquire a false consciousness and one of the main forms of learning is emancipatory learning, which is the process of "emancipation from seemingly 'natural' constraint" (Habermas, 1972, p. 311).

Thus it may be seen that in learning theory people can come to themselves, see the world differently and be emancipated from the structures into which they are born. Or, in other words, "he came to himself" (Luke, 15:17), he saw the world differently and changed direction, which is the meaning of the Greek work μετανοω, to change one's mind, to see things differently or to be converted.

Growth and development

For Dewey (1916), education is growth. By this he meant that life itself is a process in which human beings develop and grow because it is a process of having new experiences, new learning and continuous transformation of experiences and systems of meaning. There is a volume of literature on the stages of adult development and it is significant that learning is not always seen as crucial because it is taken for granted within the process. Gradually there is also emerging a literature of faith development in which Fowler (1981) relates faith development to the quest for meaning. At the very heart of growth lies certain forms of learning—learning that is reflective, learning that is encouraging human autonomy and responsibility in thought and action. Indeed, learning from the experiences of living is at the very foundation of growth. Learning is growth and maturation. There can be no maturation without learning, although there can be physical growth merely through imbibing food and drink. But "man shall not live by bread alone but by every word that proceeds from the mouth of God" (Matt. 4:4). That is, man is matured by learning, and in this case, it is learning from the established religious answers to those questions of meaning.

It was pointed out earlier that an intrinsic part of some learning experiences is reflection/meditation and there are many accounts in religious literature of the mystics who spent their time contemplating the mysteries of the world in order to mature and seek holiness. For other religious people, contemplation is not the answer to Christian maturity—living a good life is more important and for them there may apparently be little time in their lives to spend in contemplation. However, recent learning theorists have begun to recognize that there is a process of reflection-in-action (Schon, 1983), which itself suggests that the good life lived may also be underpinned with the process of learning from experience. Freire (1972a, pp. 56–57) suggests:

> Problem-posing education affirms men as beings in the process of *becoming*—as unfinished, uncompleted beings in and with a likewise unfinished reality. Indeed, in contrast to other animals who are unfinished, but not historical, men know themselves to be unfinished; they are aware of their incompleteness and this awareness lies at the very roots of education as an exclusively human manifestation. The unfinished character of men and the transformational character of reality necessitate that education be an ongoing activity.
>
> (Freire's italics)

For Freire, then, a particular form of education, and of learning, is important for the growth and development of the human being, so that the human being can be and become in this world.

Utopia

What should be the outcome of learning? Perhaps the quotation from Paulo Freire (1972a) begins to provide an answer when he discusses the idea of an unfinished reality. Elsewhere, he (1972b, p. 51) continues with this theme when he writes:

> It is as conscious beings that men are not only *in* the world, but *with* the world, together with other men. Only men, as 'open' beings, are able to achieve the complex operation of simultaneously transforming the world by their own action and grasping and expressing the world's reality in their creative language.
>
> (Freire's italics)

For Freire, human beings have both to grasp and understand creatively this complex reality of the world but also they have to transform it, to humanize it in the way that "it reveals the presence of men" (ibid., p. 55) who have grown and are capable of creating a utopia on earth. This, then, is the human ideal—throughout history humankind has looked to the future, a metahistorical future, when the world will be utopian—be it heaven on earth, the Kingdom of God or the classless society.

Molding humankind

There is a paradox to this analysis which is contained in this final section. Once the self has formed and the mind become a relatively independent entity it is able to contemplate the very process by which it was formed. It is able to be critical of the very culture that has made it what it is and being itself becomes problematic. The restless search for meaning has begun, but for others there is another process: if there are potential learners then there might even be teachers. Often they start with another approach to learning; Freire calls it the banking approach to education and elsewhere it has been called "education from above" (Jarvis, 1985). This is when the information to be learned is presented to people in a fixed curriculum and in an authoritative manner. Then, the learning does not start from disjuncture or from questions of why, then there need be no reflection, only an endeavor to memorize what has been given.

Much education is like this and the processes which have been described above may be viewed from a different perspective. There is no disjuncture until it is deliberately created, there is no question before an answer is given, there is no freedom to reflect, only the opportunity to memorize, and there is no independent growth, only an acceptance of the answers which are provided. The freedom of the quest for meaning is replaced by a certainty that is provided by others which as Fromm suggests might actually intrude into the quest and hinder it. But as he (1984 ed.) writes elsewhere, there is a fear of freedom and a need for authority in many people and so they welcome the answers that are provided and sometimes they cling to them. This is not to suggest that there is not a place for teachers—there certainly is—but the role might require some form of reconceptualization within the context of humankind's quest for meaning.

Some analysts see this as a process of cultural and social reproduction (Bourdieu and Passeron, 1977), and reproduction is a much lesser form of creation if it is creative at all. The outcome is a molded person. But this raises questions about the nature and morality of teaching, which is being considered in another paper. Since oftentimes teaching is an imposition of thoughts and ideas upon another person and since they do not necessarily stem from the learner's questioning process, they have to be presented with care, but without care and consideration the teaching process might well be regarded as one of symbolic violence (Bourdieu and

Passeron, 1977). Then it is the process of invading the person in order to mold and reproduce a person, like everybody else, so that people fit into the machine—cogs in a complicated machine—which was part of the question raised at the outset of this paper.

All who proclaim, whether teacher or preacher, have to be aware of this criticism and also be aware that in seeking to mold individuals, a very dangerous and responsible undertaking has been embarked upon: the making of the person in the image of the person. But in order to do it either learning has to be seen from within the behaviorist approach or the person has to be seen as mindless and malleable and irresponsible.

Conclusion

This paper started with a question: to what extent is learning itself a religious process and that question must now be answered. Is learning a religious phenomenon? Clearly it may be but in some cases it may not be. Perhaps it is important to separate the elements in order to elaborate on this conclusion. Learning has two elements: a process and a content. The process might be regarded as religious in certain situation, irrespective of whether the content is religious or not. However, there may be times within a religious context that the teaching and learning process may not be religious, even though the content may be. Such a conclusion raises other issues and just two of these are touched upon here.

It is clear from the above discussion that learning is fundamentally about the human being and, therefore, such definitions of learning that do not take the human person into account contain implications for humanity that require a great deal of consideration. This raises fundamental questions about the nature of some of the most widely cited definitions of learning itself and about many of the practices of teaching and learning.

One other point that needs to be made is that because learning is about the achievement of personhood and even utopian ideals, it requires a great deal of consideration from those who purport to speak on behalf of religious organizations—but as yet, unfortunately, there is no theology of learning.

In order to live life to the full human beings have to learn that underlying all meaningful living lies learning and the search for meaning is itself a learning quest, one that might be inhibited if answers that claim a degree of certainty are taught, discovered or professed. This is one of the religious paradoxes of learning and so the question—why?—may never be answered with certainty, if human beings are to achieve the fullness of their own humanity.

References

Berger, P. 1966, *Invitation to Sociology*. Harmondsworth, Penguin.
Boud, D., Keogh, R., and Walker, D. 1985, *Reflection: Turning Experience into Learning*. London, Kogan Page.
Bourdieu, P. and Passeron, J-C. 1977, *Reproduction—in Education, Society and Culture*. London, Sage.
Dewey, J. 1916, *Democracy and Education*. New York, The Free Press.
Dewey, J. 1958, *Experience and Nature*. New York, Dover Publications.
Douglas, M. 1966, *Purity and Danger*. Harmondsworth, Penguin.
Fowler, J. W. 1981, *Stages of Faith*. New York, Harper & Row.
Freire, P. 1972a, *Pedagogy of the Oppressed*. Harmondsworth, Penguin.

Freire, P. 1972b, *Cultural Action for Freedom*. Harmondsworth, Penguin.
Fromm, E. 1949, *Man for Himself*. London, Routledge & Kegan Paul.
Fromm, E. 1984, *The Fear of Freedom*. London, ARK Books.
Gutierrez, G. 1974, *A Theology of Liberation*. London, SCM Press.
Habermas, J. 1972, *Knowledge and Human Interests*. London, Heinemann.
Heidegger, M. 1962, *Being and Time*. London, SCM Press.
Hilgard, E. R. and Atkinson, R. C. 1967, *Introduction to Psychology*. New York, Harcourt, Brace & World, Inc.
Holy Bible. Revised Standard Version. London, Nelson.
Jarvis, P. 1983, Religiosity: Man's Responses to the Problem of Meaning, *Bulletin of the Institute of Worship and Religious Architecture*. Birmingham, University of Birmingham.
Jarvis, P. 1985, *The Sociology of Adult and Continuing Education*. London, Croom Helm.
Jarvis, P. 1987, *Adult Learning in the Social Context*. London, Croom Helm.
Luckmann, T. 1967, *Invisible Religion*. London, Collier-Macmillan.
Mezirow, J. 1978, Perspective Transformation in *Adult Education*, Vol. XXVIII, No. 2.
Schon, D. 1983, *The Reflective Practitioner*. New York, Basic Books.
Schutz, A. and Luckmann, T. 1974, *Everyday Structures of the Life World*. London, Heinemann.
Strauss, A. ed. 1964, *George Herbert Mead on Social Psychology*. Chicago, University of Chicago Press.

CHAPTER 7

THE SPIRITUAL DIMENSION OF HUMAN LEARNING

Originally published as 'The Spiritual Dimension of Human Learning' in R. Mark *et al.* (eds) (2007), *Proceedings of SCUTREA Conference*, Belfast: School of Education, pp. 238–45. Cross-references refer to the original publication.

In this chapter I want to argue that learning is an aspect of the human condition and that religion is a reflection of this condition so that we all have the potential to acquire spiritual answers to our human questions but since I want to differentiate the spiritual from spiritualism, it is important from the outset to clarify our terms and to contextualise the argument and so the first part of this paper sets to scene. Thereafter, we examine a number of aspects of human experience from which we can learn but for which we cannot discover empirical answers.

Setting the scene

While the terms religion and spiritual are separate concepts they are frequently used in an interchangeable manner and so we start by exploring the definition of religion. Fundamentally, there are a number of ways of defining religion in the most general rather than in confessional terms: two of which predominate – which might be called functionalist and existential.

The functionalist definition of religion is epitomised by Emile Durkheim (1915, p. 47):

> A religion is a unified system of beliefs and practices relative to sacred things, that is to say, things set apart and forbidden – beliefs and practices which unite into a single moral community called a Church, all those who adhere to them.

This functionalist definition has come in for considerable criticism in recent years for many reasons, but mainly because functionalism has itself been under attack, e.g. functionalist definitions only include those elements of the phenomenon that perform the functions specified in the definition. Consequently, with the decline in some forms of institutionalised religion – a single community – fundamental to this definition, it is argued that religion itself has declined whereas we actually find religion at the heart of many agendas from those of George Bush and other forms of fundamentalism, to the Christian efforts to overcome apartheid in South Africa and the Muslim efforts to halt westernisation in the Middle East. Nevertheless, this is a definition that faith communities can accept.

However, there is another way of approaching religion and this can be seen in the work of Max Weber (see Gerth and Wright Mills, 1948, pp. 267–359) where religion is treated as an existential phenomenon. In many ways this approach is epitomised by such writers as Berger (1967, p. 26) who suggests that 'religion is a human enterprise by which a sacred cosmos is constructed'. Kolakowski (1982, p. 194 – cited from Bauman, 1998, p. 58) also adopted a similar existentialist perspective when he suggested that religion is 'the awareness of human insufficiency, it is lived in the admission of weakness'. There is a problem with this latter type of approach that is typified by a 'god of the gaps' philosophy but if we accept that the human condition is one in which we will never have empirical answers for all our questions although we might try to find rational ones, then we can see that such a problem is misplaced. This might be seen to be part of the post-modern agenda yet we might claim with Milbank (1992, p. 37) that not only is there

> no 'purely human' space which stands disclosed once we are free of the burden of religious illusion . . . (but) a more important consideration may be that there is no purely *secular* space, outside of constitutive opposition of this term to that of 'the sacred'.

Basically, religion, according to existentialist approaches is any coherent set of answers to the questions that cause us ultimate concern. This definition suggests that all human beings are potentially religious, even if they are not committed believers of any creed, but such a definition does give rise to the conceptual problem of the spiritual.

The *Concise Oxford Dictionary* offers four similar definitions of the spiritual:

- of or concerning the spirit as opposed to matter;
- concerned with sacred or religious things; holy; divine; inspired (the spiritual life; spiritual songs);
- (of the mind etc.) refined, sensitive; not concerned with the material;
- (of a relationship etc.) concerned with the soul or spirit etc., not with external reality (his spiritual home).

While all of these definitions seek to capture the idea of the spiritual, they actually omit the precise element that concerns me here, which is its relationship to personal knowledge. In this sense, spiritual knowledge is knowledge that cannot be proven by empirical scientific methods but may be legitimated through both rational argument and pragmatic life style. This perspective is almost captured by the definition of the term spirit: 'the intelligent non-physical part of a person' (*Concise Oxford Dictionary*). One implication of this approach to the spiritual is that many so-called New Age spiritualities (see Woodhead and Heelas, 2000, pp. 110–168) can be included within it although the emphasis on rational argument and pragmatic life style also excludes some of them.

This meaning of 'spiritual' is individual and captures not only knowledge but also attitudes, beliefs and ethical values and it is not only cognitive but also emotive (Otto, 1927), and so there is a sense in which it also captures the idea of human volition and reflects our subjective identity: it is individualistic and subjective and overlaps with the concept of religion. But such approaches to religion as Berger's can incorporate both an individual spiritual and a social – a public and a private – understanding of religion. And as only certain forms of traditional institutionalised religion – public religion – have apparently declined, although even this is debatable (see Bernstein 2005, pp. 95–119), the emphasis on spirituality is a clear demonstration of the significance of the private in post-modern society and also the fact that so-called material and scientific claims do not provide answers to many questions life raised for most individuals so that the so-called secular space has actually been occupied by humanist, even spiritual, answers.

Religion, private or public, ultimately begins with the person and the person's response to the questions of human living – it is existential. In precisely the same way, human learning is an existential phenomenon in which learning is seen as the process by which individuals give or are given an explanation of the disjunctural experiences (those in which the current level of understanding does not allow a taken-for-granted response to a current experience) of everyday life. In this way they are learned explanations, transformations of any individual experience into knowledge and so on. Experiences occur in two different types: primary experiences occur through the senses and secondly experiences are cognitive. They both occur at the intersection of individuals' inner life-world with the wider social or empirical world and when they are unable to take the external world for granted and act in an almost unthinking manner. It is this that I have called disjuncture and it is the point at which learning begins. This can occur at any stage in the life span, although young children probably experience more disjunctural situations, especially primary ones, than do older persons for whom the majority of experiences may be cognitive.

Lifelong learning is:

> The combination of processes throughout a life time whereby the whole person – body (genetic, physical and biological) and mind (knowledge, skills, attitudes, values, emotions, beliefs and senses) – experiences social situations, the perceived content of which is then transformed cognitively, emotively or practically (or through any combination) and integrated into the individual person's biography resulting in a continually changing (or more experienced) person.
>
> (Jarvis 2006, p. 134)

In a sense, we are dealing with the human condition, which is one that cannot be fully understood by rational thought or empirical/scientific research – but a part of that condition is that it demands answers to the questions that arise from existence itself. In this sense, it can be argued that curiosity is innate – all children, for instance, go through a period of asking the question 'Why?' An aspect of the human condition is that we are not born with answers to the questions of our existence and so, as part of our humanity, we seek to discover them – some of which may be empirical and provable whilst others have no empirical answer but they may well be rational and pragmatic, so that I want to differentiate those explanations that have empirical or potentially have empirical explanations from those which may never have empirical answers, which I want to call spiritual. Here I concede that this is not a clearly demarcated division, it is a fuzzy line, so that disputes may arise at this point as to whether some answers should be included in the one or the other side of the hypothetical line, but what is clear is that there are 'answers' on both sides of the line! In all cases we learn from the experiences of our human condition and that some elements of the process of learning can give rise to spiritual answers as well as scientific ones. In the following section I want to explore five of these elements.

The spiritual dimensions of human learning

In this section I want to explore: the idea of learning itself; disjuncture and experience; aspects of reflection; meaning; self-identity.

Human learning

It is almost impossible to conceptualise a human being who has never learned since learning epitomises our humanity and, in a similar manner, it is as impossible to think of a time when the human being stops learning. Learning is intrinsic to our humanity – it is world-forming (Heidegger cited from Agamben, 2002, p. 51), but, as Luckmann (1967) suggests, when we do transcend our biological nature then a religious experience occurs. In this sense our learning is religious. But this raises another question – if we continue to grow and develop as a result of our learning, then humanity is an unfinished project and so we are confronted with an unanswerable question when we ask: what is the end of our learning? What then is the end of our humanity? Why are we here? Are we here just to keep on learning? No answer, secular or sacred, can provide a satisfying response to these questions and so if we ask them, we are confronted with an unanswerable: a void that reflects the human condition itself. This 'nothingness' points us beyond the scientific and empirical to perhaps a spiritual space, but once it has done this we can learn little more about the unfathomable mystery of human learning itself.

Disjuncture and experience

Our lives comprise a series of experiences made up in such a way that our biography appears as continuous experience added to by each unique episode of learning which we call an experience. But each of these unique episodes begins with the same type of question that we posed in the previous paragraph: Why has this occurred? How do I do this? What does this mean? And so on. It can be cognitive, emotional or a combination of the two: it is this that I call disjuncture. While we learn to live with our ultimate disjunctural questions we are frequently confronted with less ultimate ones that stimulate our learning or which leave us in a state of having learned once again that we do not know all the answers to our questions. Consequently, we can see that it is disjuncture itself that drives learning – it is emptiness and void that underlie our need to learn, for our learning is the continuous attempt to establish harmony between our experience and our understanding of the world. In this sense, it reflects our need to discover answers that enable us to live both in harmony with our environment and with ourselves. But we sometimes feel the need to reach out beyond our taken-for-granted, beyond our everyday, since there are still more things to learn and to do – for a paradox of our responding to our disjunctural experiences is that we are immediately confronted with new disjunctures – for life is a journey to we know not where.

Experience is a problematic concept since we have both primary and secondary experiences – primary ones are sense experiences and secondary ones are cognitive. Each of the five senses (sight, smell, sound, taste and touch) can be the start of a learning experience. Children seek to give meaning to their sense experiences and we might wonder why they do this since no fact or artefact has intrinsic meaning, but as we have pointed out already the very process of human learning is an element of the human condition in which we endeavour to give meaning to the apparently meaninglessness. Children give names to the artefacts with which they play which are the names approved by our culture, but it is these sense experiences that can take us beyond the cognitive to the emotional: What a gorgeous sound! How beautiful is this scene! What a tranquil moment! And so on. In these situations the experience is disjunctural because the beauty, tranquillity, etc., take us outside of our taken-for-granted world and we are confronted with the extraordinary – something that has no meaning or explanation in itself but it is something so extraordinary that we want to hang on to it for as long as we can – a magic moment – yet, paradoxically, we know that we can give no empirical meaning to it.

It is with experience itself that was James' (1960) starting point for religious experience – 'individual men in their solitude'. What James is saying here is that these experiences occur to the individual not that meaning is given to them in isolation from previous knowledge and we do not have to be a mystic isolated in the desert somewhere to have them but we do need the time to concentrate upon the mysteries the experience, a process that Crawford (2005) referred to as attentive experiencing.

Reflection

It is here that attentive experiencing becomes contemplation – a form of reflective learning that I have discussed in all my models of learning from the very first (Jarvis, 1987). But that reflection need not be the cold rational learning of modernity; it might well be wonder at the mystery of the experience (Otto, 1927), the admiration, even the worshipful attitude, of the believer. Reflective learning can take the learners outside of themselves providing that they have the time to think about their experience – a point that Crawford makes very strongly. Through reflection we learn but our answers might merely reveal that the world in which we are learning is itself a mystery that is slowly being uncovered by science but that beauty, awe, wonder are emotions that can take us beyond the scientific to make us aware of the non-material dimensions of human existence.

Meaning

Learning is a process of meaning making but writers, like Mezirow (1991), regard it as a process of transforming meaning while I regard learning as a process of transforming experience and giving it meaning as well as transforming of meaning into new meaning. The search for meaning is a paradoxical experience (Jarvis, 1992) from the moment we discover a meaning it leads to new questions, and so on. As soon as we begin the endeavour we realise that there is no intrinsic meaning to existence itself and that we have to give it meaning – something that has been recognised from time immemorial. In the creation myth, recorded just a few hundred years before the beginning of the Christian era, Adam gave names to the animals or to interpret the myth human-kind gave meaning to the world. Every meaning that we produce gives rise to further questions about Being itself for, like learning, the human condition is always a journey that appears to have no end. Meaning is transient and a matter of belief since there is no empirical answer to the question of meaning itself.

Self-identity

The outcome of every learning experience is that it is incorporated into our identities: through our learning we are creating our biographies. We are contin-ually becoming – an existential being: but what we are becoming and why we are becoming remain the problematics of existence itself. Our identity is neither an empirical nor a scientific phenomenon – it is not intrinsic to our body but is constructed as a result of our being and acting and from our learning. Indeed, we become selves but Chalmers (1996), amongst other philosophers, concludes that the selves that we have are not merely psychological selves residing in the brain but that there is a metaphysical self that occurs beyond it. Significantly, once we enter the debate about the brain and the mind, some of the more 'scien-tific' theories of learning, such as behaviourism and information processing, appear unsustainable philosophically. To be able to claim an identity is to make a spiritual statement for 'I' have become myself as a result of my learning.

Amongst the four aims of lifelong learning in the European Commission (2001) policy document is that of fulfilling our human potential: one that is rarely discussed in depth since the word 'potential' is itself a problem. Potential seems to suggest that there is an innate set of abilities that can be drawn out from us as we learn but it is a restrictive concept. But the nature of our humanity is potentiality itself (Agamben, 1990, p. 42). If we can keep on learning we can transcend totality, in Levinas' (1991) sense, and he argues that in relationship with others, which is the beginning of religion, we can learn to reach towards infinity:

> To approach the other in conversation is to welcome his expression, in which at each instance he overflows the idea a thought would carry away with it. It is therefore to *receive* from the Other beyond the capacity of the I which means exactly: to have the idea of infinity. But this also means: to be taught. The relation with the Other, or Conversation, is a non-allergic relation; but in as much as it is welcomed this conversation is teaching (enseignment). Teaching is not reducible to maieutics; it comes from the exterior and brings me more than I contain. In its non-violent transitivity the very epiphany of the face is produced.
>
> (Levinas, 1991, p. 51 – italics in original)

So then in a learning relationship we can transcend ourselves and reach towards infinity.

Conclusion

Learning is more than the change of behaviour or the transformation of meaning as a result of experience; it is the transformation of the experience itself and maybe also its meaning – it is fundamental to human living and being; it is becoming itself and this it points us to a mystery that is Being itself and so it is a religious or spiritual process.

References

Agamben G (1990) *The Coming Community* Minneapolis: University of Minneapolis Press
Agamben G (2002) *The Open* Stanford: Stanford University Press
Bauman Z (1998) Post-Modern Religion? In Heelas P (ed) *Religion, Modernity and Post-Modernity* Oxford: Blackwell
Berger P (1967) *The Social Reality of Religion* London: Faber & Faber
Bernstein R (2005) *The Abuse of Evil* Cambridge: Polity Press
Berry P and Wernick A (eds) *Shadow of Spirit: Post-modernism and Religion* London: Routledge
Chalmers D (1996) *The Conscious Mind* Oxford: Oxford University Press
Concise Oxford Dictionary (1996) Oxford: Oxford University Press (CD ROM)
Crawford J (2005) *Spiritually Engaged Knowledge* Aldershot: Ashgate
Durkheim E (1915) The *Elementary Forms of Religious Life* London: George Allen & Unwin
European Commission (2001) *Making a European Area of Lifelong Learning a Reality* Brussels; European Commission COM (2001) 678 final
Gerth H and Wright Mills C (1948) *From Max Weber: Essays in Sociology* London: Routledge & Kegan Paul
Heidegger M (1962) *Being and Time* New York: Harper & Row
James W (1960) *Varieties of Religious Experience* London: Fontana
Jarvis P (1987) *Adult Learning in the Social Context* London: Croom Helm
Jarvis P (1992) *Paradoxes of Learning* San Francisco: Jossey-Bass
Jarvis P (2006) *Towards a Comprehensive Theory of Human Learning* London: Routledge
Kolakowski L (1982) *Religion: If There is no God . . . On God, The Devil, Sin and Other Worries of the So-called Philosophy of Religion* London: Fontana
Levinas, E (1991[1969]) *Totality and Infinity* AH Dordrecht: Kluwer
Luckmann T (1967) *Invisible Religion* London: Macmillan
Mezirow J (1991) *Transformative Dimensions of Adult Learning* San Francisco: Jossey-Bass
Milbank J (1992) The Post-modern Agenda in Berry P and Wernick A (eds) *Shadow of Spirit: Post-modernism and Religion* London: Routledge
Otto R (1927) *The Idea of the Holy* Harmondsworth: Penguin
Woodhead L and Heelas P (eds) (2000) *Religion in Modern Times* Oxford: Blackwell

PART 3

LEARNING AND DOING

CHAPTER 8

LEARNING TO BE AN EXPERT
Competence development and expertise

Originally published as 'Learning to Be an Expert and Competence Development' in K. Illeris (2009), *International Perspectives on Competence Development*, London: Routledge, pp. 99–109. Cross-references refer to the original publication.

An expert is one who 'has extensive skill or knowledge in a particular field' or someone who is 'skilful or knowledgeable' (*Collins English Dictionary* 1979). Perhaps the dictionary should also have offered the possibility that an expert is both skilful and knowledgeable. Yet it would be true to say that for a number of years the word 'expert' has fallen into something like disrepute as terms such as 'competence' have dominated the vocabulary of political correctness. On the other hand, in the circles of Human Resource Development, 'expertise' seems to be more centrally placed than 'competence', at least in the USA (Swanson 2001).

But we have all been witnesses to deskilling as the world of technology has intruded into the worlds of production and service. It has changed the nature of work and, therefore, of work preparation. Even Lyotard (1984: 48) wrote about higher education and the higher professions:

> In the context of delegitimation, universities and institutions of higher learning are called upon to create skills, and no longer ideals – so many doctors, so many teachers in a given discipline, so many engineers, so many administrators, etc. The transmission of knowledge is no longer designed to train an elite capable of guiding the nation towards its emancipation, but to supply the system with players capable of acceptably fulfilling their roles at the pragmatic posts required by its institutions.

But, despite this emphasis, we have not destroyed the need for experts, although we have wrongly downplayed it in recent years, as I want to argue here. If we carefully examine the new workforce, we can see that there are many who have been deskilled, those whom Reich (1991) called the routine production workers, whose employment involves operating technology that has removed the skill from the production processes; they can be trained to operate the machinery and with every new piece of technology they can be updated and once they have learned it, then they go and operate it. They are the flexible workforce since they can be trained to operate almost any piece of machinery. In addition, those who do the routine manual and service but non-technological jobs also need to be competent and can be trained to be so. But there are still other types of workers who have just as great a need of expertise (both knowledge and skills) as they have ever had, and there are at least three types of worker who fall into this category: the professionals, the crafts and trades people and those who work with people (managers and sales people). This is not a matter of dividing the workforce into those who need knowledge and those who need skills – it is about dividing it between those who need expertise and those who need competence. Both of these may be understood as a potential – for work and for life in general, but whereas competence has more the nature of a general potential in a broader field, expertise is rather involving specific knowledge and skills in a specific subject or area. My concern in this chapter is with those who need expertise and I want to focus on three aspects underlying the process of becoming an expert – the nature of knowledge, practice and learning – and in the final section I want to examine some implications of this for vocational education.

The nature of knowledge

Knowledge has been traditionally regarded as theoretical, objective and an unchanging truth, but in recent years this has been recognized as misleading. Objectively, there are data and information but they are not necessarily unchanging. They are objective in as much as they can exist outside of and beyond the knowledge of those people who do not know. Data and information are the knowledge of those who propound them but they only become other people's knowledge when they have been learned subjectively. Then they become knowledge and as knowledge develops through experience and practice it might assume the form of wisdom – knowledge and wisdom are learned – much is actually learned by doing rather than just by thinking. We will return to the nature of learning below – but in the first instance, we see that the transmission of data and information are part of the curriculum of vocational education but knowledge and wisdom cannot be taught, only learned. This distinction between objective and subjective knowledge is fairly recent and traditionally scholars have not separated objective and subjective knowledge in this way but rather just referred to it all as knowledge – but not all knowledge carries equal status or significance.

But as early as 1926 the German sociologist Max Scheler (Stikkers, 1980: 76) began to classify knowledge into seven types based upon their speed of change:

- myth and legend – undifferentiated religious, metaphysical, natural and historical;
- knowledge implicit in everyday language – as opposed to learned, poetic or technical;
- religious – from pious to dogmatic;
- mystical;
- philosophic-metaphysical;
- positive knowledge – mathematics, the natural sciences and the humanities;
- technological.

Scheler regarded his final two forms of knowledge as the most artificial because they changed so rapidly, whereas the other five are more embedded in culture. We might dispute with Scheler about many aspects of this typology, including the fact that the humanities are coupled with mathematics and the natural sciences – indeed, I would place them in the same category as philosophical and metaphysical knowledge. While his analysis was over-simple, he did make it nearly one hundred years ago. Nevertheless, he makes the point clearly that many forms of positive and technological knowledge change rapidly – he suggested 'hour by hour' – but that was in 1926 and now it might be minute by minute! Consider how quickly the mobile phone or the personal computer, for instance, get out of date and how often there is pressure to purchase a new one in order to get up to date, even though we may not need it. Think of the amount of research and new knowledge necessary to produce these new commodities for this knowledge economy. Not all scientific knowledge changes rapidly: the speed of light, for instance, has not changed, whereas our understanding of the nature of light has changed. Hence, Scheler's typology, while useful for our discussion only represents some aspects of our understanding of the complex nature of knowledge itself. While he was not totally correct, his artificial forms of knowledge are related to the dominant forms of knowledge in the knowledge society and it is these that workers have to know, even to produce.

It is those societies that are at the centre of economic globalization that might be seen as knowledge societies: it is these that Daniel Bell (1973) first called the post-industrial societies. For him, knowledge is the fundamental resource for such societies, especially theoretical knowledge (Bell 1973: 14) and, as Stehr (1994: 10) pointed out, when these societies emerge they signal a fundamental shift in the structure of the economy, since the primacy of manufacturing is replaced by knowledge. It is not knowledge per se that is significant to the knowledge society but scientific – including social scientific – knowledge (Stehr 1994: 99–103) since it underlies production of new commodities and services and, consequently, has economic value. Knowledge in itself has no intrinsic value; it is only its use-value as a scarce resource which is significant. Indeed, certain forms of new knowledge are a scarce resource and usable in the production of goods and services for the market of consumption. Every marginal addition to the body of scientific knowledge is potentially valuable in the knowledge economy.

If some forms of knowledge are changing so rapidly, the question needs to be asked, how do we know that they are true? It was Lyotard (1984) who answered this question when he referred to performativity, that is that useful knowledge works – it has use-value. Knowledge then is not just something that exists in the mind, it has got to work in practice. Practical knowledge has become a dominant form of knowledge in the work place – and this again is something that is learned rather than taught, although teaching can play some part in the process. Since there is a great emphasis on practical knowledge, curricula have to be more practical than in previous years, although universities especially have not traditionally concentrated on the practical aspects of the knowledge that they have taught, and so when they are teaching practical subjects they need to recognize that they should teach not only *knowledge that* but also *knowledge how*. But even *knowledge how* is not the same as *being able to* and there is no conceptual relationship between the two – *being able to* is learned in practice while neither *knowledge how* nor *knowledge that* are learned exclusively in practice.

However, Stehr's assertion about the knowledge economy utilizing artificial, or rapidly changing, knowledge is correct and it has at least two implications that concern us here: first, these artificial forms of knowledge soon become out of date so that initial vocational preparation must focus on the short term and, second, there is a tendency to omit those other cultural forms of knowledge, such as moral knowledge, from our considerations as insignificant for vocational preparation since they apparently have no use-value. We will return to both of these points, but before we move on we can see that each of these three types of worker needs a practical knowledge base in order to function in practice, even though the new worker remains a novice at the outset. However, it must be emphasized that the knowledge economy demands, even if it does not need such, highly qualified novices when they embark upon their careers (Livingstone 2002). I do not want to discuss this point here, but it is one of the un-debated discourses of the knowledge economy that requires more consideration.

The nature of practice

Traditionally, it was assumed that the knowledge learned in the classroom could be applied to practice and we used to talk about practice being the application of theory. But gradually over the past two decades we have learned that there is a major gap between theory and practice and when I wrote *The Practitioner-Researcher* (Jarvis 1999), I assumed that practice preceded the practitioners' own theory – or rather their own practical knowledge. Practice is the process of transforming *knowledge that* and *knowledge how* into *being able to* – itself a process of learning. We all learn by doing – doing is an indication of being and intention.

However, the process of learning to be able is a much more complicated process than merely applying theory to practice as Nyiri (1988: 20–21) made clear:

> One becomes an expert not simply by absorbing explicit knowledge of the type found in text-books, but through experience, that is, through repeated trials, 'failing, succeeding, wasting time and effort . . . getting a feel for the problem, learning when to go by the book and when to break the rules'. Human experts gradually absorb 'a repertory of working rules of thumb, or "heuristics", that combined with book knowledge, make them expert prac-titioners'. This practical, heuristic knowledge, as attempts to simulate it on the machine have shown, is 'hardest to get at because experts – or anyone else – rarely have the self-awareness to recognize what it is. So it must be mined out of their heads painstakingly, one jewel at a time.' [All quotations from Feigenbaum and McCorduck 1984]

As the years go by the experts not only gain knowledge and skills, they gain wisdom, which can be regarded as:

> the ego's increasing capacity to tolerate paradox. This same capacity char-acterizes the mature defenses, which can maintain a creative and flexible tension between irreconcilables and allow conscience, impulse, reality, and attachment all to have places at the center stage.
>
> (Vaillant 1993: 328)

But this process of gaining expertise and wisdom is not something that happens in a short period of time. Through these complex learning experiences, novices might move gradually towards the status of expert, a process which was first discussed by Dreyfus and Dreyfus (1980). They posited that a learner goes through five stages in becoming an expert: novice, advanced beginner, competent, proficient and expert (cited from Benner 1984: 13; see also Tuomi 1999: 285–340). But it was Aristotle who focused on this practical knowledge – which he called practical wisdom – something that could only be learned with the passing of years. In precisely the same way, more experienced workers might continue to learn and continue to develop new knowledge through the process of practice. But there is no short timescale on this process – Benner (1984: 25) suggests that competence in nursing (the field of her own research) might come after two or three years of practice, and proficiency between three and five years (p. 31). However, this raises quite major questions when we recognize the speed of change of artificial knowledge – some of the knowledge learned in the classroom might already be out of date before the practitioner has become an expert. Indeed, practice itself is not static but rapidly changing so that practitioners are not simply using knowledge gained in the classroom or in any form of initial vocational education. Indeed, they may reach a stage where they have to innovate within their own practice or, in other words, where they create new knowledge and new ways of doing things and their expertise means that they also need to be creative – they become experts. There are at least two implications of this: first, we have to be aware, not every practitioner moves through this progression – for some, each procedure is the mere repetition of the previous one so that we can say that some practitioners have twenty-five years of experience while others have one year of experience twenty-five times; second, the expert can become frustrated by the rules of bureaucracy and job satisfaction can decline if the expert practitioner feels frustrated (Jarvis 1977) and this can be especially problematic in a litigation-orientated society.

Practitioners also have to gain that wisdom that Vaillant (1993: 328) wrote about in order to practise in this type of situation – the ability to 'maintain a creative and flexible tension between irreconcilables and allow conscience, impulse, reality, and attachment all to have places at the center stage' of practice, since these go with expertise. Immediately we see that practice is no longer just a matter of knowledge and skill, it is about the practitioner being confident, creative, having the right impulses, commitment, and so on. But more than this – in practice, practitioners work with others – patients, clients, colleagues and so on. It is a social activity and while expertise is very important, Maister (cited in Daloz *et al.* 1996: 25) wrote that 'Your clients don't care how much you know until they know how much you care'. In other words, practice is a moral undertaking; it is about trust and respect for others. Practice is ultimately about the nature of the practitioners themselves. Practice is about the person – as practitioner. This points us to a broader understanding of vocational education since it is about developing the person as well as teaching knowledge and skills. But before we examine this, we see one other thing – *being able to* is not something that can be taught, it has to be learned but it is even more than this – *being able to* is about *being* itself, but before we turn to this we now need to look at the nature of human learning.

The nature of human learning

Being able to is not something that can be taught, neither is expertise nor wisdom – but neither it nor they can be learned and learning is not something that is restricted to the classroom or the lecture theatre – learning is something that can happen anywhere and at any time. Consequently, at the heart of our concern lies the understanding of the learning process, which is itself a very complex process – but one that we take for granted. Learning is *the combination of processes whereby the whole person – body (genetic, physical and biological) and mind (meaning, knowledge, skills, attitudes, values, emotions, beliefs and senses) – experiences a social situation, the content of which is then transformed cognitively, emotively or practically (or through any combination) and integrated into the person's individual biography resulting in a changed (or more experienced) person.*

This is a much more complex definition of learning than usually suggested and more complex than the one that I posed when I originally sought to understand the learning process (Jarvis, 1987) and even different from the one which I used when I examined learning much more fully elsewhere (Jarvis, 2006). It is the one which I have later developed further (Jarvis, 2008). Basically, however, four things happen during the learning process: a sensation (physical, emotional, attitudinal, etc.) is changed into 'brain language', the experience that the person has on receiving the stimulus is transformed, the person is changed from one state to another and the person s relationship with the life-world is changed from harmony to disjuncture and gradually back to a new harmony provided the external world does not change (which is debatable). I have depicted this process in the two diagrams below.

In Figure 8.1, following Schutz and Luckmann (1974), we take our life-world for granted (box 1), and we live in the flow of time (what Bergson called *durée*) but when we cannot take our world for granted we experience disjuncture or have some sensation or stimulus that causes us to experience disjuncture (box 2). Through the learning process we transform the sensations (box 3) and then we seek to practice the resolution (box 4) which may be much more than just performance since we are not mindless individuals, and this may, after many attempts, lead us to a new harmony with our life-world – provided other factors in the life-world have not altered.

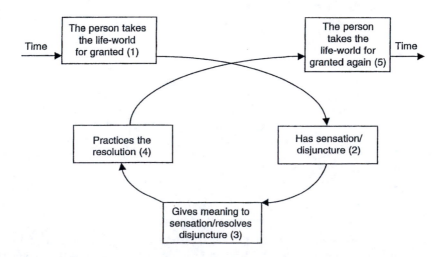

Figure 8.1 The transformation of sensations in learning.

Learning, however, is still more complicated than this first diagram suggests, as the second diagram illustrates because it involves the person of the learner (see Figure 8.2).

In this second diagram, we can see the other aspect of the learning process that occurs simultaneously with the first – the learner is transformed: the learners in the life-world (box 1_1) have an experience (box 1_2) – that can occur in the classroom or the workplace, or elsewhere – which is constructed as a result of our perception of the situation and our previous learning, and it is the content of this experience which is transformed, and we undertake learning (box 6) through our thinking, our doing and our emotions (boxes 3, 4, 5) and as a result of this learning the whole person (body, mind, self, life-history) (box 6) is changed. It is this changed person (box 1_2) who has future experiences and continues to be changed as the practitioner gradually becomes an expert.

When we move from the classroom to the field of practice we actually move from the taken for granted to a new situation (box 1) which is disjunctural since it is another situation and we do not know precisely what to do in it and so we try to resolve the disjuncture by utilizing the *knowledge that* and the *knowledge how* that we have learned, and by so doing we begin to learn *to be able to* – but this is a new learning experience. Through practice (boxes 3, 4 and 5), we gradually learn the knowledge, skills and attitudes, etc. necessary to be able to take our practice situation for granted (box 6). This is where the danger occurs

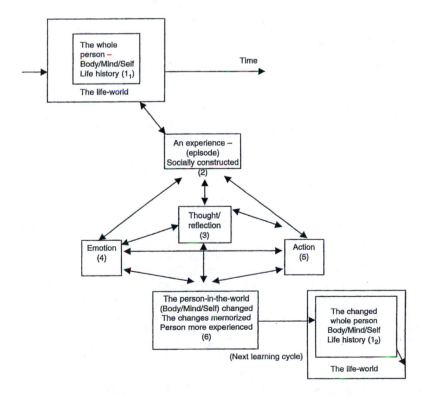

Figure 8.2 The transformation of the person through learning.

in practice – we can then just take our practice situation for granted and perform our practice unthinkingly, or else we can see each situation as unique, each differing slightly from the last, and so we make each one disjunctural and we adapt our practice accordingly, or as Nyiri says 'through repeated trials, "failing, succeeding, wasting time and effort . . . getting a feel for the problem, learning when to go by the book and when to break the rules" ' we learn to perfect our practice, even to innovate upon it and produce that new knowledge and skill that we discussed earlier. During this process, we are changed (box 6) and perhaps we grow in wisdom pre-consciously during the process.

Competence is, in a sense, when the practitioners acquire the necessary expertise to fit into the social situation and begin to take their situation and practice for granted. Becoming an expert is when they continue to create their own disjuncture in the practice situation in order to enhance their expertise beyond that of merely fitting in'. It is this trying to reach beyond the 'taken for granted' that distinguishes the expert from one who merely has competence or expertise – this is when creativity begins and it is built upon the solid foundation of expertise. Once they reach this state they begin to realize just how much more there is to learn – the beginning of wisdom is the realization of ignorance. But the significant point is that it is the whole person – body and mind – who is changed and who acquires expertise and wisdom as a result of all that trial and error learning in practice, especially if it is coupled with continuing vocational education – but both wisdom and this level of expertise cannot be taught – they can only be learned in practice.

Some implications for vocational education

Thus far we have looked at the nature of knowledge, practice and learning and we can see that this analysis has certain implications for vocational education: I want to look briefly at four here: the short and the long term; the learner; learning in practice; preparing the manager/supervisor.

Short and long term: Traditional vocational education has a short-term end-product only for the routine production workers who can acquire competence to operate technology or to perform their routine roles within the employing organization. For all other workers, vocational education should be seen within a longer time frame and this means that we have to recognize not just the demands of the occupational role but the demands of the practice within which that role is performed. Once we do this we have to look at the wider types of knowledge and skill that are necessary. We have, for instance, highlighted the need for moral knowledge for those who deal with people either as clients or as colleagues and this demands more than mere instrumentality. But this is only an illustration of the way that we need to think about the breadth of initial preparation and prepare workers to be able to learn beyond competence.

The learner: Many approaches to learning are concerned with the way that the information is processed or the behavioural outcomes of the learning process, but in the model of learning that I have suggested I have focused on the learners themselves. Most theories of learning are, I believe, quite deficient in this in a number of different ways, as I have argued in *Towards a Comprehensive Theory of Human Learning* (Jarvis 2006) where I have focused on the person of the learner. The learner is both mind and body and in learning and in practice the one does not operate without the other. This also calls into question the emphasis on the concept of competence with its behavioural implications and also information processing with its emphasis on the brain as a glorified computer. The expert is more than a functionary responding to the demands of the system – the expert is a significant person in society using expertise and knowledge to transcend the system and enrich the lives of all who live in society. We need to understand the nature of personhood and learning if we are to be of service to those with whom we work; we need to value the person of the learner and this is more than human resource development – it is about personal growth and development. At the heart of our concern is respect for the personhood of people as we help them develop all of their abilities. Ultimately, we are all involved in *learning to be* as well as *learning to do* and *learning to know* – this chapter is about *learning to be an expert*.

Learning in practice: We have to recognize that if we want experts, and wise ones at that, we have to prepare workers to understand that the practice into which they are going is a constantly changing one where new demands are being made on them all the time and that they also have to make new demands upon themselves so that they have to be prepared to learn new practices, to learn to enhance their existing ones, and so on. They have to learn how to learn, which means that new types of teaching and learning techniques have to be incorporated into the vocational training programme. New knowledge, new skills, new teaching and learning techniques – this points to the fact that vocational education needs itself to be undergoing continuous change and the importance of work-based learning needs to be recognized and, in addition, we have to help educational institutions to recognize and accredit such work-based learning programmes. However, programmes of this nature require higher educational institutions to continue to adapt their understanding to accreditation and place even more significance on the relationship of practice to theory. We have to recognize the complex process of learning in practice and help those who are undertaking it.

Preparing the manager/supervisor: Since the workplace is a site of learning, those who supervise need to be involved in the workers' learning. Consequently, managers and supervisors should to be taught how to be mentors of work-placed learning. This then is part of their continuing professional development and the concept of management needs to undergo some transformation as we develop teams who need to learn to work together.

Conclusion

Vocational education is now far removed from training and the old debates about knowledge and skill, and the policy implications of these changes have to be taken into account from the outset. In this depersonalized society, we need to re-emphasize the place of the person and we need to re-conceptualize learning away from the rather sterile debates about lifelong learning that occur in policy documents and learn what it really means for whole people to learn. Perhaps the focus of our vocational education needs to come from the UNESCO report *Learning: The treasure within* (Delors 1996) in which there are four pillars of learning – to be, to do, to know and to live together. Here we begin to grasp what it means for people to learn – primarily learning to be, so that we can also learn to know, to do and to live together wisely and with expertise.

Acknowledgements

This chapter was originally presented as a paper at the Hong Kong Council for Vocational Education and has subsequently been revised for this publication.

References

Bell, D. (1973) *The Coming of Post-Industrial Society*. New York: Basic Books.
Benner, P. (1984) *From Novice to Expert*. Menlo Pack, CA: Addison Wesley.
Collins English Dictionary (1979).
Daloz, L., Keen, C., Keen, J. and Parks, S. (1996) *Common Fire*. Boston, MA: Beacon.
Delors, J. (1996) *Learning: The treasure within*. Paris: UNESCO.
Dreyfus, S. and Dreyfus, H. L. (1980) A five stage model of the mental activities involved in directed skill acquisition. Unpublished Report: University of California at Berkeley.
Feigenbaum, E. A. and McCorduck, P. (1984) *The Fifth Generation*. New York: Signet.
Jarvis, P. (1977) Protestant ministers: job satisfaction and role strain in the bureaucratic organisation of the Church. Birmingham: University of Aston. Unpublished PhD thesis.
Jarvis, P. (1987) *Adult Learning in the Social Context*. London: Croom Helm.
Jarvis, P. (1999) *The Practitioner-Researcher*. San Francisco: Jossey-Bass.
Jarvis, P. (2006) *Towards a Comprehensive Theory of Human Learning*. London: Routledge.
Jarvis, P. (2008) *Learning to Be a Person in Society*. London: Routledge.
Livingstone, D. (2002) Lifelong learning in the knowledge society: a North American perspective. Reprinted in R. Edwards, N. Miller, N. Small and A. Tait (eds) *Making Knowledge Work: Supporting lifelong learning (Vol 3)*. London: RoutledgeFalmer.
Lyotard, J-F. (1984) *The Post-Modern Condition: A report on knowledge*. Manchester: Manchester University Press.
Nyiri, J. C. (1988) Tradition and practical knowledge. In J. C. Nyiri and B. Smith (eds) *Practical Knowledge: Outlines of a theory of traditions and skills*. London: Croom Helm.
Reich, R. (1991) *The Work of Nations*. London: Simon & Schuster.
Schutz, A. and Luckmann, T. (1974) *The Structure of the Life World*. London: Heinemann.
Stikkers, K. (1980) (ed.) Scheler, M. ([1926] 1980) *Problems of a Sociology of Knowledge*. London: Routledge & Kegan Paul.
Stehr, N. (1994) *Knowledge Societies*. London: Sage.
Swanson, R. A. (2001) *Foundations of Human Resource Development*. San Francisco, CA: Barrett-Koehler Publishers.
Tuomi, I. (1999) *Corporate Knowledge: Theory and practice of intelligent organizations*. Helsinki: Meraxis.
Vaillant, G. E. (1993) *The Wisdom of the Ego*. Cambridge, MA: Harvard University Press.

CHAPTER 9

PRACTITIONER RESEARCH AND THE LEARNING SOCIETY

Originally published as 'Practitioner Research and the Learning Society' in P. Jarvis (1999), *The Practitioner-Researcher*, San Francisco: Jossey-Bass, pp. 159–68. Cross-references refer to the original publication.

Throughout this book, there has been a recognized interrelationship between research and learning; indeed, in Chapter Eight especially we noted how reflective learning and action research became almost interchangeable concepts at one point. Consequently, the relationship between the practitioner-researchers' research and the learning that occurs in practice does require some exploration. In this chapter we undertake this journey and explore the idea that the emergence of practitioner-researchers is a symbol of the development of the learning society. The chapter has five sections: the first briefly explores the idea of the learning society, the second analyzes the relationship between research and learning, the third examines the emergence of practitioner-researchers in the learning society, the fourth looks at the process of democratizing research, and the fifth explores the relationship among learning, research, and scholarship.

The idea of the learning society

The learning society is a metaphor to describe the type of society in which we live, and here I want to examine three different interpretations of it: as a futuristic and a rather idealistic concept, as a learning market, and as a reflexive society. I want to show how this book's argument reflects the fact that we do live and practice in a learning society of a reflexive nature, although some of the ideas from the first two interpretations are also relevant to our discussion.

The learning society as futuristic

When Hutchins (1968) wrote his classic book on the learning society, he looked to the future and suggested that the learning society "would be one that, in addition to offering part-time adult education to every man and woman at every stage of grown-up life, had succeeded in transforming its values in such a way that learning, fulfilment, becoming human, had become its aims and all its institutions were directed to this end" (p. 133). For Hutchins, education would come into its own, and the new learning society would be the building of a new Athens, made possible not by slavery but by modern machines. It was the realization of the computer revolution that led Husen (1974) to very similar conclusions. He argued that "*educated ability* will be democracy's replacement for passed-on social prerogatives" (p. 238). This is something to which we will return later in this chapter. He thought that the knowledge explosion would be fostered by a combination of computers and reprographics, and he foresaw the possibility of *"equal opportunities* for all to receive as much education as they are thought capable of absorbing" (p. 240).

More recently, a similar position has been adopted by Ranson (1994), who has suggested that "there is a need for the creation of a learning society as the constitutive condition of a new moral and political order. It is only when the values and processes of learning are placed at the centre of the polity that the conditions can be established for all individuals to develop their capacities, and that institutions can respond openly and imaginatively to a period of change" (p. 106). Ranson approached the subject starting with school education rather than with an adult or lifelong education framework. It is futuristic and rather idealistic. Boshier (1980), while still looking forward to a learning society, actually started from the position of an adult educator and recognized that this new society is about more than school education. He explored the post-school institutions in New Zealand to discover the structural basis of such a society— but it was still an educational phenomenon.

In a sense, each of the theorists discussed here foresaw an educative society. Significantly, all these theorists start their analyses with one part of the public institution, and for them the learning society remains an ideal that will be real- ized only when the more public institution of education has been reformed. What we have seen in the emergence of the practitioner-researcher has been that a great deal of the learning and the research is practice-based, and so far we have made little reference to the educational institutions.

The learning society as a learning market

Contemporary society is also a consumer society, and the history of consum- erism can be traced back to the eighteenth century (Campbell, 1987). Any anal- ysis of the market requires consumers. Clearly there can be no market economy unless there are consumers who want to purchase the products that are being produced. Advertising plays on imaginary pleasure—and shopping can be fun. Now, as Usher and Edwards (1994) point out, one of the features of contempo- rary society is that of experiencing—it is a sensate society. This is not new, as Campbell has shown, but it is the type of society in which the longings of the imagination can be satisfied through consumption, and the basis of advertising is thus the cultivation of desire.

When learning is equated with education in people's minds, they tend to remember unpleasant experiences at school, when it might not have been fun to learn, and this can cause them to erect a barrier to further education—a barrier that every adult educator has sought to overcome. But now that learning has become separated from education in many people's minds, learning can become fun. Now people can read books, watch television, listen to the radio, surf the World Wide Web, work on their personal computers, discuss with other people through electronic mail, and acquire and exchange information in many other enjoyable ways. Today it is possible to learn all the things people have ever wanted to know by attending learning groups, using multimedia personal computers and the Internet, and so on. But the providers of these learning mate- rials are now not all educational institutions, and educational institutions are having to change their approach rapidly to keep abreast with a market generating information about all aspects of life every minute of the day. People can now choose the medium they are going to employ to receive their information. There are no age limits. Knowledge production has become an industry, cultivating the desire of people to learn so they can take part in contemporary society. This is now a fundamental motivator behind advertising campaigns.

The information society is a market for information. Providers are manu-facturing and selling a wide variety of learning materials. This has created a paradoxical situation: although learning is a private and individual process, one of the features of the market is that the consumption of learning has to be public—conspicuous consumption. Educational institutions make public this private activity; it is part of their institutional business. They grant credit for learning from life experience and thus bring this private learning into the pseudo-public sphere of education (Jarvis, 1996). Because educational qualifica-tions are important for practitioners seeking career advancement, they are engaging in additional study to gain credit. This in turn means that the private learning they formerly undertook to improve their practice for themselves and their clients is now becoming the action research project that constitutes part of their continuing education.

Driven by the desire of producers to provide a learning commodity that can be purchased and by educational institutions that can grant credit for private learning, the learning society as an information market has inadvertently fueled the increase in practitioner-researchers because practitioners need these qualifi-cations for career advancement.

The learning society as a reflexive society

Reflective learning and reflective practice have become common-place ideas since Schön (1983). But reflective learning is itself a sign of the times; underlying it is the idea of reflexive modernity, which we briefly mentioned at the start of this book. Giddens (1990) and others have argued that reflexivity is funda-mental to the nature of modernity, which overrode all forms of tradition. Giddens wrote:

> The reflexivity of modern social life consists in the fact that social practices are constantly examined and reformed in the light of incoming information about those very practices, thus constitutively altering their character. We should be clear about the nature of this phenomenon. All forms of a social life are partly constituted by actors' knowledge of those forms. Knowing "how to go on" . . . is intrinsic to the conventions which are drawn upon and reproduced in human activity. In all cultures, social practices are routinely altered in the light of ongoing discoveries which feed into them. But only in the era of modernity is the revision of convention radicalised to apply (in principle) to all aspects of human life [pp. 38–39].

Society has become reflexive, and the knowledge that people acquire is no longer certain and established forever—its value lies in its enabling them to live in this rapidly changing society. The pace of change is now so rapid that every-body is required to learn new things regularly just to keep up. Much of this learning is individual and private, but some of it is more public. This is very clearly the case with the knowledge-based occupations, as we have seen. For instance, practitioners are required to keep abreast with the changes occurring within their occupational field. Hence there has been a mushrooming of vocational qualifications, especially at the advanced-degree level. This tremendous growth in new information and the very rapid changes that are occurring in society reflect the idea that the learning society is intrinsic to modernity.

From the perspective of rapidly changing knowledge, there is a fundamental shift in the conception of knowledge itself, from something that is certain and true to something that is fluid and relative. Underlying this form of society is experimentation, which itself leads people to reflect continually on their situation and on the knowledge they possess to cope with it. The need to learn new knowledge is pervasive, but learning new things and acting on them always contains an element of risk. Paradoxically, learning is also a reaction to risk— the risk of not always knowing how to act in this rapidly changing world. Reflexivity is a feature of modernity (Beck, 1992). Reflective learning is a way of life rather than a discovery made by educators and something to be taught in educational institutions. The learning society, then, according to this interpretation, is not a hope for the future but an ever-present phenomenon of the contemporary world. This is the very same case made in our discussion of the uniqueness and transitory nature of practice: reflective learning in practice is a symbol of the learning society.

Learning and research

The reflexive society is a rapidly changing one; practitioners cannot always presume upon their practice situations, so they sometimes face disjuncture. Disjunctural experiences are often ones in which individuals ask why or how. These are the questions that commence the learning process; unsurprisingly, they are also the questions that commence the research process.

Cohen and Mannion (1985) made the point that there are three ways by which humans seek the truth: experience, reasoning, and research. I have suggested that learning is the process of creating and transforming experiences into knowledge, skills, attitudes, values, emotions, beliefs, and the senses: indeed, reasoning might also be such a process. Research is also a process of transforming experience, sometimes through a reasoning process, but often through much more controlled methods and techniques. Indeed, it is a process of learning—it is a form of learning, but it is not so broad as learning itself. Research has, as I argued in Part Three, rigorous methods of discovering and analyzing data. It is a restricted form of learning employing these methods. Even so, it is still learning.

We can go further and suggest that the methods we discussed in Part Three are those that enable us to get as close as possible to understanding the unique and transitory nature of the experiences of the practitioners, so that these forms of research reflect the reflexive society. The research I have described in this book is therefore a phenomenon that we might well expect to occur in the learning society. Research itself is intrinsic to the learning society.

Practitioner-researchers and the learning society

Practitioner-researchers, as we have argued, are a new breed of practitioner. They have emerged at this time because practice is changing rapidly, and we can no longer assume that research conducted in the past is replicable in the future. In addition, because knowledge is now relative and changing rapidly, it is essential for knowledge-based workers to keep pace with these changes and to continue their education. Nearly every master's degree requires producing a research dissertation, which has helped to generate more practitioner-researchers.

All of these phenomena are characteristics of reflexive modernity; they are all part of the learning society. Thus we can claim that the emergence of the practitioner-researcher role is a symbol of both late modernity and of the learning society in its reflexive form.

Democratization of research

Research has traditionally been associated with the empirical and the scientific, a realm of high-status knowledge, and researchers were automatically treated as people from the upper echelons of the learned society. Indeed, this high status is reflected in the fact that, as McNiff (1988) has rightly claimed, "the epistemology of the empiricist tradition is that theory determines practice. Teachers are encouraged to fit their practice into a stated theory (p. 13). But this perspective has now been called into question; we have seen that not all theory need relate to practice, and theory that does has the value only of hypothesis rather than of determination. Consequently, the function of control and its associated high status has been undermined. Neither research nor the researchers can now be distanced from everyday practice and ordinary practitioners, as they were in the past. Indeed, practitioner-researchers have broken down the boundaries.

The boundaries of society have become more open; more people can penetrate the apparent mysteries of "scientific" research, and research itself has become much more a part of everyday practice. Lyotard (1984) makes a similar point about education as a whole: "The transmission of knowledge is no longer designed to train an elite capable of guiding a nation towards its emancipation, but to supply a system of players capable of acceptably fulfilling their roles at the pragmatic posts required by its institutions" (p. 48). This is precisely the point I have made about a great deal of practitioner-researchers' research. It is regarded by managers as an essential tool in providing data for them make their decisions. Research, overall, is now about helping the system, organization, or practice improve its performance—which is precisely what action research claimed. Research, then, is no longer only a function of the elite, by the elite, for the elite. Research has been democratized. Practitioner-researchers are now part of the knowledge workforce—perhaps more than one-third of the workforce (Reich, 1991). The learning society is a "flatter" society with fewer layers in its hierarchy, and although it is not entirely democratic, its openness does at least allow people to cross the boundaries of the social strata. Practitioner-researchers do this, and research itself has become a more democratic phenomenon, the outcomes of which can be used more broadly in society.

Research and scholarship in the learning society

The intellectuals did legislate for what was regarded as correct practice, as McNiff (1988) correctly points out, but now that role has changed (Bauman, 1992). Intellectuals have to find a new role in a society that has displaced them politically with managers and allowed their elite research functions to be appropriated and expanded by practitioner-researchers. Now the scholars comment on society from a distance, or as Bauman so beautifully puts it: "The House of Solomon is now placed in a prosperous suburb, far away from ministerial buildings and military headquarters where it can enjoy in peace, undisturbed, the life of mind complete with a not inconsiderable material comfort" (p. 16). Bauman goes on to point out that "contemporary intellectuals must stick unswervingly to the Western injunction of keeping the poetry of values away from the prose of bureaucratically useful expertise" (pp. 16–17). In other words, scholarship contributes to the metatheory in a world where the "useful expertise" is practical and the practitioner-researchers' research focuses on the pragmatic. It is this type of research that provides the basis of policy decisions in a managerial world.

Such academic scholarship, as we have seen, still serves as an important function in both the preparation and the continuing education of practitioners, but its function is now of a more hermeneutic nature—interpreting the developments of practice, highlighting some of the potential pitfalls, and giving advice to the practitioners, the policymakers, and occasionally the politicians.

Herein lies one of the other significant distinctions between theory and metatheory: theory is knowledge of practice; it provides hypotheses for practice, and in this sense it is practical. Metatheory is knowledge about practice and interpretative, and in this sense cannot, and should not, be applied directly to practice.

Conclusion

Practitioner-researchers and their research are a sign of the times. Practitioner-researchers are an intrinsic part of the learning society, responding to the changes with practical knowledge that enables them to cope with the changes. Their research illustrates that in the learning society, many of the research projects need to be small, local, and practical, producing both a personal theory and information about practice.

Can we say that practitioner-researchers are the successors of the scholars whose learning and research have produced the meta-theory and the informed comment on the system? Perhaps it would be incorrect to suggest that practitioner-researchers have actually replaced them, although it would be true to say that some of the scholar's functions have been taken over by practitioner-researchers. Even so, a great deal of practitioner-researchers' work is local and specific; the scholars still take a broader perspective and are still able to place the local and specific into a larger context. Consequently, their role is still important, and it is still necessary for practitioner-researchers to understand metatheory and its functions. Metatheory remains part of the curriculum for initial preparation, but perhaps it has an even greater role in the continuing learning of practitioners.

Clearly, however, the concept of the learning society also involves the providers of learning opportunities, especially the professional schools and universities. In the final two chapters of this book, we explore some of the implications of this discussion for providers of learning.

References

Bauman Z (1992) *Intimations of Post-Modernity* London: Routledge
Beck U (1992) *The Risk Society* London: Sage
Boshier R (1980) *Towards the Learning Society* Vancouver BC: The Learning Press
Campbell C (1987) *The Romantic Ethic and the Spirit of Consumerism* Oxford: Blackwell
Cohen L and Mannion L (1985) *Research Methods in Education* London: Croom Helm
Giddens A (1990) *The Consequences of Modernity* Cambridge: Polity Press
Husen T (1974) *The Learning Society* London: Methuen
Hutchins R (1968) *The Learning Society* Harmondsworth: Penguin
Jarvis P (1996) Public Recognition of Lifetime Learning *Lifelong Education in Europe* Vol 1 No 1 pp. 10–17
Lyotard L-F (1984) *The Post-Modern Condition: A Report on Knowledge* Manchester: University of Manchester Press
McNiff J (1988) *Action Research: Principles and Practice* London: Macmillan
Ranson S (1994) *Towards the Learning Society* London: Cassell
Reich R (1991) *The Work of Nations: Preparing Ourselves for Twenty-First Century Capitalism* New York: Simon & Schuster
Schon D (1983) *The Reflective Practitioner* New York: Basic Books
Usher R and Edwards T (1994) *Postmodernism and Education* London: Routledge

PART 4

TEACHING

▬

CHAPTER 10

ETHICS AND TEACHING
Exploring the relationship between teacher and taught

Originally published as 'Ethics and Teaching: Exploring the Relationship between Teacher and Taught' in P. Jarvis (ed.) (2006), *The Theory and Practice of Teaching*, second edition, London: Routledge, pp. 39–52. Cross-references refer to the original publication.

In recent years there has been a growth in the study of ethics and teaching (Jarvis, 1997; Freire, 1998; Palmer, 1998, Macfarlane, 2004, *inter alia*). In another sense, Levinas' (1991a) study on *Totality and Infinity* is also an ethical study about learning in relationship throughout which he referred to teaching. I want to use some of the ideas in this study to explore an ethical approach to teaching based upon the nature of the relationship between teachers and taught, as I did in *Ethics and the Education of Adults in Late Modern Society* (Jarvis, 1997). Underlying this is Buber's (1959) profound study *I and Thou*. However, using Levinas' terminology I want to divide this chapter into three sections: teaching and the stranger – lecturing; teaching and totalising – managing the system; teaching and infinity – sharing and expanding. Each section contains an ideal type picture of a form of teaching, together with its strengths and weaknesses.

Teaching and the stranger: lecturing

In Chapter 2 of this book we used a word picture of a professor performing in a large lecture theatre; the lecturer was far removed from the students and they came to listen to the pearls of wisdom that he uttered from afar. This is not an unusual description – lecturers and the large lecture hall crowded (perhaps) with students wanting to learn the knowledge that is to be presented. Indeed, with the curtailment of funding in higher education in a number of countries, this is a form of teaching that will remain a popular form of knowledge presentation for years to come. Even more so, in distance and e-teaching there is a real possibility that similar forms are emerging in which the lecturers are far removed from the learners and have no personal relationship with them. Lecturing, then, does not only occur in a large lecture hall with the lecturer standing performing before a large audience; it occurs within the much more confined space of the class room. Lecturers are didactic teachers who expound their theme and, having done so, they have completed their task and with clear conscience they can leave the class room. Colin Griffin has dealt with didactic teaching in Chapter 6 of this book and so we need not explore this is great detail here.

Nevertheless, it would be true to say that in lecturing, the teachers can remain true to themselves and to their understanding of the truth. They have had time to think through the information that they present, to know that they have read and studied the latest research on the subject and that what they present is true to their understanding of it. Teaching is about the presentation of information for students to learn. Consequently, two moral elements dominate this approach to teaching: that lecturers should be true to their discipline, and that they should be true to themselves. Indeed, it is a categorical imperative that they do this and to do less is to fall far short of the ethical demands of professionalism in teaching. In this sense, lecturers can present their best understanding of the information and construct their argument in a most logical manner so that the learners can see the validity of what they are being taught. Learners have an opportunity – no, a moral responsibility – to learn what they are taught so that they can use it appropriately thereafter, including in examination settings.

One of the advantages of this approach is that lecturers can prepare their notes, overhead slides or PowerPoint presentations and handouts and present the material in as professional a manner as they know. This reflects the authority and expertise of the teacher. Indeed, it is also a most useful method for novice teachers – all the information is prepared and as long as the lecturers keep to their notes, they are safe. Indeed, when I used to train educators (both school teachers and lectures in all forms of professional and adult education) I used to say to them – if you are not confident of your subject or yourself, prepare a lecture, go into the class room and deliver it and get out before anybody asks you questions that might reveal your ignorance. Lecturing can be the novice teacher's survival kit: but if lecturers are confident then they might be better teaching their subject!

The point about this situation is the social, and sometimes the physical, distance that exists between lecturers and their students. Lecturers are presenting their material without interacting with the students – there is no I–Thou relationship, but an I–It one, where the 'It' is the class or the group. Levinas would see this situation as one in which the lecturers are free, at home in their own world, and they can identify themselves as lecturers simply by their performance. The students do not really disturb the freedom of the lecturer and have no power over them – they are 'strangers'. As strangers, they can make no demands on the lecturers. In precisely the same way, strangers are free; free also from the lecturers, although the students are not free from the demands of the educational system of which the lecturer is a representative. In order to enter relationship but not to destroy the strangers' otherness or self, or the lecturers' own sense of self, they need to enter into conversation with each other and genuine conversation cannot be carefully planned like a lecture presentation; indeed, by its very nature, lecturing is one-way communication devoid of conversation.

Naturally this is an ideal type, but it depicts something about the nature of lecturing but what happens when the strangers seek to enter conversation with the lecturers? Now they impinge upon the freedom of the lecturer and Levinas (1991a, p. 43) writes: 'We name this calling into question of my spontaneity by the presence of the Other ethics'. For Levinas, ethics begins when we experience the other personally and so, in some way, we are no longer totally free even if we have ever been so. Elsewhere in his work (Levinas, 1991b, pp. 14–15), he suggests that this personal relationship is not merely cognitive but emotive, being vulnerable in relationship with the other. I think that Levinas under-emphasises the ethics of strangers co-existing without entering into relationship. He also under-emphasises the ethics of being true to oneself, like the professional ethics that demands that the lecturers always give their best presentation. Even so, when the stranger becomes a face, a person with whom we can enter relationship through conversation, then different ethical demands are made upon both *ego* and *alter*. Indeed, Levinas (1991a, p. 40) actually goes so far as to suggest that 'the bond that is established between the same and the other without constituting a totality' is religion – but to discuss this here is beyond the brief of this chapter.

In entering a relationship, face to face, each still have to respect the other's sense of being, self-hood and freedom. In the relationship itself there are tremendous challenges and also great potentialities, but they can only be realised in the flourishing and yet respecting the other in the relationship itself. Striving after the richness of this relationship, Levinas claimed, lies at the heart of humanity itself, it is our human desire, and part of the argument of this chapter is that teaching can only occur in human relationship when we can strive to achieve that potentiality but there is a real possibility that we, as teachers, might produce a different outcome if we become totalisers.

Teaching and totalising: managing the system

The totaliser reflects the world as we currently know it and this is Levinas' starting point. His question is how can we transcend this world? How can we reach to that something beyond it and embark upon a journey that has no end, which I argue is the ethical ideal of teaching and we will return to this in the next section of this chapter. But first, what is totalising and how does it manifest itself in teaching? The totalisers live in a world dominated by social systems which are objective and rational; it is a world that subordinates the individual (domesticates, is a word sometimes used) and, in one sense, ensures that the stranger will never become a face that can be taken seriously. Wild, in his excellent Introduction to this book, summarises this position:

> To be free is the same as to be rational, and to be rational is to give oneself over to the total system that is developing in world history . . . All otherness will be absorbed in this total system of harmony and order.
>
> (Levinas, 1991a, p. 15)

This is a system which demands that individuality be subjugated to the group, which is neutral and impersonal, rational and objective. Naturally, this is an ideal type and reflects Wrong's (1961) well-known argument of the over-socialised view of human beings. Wrong argued that humans are not so totally socialised, but the point behind Levinas' argument is that by subjecting human beings to such relationships we fail to recognise their individuality and realise the rich potential of human relationship. While teaching should not be a profession that over-socialises, or indoctrinates (see Wilson, 1964; Snook, 1972), there is certainly more than a danger that totalising tendencies emerge and the human face that sometimes appears is lost in strangerhood as the social system dominates and teachers become too busy for their students, as they have to complete the paperwork or prepare for yet another inspection, or for a variety of other reasons which reflect the type of society to which Levinas is opposed. Wild (Levinas, 1991a, p. 17) writes: 'It is outwardly directed but self-centred totalising thinking that organizes men and things into power systems, and gives us control over nature and other people. Hence it has dominated the course of human history.'

Totalitarian thinking looks to the objective system, to rational means and ends, to power and control and to seeking harmony or conformity with the established procedures and in different ways perhaps we, as teachers, incorporate totalistic thinking in our daily practice. The totaliser takes away the other's freedom, sometimes unthinking, and this can occur through a variety of ways during teaching and learning. I want to suggest just five ways here by way of illustration: the aims and objectives, method, content, assessment of teaching and, finally, by lecturers being over-protective, shepherding or even 'mothering' the students.

Aims and objectives

The aims of education constitute a major philosophical discussion which is beyond the remit of this chapter but it is worth noting the position adopted by MacIntyre (1964), as a representative of many who would seek to locate education outside the social system in some way or another. MacIntyre wrote:

> I hope it is clear . . . that the values of rational critical inquiry seem to me to stand in sharpest contrast to the prevailing social values. The task of education is to strengthen the one and weaken the other. Above all the task of education is to teach the value of activity done for its own sake.
>
> (1964, p. 21)

Despite this hope, it is commonly accepted by sociologists that education acts as a means of social and cultural reproduction (Bourdieu and Passeron, 1977), and the more radical Althusser (1972) claimed that education is a powerful state ideological apparatus. The aims of education seem to be at odds with its functions and perhaps we can begin to see the reason why when we look at just one common educational practice – the setting of objectives. Both when a course or module is prepared and when a lesson is prepared, it is commonly expected that the preparation should record the objects of the programme or the session and these are expected to be written as behavioural objectives, for example, 'At the end of this session the students will have learned . . .'. This is both a false statement and a revealing assumption! The false statement is that prediction is a most problematic concept, especially when it comes to predicting human behaviour. It might be more correct to write, 'At the end of this session, the teacher anticipates covering the following topic(s) . . .'. But the revealing assumption is that teachers can not only transmit material but that we assume that the students will learn it in a way that the teachers expect. This suggests an authority of the teacher to control the learning processes of the students and that they will accept what they are taught uncritically. Both of these points need further discussion:

> *The authority of the teacher*: The teachers' authority should be as experts in the subject matter being presented and also as experts in the ways in which it is presented – but the teachers do not have the authority over the learners to such an extent that they can control their thought processes. Indeed, that would be indoctrination.
> *The students' accepting what they are taught*: Learning is a very complex process (see Jarvis, 2005) in which we learn knowledge, skills, beliefs, attitudes, values, emotions and the senses even though we tend only to assess

one or at most two dimensions of this process. Moreover, we often tend to look only for the 'right' answer in that dimension. But to learn critically, creatively, thoughtfully, meaningfully, and so on, is much more complex and if we merely accept what we are told we are in denial of our humanity. Indeed, Nietzsche (Cooper, 1983) suggested that to accept passively what we are told is an act of inauthenticity. But more than this, if teachers expect to create such learning situations they are seeking to take away the students' right to disagree and this is morally unacceptable since it denies their humanity.

Clearly the way that behavioural objectives are used shows that for many teachers, they have not pursued their rationale to its logical conclusion but once we do we can see that underlying them is an untenable ethical position, as well as a completely impractical one. What is clear from this discussion and will become clearer as we develop this chapter is that it is the person who learns (we do not teach education, sociology or mathematics, etc. – we teach students education, sociology, mathematics, etc.) and this is fundamental to our ethical understanding of teaching – if we seek to control, indoctrinate or deny the learners' humanity in any way the students remain strangers with whom we do not really enter into conversation.

Does this mean that we should have no objectives when we teach? Clearly not – aimless activity is not necessarily a good use of time, but we should be more prepared to look at expressive objectives in which the learners assume a much more significant place.

Teaching methods

Teaching involves conversation, or to put it in a more commonly used jargon – dialogue. There are two forms of dialogue that should follow from good teaching: dialogue between teacher and taught and dialogue between taught and taught, depending on the teaching method being used. Consequently, an initial base line to judge on the ethics of teaching is the extent to which the method chosen encourages dialogue – encourages a situation in which all who speak are listened to.

Now it has to be acknowledged that the teaching role does inhibit this relationship from developing and that even as it does, there is frequently a residue of the authority of the role present in the conversation. But being an authority is not the same as being in authority and if teachers have to utilise the authority of the role in order to teach, then there is a sense in which they need to reflect carefully upon the way that the role is being performed or even their preparation for the role – there may be classes in which role authority is useful but they are fewer than we might assume. There are many books that demonstrate how role authority can be overcome and respect for teachers take its place (see Palmer, 1998, *inter alia*). Being an authority should command the respect of those who seek to learn the topic under consideration.

I am not advocating here that every session should be dialogue all the time and I know that there are many occasions when we want to enter conversation with the learners that the class can be dominated by one or two loquacious students. Yet if we enter a genuine dialogue with the class as a whole, it will often curtail excessive involvement of one or two students. But there is also a place for us to take the talkative learners aside and discuss quite openly with them about their involvement within the group – but it should be done quietly in private, still respecting the personhood of the student. However, this does mean that we need to be quite open with our classes about the methods that we are going to use and discuss with them the advantages and disadvantages, and so on. If we are open and we do enter a dialogue then we must listen to what is said to us and be prepared to learn from it – listening by the teacher is not a façade, but a genuine act of learning on our part.

There are also occasions when we put the students into groups so that we encourage them to talk to and learn from each other. Small group teaching is a very good teaching method when used wisely and well, although there are occasions when it is wrongly used and often students will be aware of it and they can be overheard making comments such as, 'Groups again!' Often when we use group teaching we, as teachers, often wonder between the groups listening to what is going on. However, Brookfield (1990, pp. 194–195) noted that sometimes such visits to the group by the lecturer controlled the group dynamics and so he stopped visiting small groups during teaching sessions. There is a sense in which the residue of the teacher's authority can inhibit genuine discussions in groups, and this should also be avoided because there is a sense in which we might be demonstrating our authority at the expense of the learners. We have to be aware of this possibility.

Indeed, we can all misuse our authority in a variety of way and perhaps Bourdieu's and Passeron's (1977) concept of symbolic violence points us in this direction. Their initial definition is quite broad:

> *All* **pedagogic action** *(PA) is, objectivity, symbolic violence insofar as it is the imposition of a cultural arbitrary by an arbitrary power.*
> (Bourdieu and Passeron, 1977, p. 5
> (italics and bold in the original))

We might want to dispute the breadth of this definition but the point underlying the definition is the totality of the culture from which we cannot escape, so that they are suggesting that whatever methods are used the learners are still forced to function within a specified cultural framework. However, if we enter negotiation, encourage critical and original thought, we might just overcome the totality of culture, which is a major part of Levinas' argument. It is, therefore, quite ethical to discuss with the class the teaching methods that we are going to employ, even to negotiate with them so that we are sure that we are always trying to enter a genuine conversation with all of our learners.

Content

It is much more difficult to discuss the content of individual sessions with students since many syllabi are set by the professional bodies or by the validating body and this is both understandable and perfectly acceptable; it is right and proper that students should learn a body of information before they qualify, but there are two points that might be made about this – the first is personal and involves the whole course while the second is much more specific.

From a personal point of view, in the early 1980s I taught a part-time Master's degree course on Adult Education in which all the students were practising adult educators, and one year I discussed with the students an idea that they should choose all the course content and teach each other while I would sit in and contribute occasionally. However, I was far from inactive during this period since each week I prepared a full set of lecture notes on the subject of their choice. The course was a great success from the students' perspective and they enjoyed it very much but the outcome was that I put the notes that I had prepared each week together and published it as a book (Jarvis, 1983) and twenty-two years later that book is still in print in its third edition (Jarvis, 2004). Allowing the students to choose both the content and the method actually proved extremely beneficial and it was ethically acceptable and the students were far from strangers – some are still my friends.

Even if we follow a prescribed syllabus, there is still a place for student involvement in the content for each session. I well remember hearing a colleague once as we came to the end of the academic year coming out of a class and saying – 'Thank goodness, I've covered the syllabus; we had to rush quite a number of things, but I got through it'. The question that might be asked about that exclamation is did he just cover the syllabus or did he teach it? There were many places during the year when he might have discussed with the students which parts they regarded as most vital, whether there were sections that they knew, whether there were some bits they would be prepared to teach themselves, etc., so that he could participate with them in the crucial, new sections, and so on. In keeping them at a distance, they remained strangers who did not interfere with his freedom to choose and whilst he may have felt ethically justified in what he did, there were many other ethical questions that demanded answers.

Assessment

Assessment is thoroughly discussed in two chapters later in the book but I want to raise two points here. The first comes from Freire:

> On this occasion our teacher had brought our homework to school after correcting it and was calling us one by one to comment on it. When my turn came, I noticed he was looking over my text with great attention, nodding his head in an attitude of respect and consideration. His respectful and apprecia- tive attitude had a much greater effect on me than the high classification that he gave me for my work. The teacher affirmed in me a self-confidence that obviously still had room to grow. But it inspired me to a belief that I too had value and could work and produce results.
>
> (1998, p. 47)

The student was a face, but so often written work is returned anonymously and the students are treated as strangers. But we are not dealing with strangers, we are working with people and so when we assess the work of individuals who are faces to us, then we should enter a dialogue with them in the assessment. We are working with people and it is people who learn and who grow and develop and so that our written comments should be rather like that school teacher cited from Freire's work: we should not just mark things wrong, for instance, so much as to ask why/how they had reached their conclusion; we should write encour- aging points and appreciate good and interesting answers, and so on. We are addressing faces not strangers through the written word.

Teaching people takes time! Often we do not have the time. The system demands that we make the faces strangers and get on with other aspects of our work. This too is our temptation, because our work is demanding and time-consuming, but we might actually discuss our difficulties with our students and treat them as faces rather than condemn them to strangerhood. However, there is another way in which we can take away students' dignity and self-hood.

The over-protective teacher

There are some occasions when teachers gain a following who hang on to their every word, and so on. Sometimes teachers encourage this; it is certainly good for our ego. But if we overstep the mark, as it were, we take from the students something of their freedom and, once again, it is not longer a conversation but an exposition in which the teachers give the students of their wisdom but not from the opposite extreme from stangerhood and we incorporate them into another system – one which revolves around the teachers and their *ego* and this also has many dangers.

In most of our teaching the stranger occasionally emerges as a face and on others the face is condemned to strangerhood. Clearly there are a multitude of factors that create these situations and we are all caught up within the system and its demands and as these demands grow so the potentialities of the face decrease. This does not mean that students will fail – after all they still have the library, the Web and each other, so that there are many other resources. If we treat them as faces, however, we might actually direct them to such resources as we discuss the demands that the system makes on us as teachers. But what does infinity offer?

Teaching and infinity: sharing and expanding

Levinas (1991a, p. 52) claims that 'The immediate is the face to face'; it is in this situation that those who interact are open to each other, and it is in conversation that each can inspire the other. Writing from the perspective of the self:

> It is therefore to *receive* from the Other beyond the capacity of the I, which means exactly: to have the idea of infinity. But this also means to be taught. The relation with the Other, or Conversation, is a non-allergic relation, an ethical relation; but inasmuch as it is welcomed this conversation is a teaching . . . Teaching is not reducible to maieutics; it comes from the exterior and brings me more than I contain. In its non-violent transitivity the very epiphany of the face is produced.
>
> (Levinas, 1991a, p. 51
> (italics in original))

Maieutics is the Socratic mode of teaching (see Chapter 7 on the Socratic method) in which Socrates implied that individuals have latent ideas which just had to be brought to the consciousness through questioning. But, Levinas claims that teaching brings something new to the learner through which the learner can grow and develop. In conversation this is a two-way process whereby each enriches the other and continues to do so for as long as the relationship is active. The idea of learning from the students echoes Freire's student/teacher–teacher/student idea – something to which he was to return throughout his life: 'Only the person who listens patiently and critically is able to speak *with* the other, even if at times it should be necessary to speak *to* him or her' (Freire, 1998, p. 110).

In the Preface, Levinas (1991a, p. 25) suggests that 'infinity overflows the thought that thinks it': it is, therefore, beyond experience. It is growth and development and yet more grow and development since human beings can transcend themselves, and reach towards an infinite capacity and achievement – it is beyond thought itself. Wild (Levinas, 1991a, p. 17) suggests, 'The former (totalisers) seek for power and control; the latter (infinitisers) for a higher quality of life. The former strive for order and the system; the latter for freedom and creative advance.'

There is a folk high school in Tennessee called Highlander and one of the things that I learned from that historic place is my ABC – Any Body Can! It is this hope that lies behind the infinitiser. At this point it might well be asked whether this is not something that most teachers want to do for their students and, to some extent, it is but the point of Levinas' argument is to ask whether we can actually transcend the system and reach to the heights of human creativity and self-hood within it. He leans to the idea that this can only truly happen through conversation in which neither imposes upon the other but each teaches the other that enables us to transcend it. It is a truly democratic process.

Clearly, Levinas' argument is open to considerable questioning in some places and in the way it is presented it is certainly centred upon the Self who needs to break away from the social system and transcend it and I do not think that he pursues how the relationship conversational relationship that points us towards infinity sufficiently far. But the ideas underlying his thinking are certainly applicable to the teaching and learning situation, since it points to the:

- all-embracing social and cultural system within which we live and which we take for granted;
- power implicit within the system for the role players (teachers);
- significance of the other (students) as persons (faces);
- importance of the interaction;
- mode of interaction;
- intentions of the participants;
- often untested and infinite capacity of human beings if they can break away from the system.

Conclusion

There are no directives in striving towards infinity, only hopes and aspirations. These will reflect both the teachers' hopes for their students but also their hopes for the world because in genuine conversation teachers' own beliefs – their own personhood – must be apparent. The more we think along these lines the more fundamental becomes the position which might best be summed up by Freire's condemnation of teaching that just conforms and does not look towards infinity:

Educative practice is all of the following: affectivity, joy, scientific serious-
ness, technical expertise at the service of change and, unfortunately, the
preservation of the status quo. It is exactly this static, neoliberal ideology,
proposing as it does 'the death of history' that converts tomorrow into
today by insisting that everything is under control, everything has already
been worked out and taken care of. When the hopeless, fatalistic, anti-
utopian character of this ideology, which proposes a purely technical kind
of education in which the teacher distinguishes himself or herself not by
desire to change the world but to accept it as it is. Such a teacher possesses
very little capacity for critical education but quite a lot for 'training', for
transferring contents. An expert in 'know-how'. The kind of knowledge
this 'pragmatic' teacher needs for his or her work is not the kind I have been
speaking of . . . It is not for me to judge, of course, regarding the value of
this knowledge in itself, but it is my duty to denounce the antihumanist
character of this neoliberal pragmatism.

(1998, pp. 126–127)

Freire in his more political way concurs with Levinas in his reflections on the
self and the world; both point beyond the totality to the infinity or to the utopian
dreams of teaching. It was this dream that led Palmer into the movement for
educational reform:

I am a teacher at heart, and I am not naturally drawn to the rough-and-
tumble of social change. I would sooner teach than spend my energies
helping a movement along and taking the hits that come with it. Yet if I care
about teaching, I must care not only about my students and my subject but
also for the conditions, inner and outer, that bear on the work teachers
do. Finding a place in the movement for educational reform is one way to
exercise that larger caring.

(1998, p. 182)

Underlying all teaching is a utopian dream, and aspiration towards infinity
and the ethics underlying the whole exercise of teaching and learning is that
together teachers and learners, who are also learners and teachers, must recognise that it is human beings (faces) who constitute the process and they are
always in the process of becoming – growing and developing – and reaching
beyond where they are now and the nurturing of this process is human care and
concern for the Other.

References

Althusser, L. (1972) Ideology and Ideological State Apparatuses in Cosin, B. (ed.)
    Education, Structure and Society Harmondsworth: Penguin
Bourdieu, P. and Passeron, J.-C. (1977) *Reproduction in Education, Society and Culture*
    (trans. R. Nice) London: Sage
Brookfield, S. (1990) *The Skillful Teacher* San Francisco, CA: Jossey-Bass
Buber, M. (1959) *I and Thou* Edinburgh: T&T Clark
Cooper, D. (1983) *Authenticity and Learning* London: Routledge & Kegan Paul
Cosin, B. (ed.) (1972) *Education, Structure and Society* Harmondsworth: Penguin
Freire, P. (1998) *Pedagogy of Freedom* Lanham: Rowman & Littlefield
Jarvis, P. (1983) *Adult and Continuing Education: Theory and Practice* London: Croom
    Helm

Jarvis, P. (1997) *Ethics and the Education of Adults in Late Modern Society* Leicester: NIACE

Jarvis, P. (2004) *Adult Education and Lifelong Learning: Theory and Practice* London: RoutledgeFalmer (3rd edition)

Jarvis, P. (2005) *Towards a Comprehensive Theory of Human Learning* London: Routledge

Levinas, E. (1991a) *Totality and Infinity* (trans: A. Lingis) Dordrecht: Kluwer

Levinas, E. (1991b) *Otherwise than Being or Beyond Essence* (trans: A. Lingis) Dordrecht: Kluwer

Macfarlane, B. (2004) *Teaching with Integrity* London: RoutledgeFalmer

MacIntyre, A. (1964) Against Utilitarianism in Hollins T (ed.) *Aims in Education* Manchester: University of Manchester Press

Palmer, P. (1998) *The Courage to Teach* San Francisco, CA: Jossey-Bass

Snook, I. (1972) *Concepts of Indoctrination* London: Routledge & Kegan Paul

Wild, J. (1991) Introduction to Levinas E *Totality and Infinity* (trans: A. Lingis) Dordrecht: Kluwer, pp. 11–20

Wilson, J. (1964) Education and Indoctrination in Hollins, T. (ed.) *Aims in Education* Manchester: University of Manchester Press

Wrong, D. (1961) The Over-Socialized Conception of Man reprinted in Wrong, D. (1976) *Skeptical Sociology* London: Heinemann

CHAPTER 11

TEACHING

An art or a science (technology)?

Originally published as 'Teaching: An Art or a Science (Technology)?' in P. Jarvis (ed.) (2006), *The Theory and Practice of Teaching*, second edition, London: Routledge, pp. 16–27. Cross-references refer to the original publication.

The ideal lecture theatre is vast, truly vast.
It is a very sombre, very old amphitheatre, and very uncomfortable.
The professor is lodged in his chair, which is raised high enough for everyone to see him;
there is no question that he might get down and pester you.
You can hear him quite well, because he doesn't move.
Only his mouth moves.
Preferably he has white hair, a stiff neck and a Protestant air about him.
There are a great many students, and each is perfectly anonymous.
To reach the amphitheatre, you have to climb some stairs, and then, with the leather-lined doors closed behind, the silence is absolute, every sound stifled;
the walls rise very high, daubed with rough paintings in half tones in which silhouettes of various monsters can be detected.
Everything adds to the impression of being in another world.
So one works religiously.

(History student, female, aged 25 –
cited by Bourdieu and Passeron, 1994, p. 1)

Academic discourse, as Bourdieu and Passeron make clear, uses a vocabulary far removed from the students' everyday experience and not well understood by them. When they try to use it, usually incorrectly, it merely reinforces the professors' perception of them as unintelligent, since they try to repeat the ideas of the professors in a language that they have not mastered. But even if they do master it, it contains only limited forms of knowledge that might, or might not, be useful to the students in their own everyday life, or even their own professional life. It is about certain forms of cognitive knowledge, omitting the other dimensions of human living and human practice. But the question that we might want to ask is – is what we have described here actually teaching? It has certainly passed for teaching in universities for a long while. But how do we evaluate it – is it because 'correct' knowledge is being transmitted or is it because the process facilitates the learning. Universities have traditionally been concerned about the former and only recently have they become concerned about the latter. Therefore, before we can seek to answer the question posed by this chapter's title we need to explore what we mean by teaching. This chapter, therefore, falls into three parts: the concept of teaching; teaching as a technology; teaching as an art.

The concept of teaching

A great deal of emphasis in contemporary education has been on learning and the learner, although concerns about teaching have continued to surface – as the Quality Assurance exercise and the emphasis in the Dearing Committee's (1997) report make clear. In the latter, we read:

> We recommend that, with immediate effect, all institutions of higher educa-
> tion give high priority to developing and implementing learning and
> teaching strategies which focus on the promotion of students' learning.
>
> (Recommendation 8)

> We recommend that institutions of higher education begin immediately to
> develop or seek access to programmes for teacher training of their staff, if
> they do not have them, and that all institutions seek national accreditation
> of such programmes from the Institute for Learning and Teaching in Higher
> Education.
>
> (Recommendation 13)

While the Dearing Committee was concerned that the image of the professor sitting high above his students had to be eradicated, the committee did not really consider the concept of teaching itself, although it did include distance educa-tion within its deliberations.

In the previous chapter we outlined the meanings to the concept given by the *Concise Oxford English Dictionary* but in order to demonstrate how even the dictionaries differ, in this chapter we record the meanings given by *Collins Dictionary*. It offers us a number of different ways of viewing teaching: to help to learn, to show; to give instruction or information; to cause to learn or understand; to teach someone a lesson. Perhaps this final one shows us something of the paradox of teaching, but the many definitions from both dictionaries illustrate that it is hard to define teaching. Indeed, Pratt (1998) offers five different approaches to it: transmission (effective delivery), apprenticeship (modelling ways of doing), developmental (cultivating ways of thinking), nurturing (facilitating self-sufficiency), and social reform (seeking a better society). Pratt is actually suggesting five different aims of teaching rather than five different conceptions of it. Nowhere does he actually offer a definition, since he recognises that people, like the dictionaries, have a variety of perspectives on the subject. Neither does he try to distil out common elements from these perspectives in order to provide a conceptual framework for understanding the concept.

Many years before this, Hirst and Peters (1970, p. 80) tried to delimit teaching by suggesting that 'teaching had to indicate or express some content, that pupils are intended to learn', and this for them was the thing that distinguished teaching from other similar activities. It certainly fits the pattern of the professor, as described by Bourdieu and Passeron, and it is also in accord with curriculum theory where content is one of its central elements, but if this is the essential nature of teaching it is hard to locate facilitation within it. In these contexts, it is perhaps no wonder that writers such as Carl Rogers (1983,

p. 119) can claim that teaching is an over-rated function. But Rogers was a teacher! But not one who sought to control the content of what is taught and so Hirst's and Peters' approach is not applicable to all forms of teaching. Perhaps, an even more inclusive definition is required.

Brown and Atkins (1998, p. 2) actually offer a simple and almost self-evident definition of teaching: it is 'providing opportunities for students to learn'. Kidd (1973, p. 292) would agree with this and he suggested that we need a noun that captures the idea of 'he (*sic*) – who-assists-learning-to-happen' – which is rather like the idea of animation. Yet this approach is not as self-evident as it might seem. For instance:

- What happens if the students do not take the opportunities – is providing them with opportunities still teaching? One could claim that it is, but Freire (1998) would claim that there can be no teaching without learning. Nevertheless, if teachers' cannot attract their learners they might be considered poor teachers rather than non-teachers. Yet poor teaching might not be the only reason why the students do not learn – it might simply be that they do not want to learn, or that they consider the subject irrelevant to their lives. It is possible to take a horse to the water but it cannot be made to drink.
- Does there have to be a relationship between the teacher and the learners for teaching to occur, as there is in the traditional classroom – or has the realignment of time and space in late modern society meant that the teacher's role has changed in dramatic ways? Clearly as teachers now prepare material on-line there can be no face-to-face relationship in these instances, but neither did the professor seated high above his students have much of a relationship with them. In on-line teaching a relationship might emerge, although its nature will have changed, and an opportunity to learn has still been provided.
- Writing a book or a journal article might be viewed as providing an opportunity to learn, but is authorship *per se* teaching? It certainly provides opportunities for learning but authors are not necessarily teachers in the formal sense of the word; they might not regard themselves as teachers, nor might they regard their writing as teaching. Yet in writing material for print-based distance education, there is an intention to provide opportunities for learning, so that certain forms of authorship are teaching. Consequently, teaching might be seen as an intended activity.

It may be seen that it is extremely difficult to get a definition that delimits teaching from other similar activities. Nevertheless, for the purposes of this chapter, teaching is regarded as an intentional activity in which opportunities to learn are provided, and this is broad enough to include all the types of teaching mentioned above. Now the question posed by the title of this chapter might be addressed.

Teaching as a technology

Since education has been an Enlightenment product, it is no surprise to find that the traditional concept of teaching has embraced many of its philosophies, such as the emphasis on an end-product, rationality, efficiency, scientific ideals of measurement and evidence, and both an empirical and pragmatic approach to knowledge. Significantly, learners were treated almost as if they were passive recipients of the information that they were receiving; they could be treated almost as inanimate objects so that the process could be likened in some way to natural science. Teaching could, therefore, be examined in the same way as material objects, so that the techniques by which knowledge was transmitted were regarded as crucial to the process. Therefore, teaching as we have traditionally known it might be regarded as the product of the era of modernity. It is an activity that had to fit this paradigm, so that this calls for a discussion of at least three aspects of teaching; the end-product of teaching, the means to the end and an assessment of the process.

The end-product

The outcome of any teaching process had to be measurable so that the emphasis on behaviourism reflected the instrumental rationality of the period. If teachers could understand how the learning process occurred they could endeavour to ensure that their activity was efficient and achieved the pre-determined outcomes. Hence scientific experiments were needed to demonstrate how individuals learned and Skinner, amongst others, was able to demonstrate this case in laboratory experiments with animals. This satisfied the scientific emphases of modernity. Consequently, the more teachers understand processes of reinforcement in learning, the more effective their teaching might become so that they achieve their specified objectives – usually behavioural in nature. Skinner (1968, p. 59) actually believed that teaching is a technology in which we can 'deduce programs and schemes and methods of instruction'. Therefore, lessons and teaching materials could be designed that provided the type of reinforcement necessary to achieve the pre-determined outcomes, that could then be measured either by behavioural change or by examination and assessment of the knowledge taught. In precisely the same way he (1968, p. 65) believed that teaching machines are devices that 'arrange the contingencies of reinforcement' and, therefore, effective distance education could use the same psychological processes as face-to-face teaching and their effectiveness could be assessed in precisely the same manner.

While there is considerable evidence that conditioning is effective, fundamental questions have to be asked about the extent to which the laboratory experiments with rats and mice can be transferred to human beings. Nevertheless, behaviourism was a product of this period, and this approach to teaching seemed self-evident and was widely accepted and is still accepted.

Means to an end

Teaching techniques are means to an end – they might be regarded as a form of instrumental rationality, and therefore fit into this paradigm of scientific modernity. In basic curriculum theory we see the logical pattern of aims of the lesson, content to be taught and, therefore, the methods to be used. Finally, in this model, evaluation occurs – of the content and of the methods selected. The choice of method bears little or no relationship to moral or philosophical principles but only to a realistic understanding of human behaviour and its effectiveness in producing the desired outcomes. This 'scientific approach' is even more pronounced in the various approaches to instructional design, which are more common in the United States than in the United Kingdom (West *et al.*, 1991; Gagné *et al.*, 1992). Here the models for designing instruction are extremely sophisticated; they provide rational processes and programmes that instructors should implement in order to make their instruction more effective. Once more, it is the technique and not the teacher that is important, so that individual instructors or the teachers are almost dispensable to the process.

Perhaps we see this even more with the use of PowerPoint presentations – I have attended conferences where there has almost been a competition for the most sophisticated PowerPoint expertise, almost irrespective of the conceptual level of its content. It is almost as if the technology has assumed a greater importance than the content or the teachers and learners.

This argument has been pursued even further when it comes to distance education, since it is possible to design the types of materials that Skinner (1968, p. 65) advocated when he suggested that 'the teaching machine is simply a device to arrange for the contingencies of reinforcement'. In another way we see teaching as no more than a transmission of knowledge to more students man a single lecture theatre would hold. Peters (1984) equated the production of distance education materials to a process of manufacture. In this, teaching was becoming efficient since it enabled one set of teaching materials to be mass-produced and used with a far greater number of learners. However, in a later work, Peters (1998) has also noted that other distance education material does take philosophical and humanistic concerns into consideration.

Nevertheless it is quite significant that in teacher training there has been a considerable emphasis placed on teaching methods – see the discussion in the next chapter. It is the method that is important rather than the personality of the teachers or of their behavioural and ideological dispositions. Teaching techniques are important, and few people would deny this, but the emphasis placed upon them reflects the era of modernity. Skinner (1968, p. 91), however, actually recognised that if these techniques are used unwisely they might inhibit learners' creativity, so that he indicated that teaching might be more than technique, as do other theorists of education. Not all objectives, for instance, are behavioural – some are expressive (Eisner, 1969), and more recently the focus has been on other elements of teaching, such as teaching style – a point to which we will return in the next section and even more so in the next chapter.

In my own work (Jarvis, 1995) I originally suggested that there are three different categories of method: didactic, Socratic and facilitative, but in this book we have added a fourth – experiential. Within this discussion, however, the ethics of teaching acquires a more significant place, a point to which we shall return below.

Evaluating the teaching process

Since the emphasis of teaching has been placed on instrumental rationality, it is little wonder that one of the ways of measuring teaching success has been on the outcomes of the process. Teachers must be effective if they produce students who gain good grades – a measurable outcome. But there is no direct evidence to indicate that the teaching process has actually been the cause of the measurable outcome! It might have been, but we do not necessarily know whether it is the teaching process, or the teachers' personality or the learners and their efforts, which help achieve the success. But there is at least one other problem: students can learn from many other sources and it might even be that poor teachers drive good students to the libraries. But so does the fear of failure! Our professor sitting on high might actually be communicating relevant knowledge but fear of failing his course might mean that his students spend hours in the libraries and then it is their study skills that are as, or more, important than the lectures that they attended.

The other way of assessing the teaching process is to observe it and in some way record it. In this numerical world, we have seen teachers graded, and in some places the grade is used in helping to determine whether, or not, teachers should be promoted. But as we know from all the research on marking essays that there is a tremendous difference between different markers and how much more is this likely to be when each teaching event is unique and when it is not really possible to re-visit the event and re-consider it? We are all aware that students' evaluations of the same lesson do not all agree, and a similar disagreement might well be found if experienced lecturers all assessed a teaching process. Indeed, many years ago we tried an experiment in a workshop when we asked thirty teachers to assess a video of someone cleaning a pair of shoes – there was considerable variation in their assessments! This is not to claim that bad teaching cannot be identified, only that it is more difficult to do than many of the over-simplistic methods that are often employed in many situations.

With distance education materials, we can only evaluate the content and the way that it is produced and presented, but the writer of the material may not actually be the person who designs the format or produces the final structure. In this sense, the writer as academic can be evaluated but the presentation of that material is a skill that might other professionals might possess, so that teaching itself becomes a team activity with at least one partner not necessarily being an academic. However, it is also clear from this discussion that distance education has changed the nature of teaching; it is about content, process and design which captures the spirit of the technological age. It is an ultimate form of manufacture; it comes much closer to being a technology and a science of production than does classroom teaching. Like other occupations, the uniqueness of the person is removed. The human relationship of the classroom is displaced by impersonal transmission of knowledge and individual learning and achieving. However, in certain forms of on-line learning we are beginning to see the possibilities of relationship and individuality emerge in distance education – it is a more human and a neo-Fordist approach to education.

What we have begun to question in each of these points is the idea that teaching is just about technique. It is a technology but is this all it needs to be to provide learning opportunities intentionally? Is the teacher merely the instrument choosing the right methods, communicating the 'correct' knowledge and getting the desired results? In this process the students are treated as passive and are moulded like materials in other production processes – but this does not exhaust the process of teaching since students need individual help, need to be motivated, and so on. Learning and teaching needs a personal relationship in order to achieve the best outcomes and this is also recognised by the fact that many distance education institutions also provide opportunities for face-to-face contact.

The art of teaching

The concentration on content and method has led many of us to say that 'I teach sociology' or 'I teach mathematics' – but this is incorrect. Actually, 'I teach people sociology' or 'mathematics', and so on. Sentences of this nature betray the values of a technological age, but they are incorrect and they also hide something of the moral basis of teaching, a point to which we shall return in a later chapter.

Brookfield (1990, p. 2) has denied the importance of the technology of teaching by suggesting that it is rather like 'white-water rafting'. In a sense the conditions in which it occurs are not controllable. In a similar manner Eble (1988, pp. 11–12) seeks to dispel at least twelve myths of teaching, although he concentrates rather more on the teaching process than on the conditions; three of his twelve myths are that:

- teaching is not a performing art
- teaching should exclude personality
- popular teachers are bad teachers.

Basically he is saying precisely the same thing as Freire (1998) when he calls teaching a human act, but he goes a little further than Freire by implying that there is something of a performance in teaching. I do not think that Freire would disagree with this. However, this aspect of teaching – teaching style – is notably absent from many teacher-training courses.

Kidd (1973, p. 295) suggests that teaching styles are often presented as dichotomies:

- permissiveness versus control
- aggressiveness versus protectiveness
- emphasis on content versus emphasis on participation.

In my own work, I (Jarvis, 1995, p. 105) have suggested that research into leadership management styles are also useful when thinking about teaching style, such as Lippett and White (1958) who suggested that there are three leadership styles: authoritarian, democratic and laissez-faire, and McGregor's (1960) Theory X and Theory Y, with the former treating learners as if they do not want to learn and the latter assuming that they are highly motivated. The recognition of teaching style is the recognition that teachers' performances as an intrinsic part of the teaching process. More works are now focusing on teaching style as well as teaching method than in previous generations – style is the about the art of teaching rather than the science. It is also about the teachers' own humanity and personality. Style clearly overlaps with method, but is still different from it. For instance it is possible to have an authoritarian facilitator and a democratic lecturer, and so on.

However, there is more to humanistic teaching than just style. This form of teaching involves a relationship, one that is necessarily moral, for all human interaction has a moral component. I have argued elsewhere (Jarvis, 1997) that there is one universal moral value – that is being concerned for the Other – and it is never wrong to care for the Other – whoever the Other is. Consequently, teachers should be concerned for their students, but students should also be concerned for their teachers. There are many books and papers that have sought to demonstrate the significance of the moral relationship in teaching (Daloz, 1988; Freire, 1998; Palmer, 1998, *inter alia*) and they recount the lengths to which teachers should go to help students achieve their own fulfilment through the processes of teaching and learning. This is the vocation of teaching. We shall return to the moral element in teaching in a later chapter.

Palmer (1998, p. 74) highlights some of the paradoxes of classroom teaching and suggests six – the classroom space should:

- be bounded and open;
- be hospitable and 'charged';
- invite the voice of the individual and the voice of the group;
- honour the 'little' stories of the students and the 'big' stories of the disciplines and the traditions;
- support solitude and surround it with the resources of the community;
- welcome both silence and speech.

Once these paradoxical and moral elements enter into the teaching and learning process, the focus is on the humanity of the learners and much of the instrumentality of teaching fades into insignificance. Teaching is about respecting the personhood of learners and teachers and enabling human beings to achieve their own potential, without imposing on them pre-determined outcomes of the teaching, although we recognise the importance of what is learned in the process. Fundamentally, teaching is a human process, in which the teachers themselves may well be the best instruments that they have in helping learners to both learn their subject and achieve their potential. We are now beginning to see recognition of this when, as in the UK recently, there have been campaigns to attract people into the teaching profession using celebrities who have proclaimed how specific teachers have most influenced them in their earlier life, and so forth. This is an implicit recognition that the emphasis on the instrumentality of the Enlightenment era, which modern teaching acquired, have always underplayed the human elements of the process – teaching is an art.

Conclusion

Like the dictionaries that offered a number of definitions of teaching, we cannot reach a definitive conclusion as to whether teaching is a technology or an art. Clearly some forms of teaching, especially those that tend to depersonalise the teaching and learning process, like the professor with whom we opened this chapter who can lecture to hundreds of students, and those other forms that lend themselves to mass production, suggest that teaching is a technology. But when teaching is face-to-face and interactive, when it is a human process then it is much more than a science – it is an art.

References

Bourdieu, P. and Passeron, J.-C. (1994) Language and the Teaching Situation in Bourdieu, P., Passeron, J.-C. and Saint Martin, M. (eds) *Academic Discourses* Cambridge: Polity Press

Brookfield, S. D. (1990) *The Skillful Teacher* San Francisco, CA: Jossey-Bass

122   *Teaching*

Brown, G. and Atkins, M. (1988) *Effective Teaching in Higher Education* London: Methuen

Collins Dictionary of the English Language

Daloz, L. A. (1988) *Effective Teaching and Mentoring* San Francisco, CA: Jossey-Bass

Dearing, R. (Chair) (1997) *Higher Education in the Learning Society* (Summary Report) London: HMSO

Eble, K. E. (1988) *The Craft of Teaching* San Francisco, CA: Jossey-Bass (Second Edition)

Eisner, E. W. (1969) Instructional and Expressive Educational Objectives in Popham, W. J., Eisner, E. W., Sullivan, H. J. and Tyler, L. L. (eds) *Instructional Objectives* Chicago, IL: Rand McNally

Freire, P. (1998) *Pedagogy of Freedom* Lanham: Rowman & Littlefield

Gagné, R. M., Briggs, L. J. and Wagner, W. W. (1992) *Principles of Instructional Design* Fort Worth: Harcourt Brace, Janovitch (Fourth Edition)

Hirst, P. and Peters, R. S. (1970) *The Logic of Education* London: Routledge & Kegan Paul

Jarvis, P. (1995) *Adult and Continuing Education: Theory and Practice* London: Routledge (Second Edition)

Jarvis, P. (1997) *Ethics and the Education of Adults in Late Modern Society* NIACE: Leicester

Kidd, J. R. (1973) *How Adults Learn* Chicago, IL: Association Press (Revised Edition)

Lippett, R. and White, R. K. (1958) An Experimental Study into Leadership and Group Life in Maccoby, E. E., Newcomb, T. M. and Hartley, E. L. (eds) *Readings in Social Psychology* New York: Holt

McGregor, D. (1960) *The Human Side of Enterprise* New York: McGraw Hill

Palmer, P. J. (1998) *The Courage to Teach* San Francisco, CA: Jossey-Bass

Peters, O. (1984) Distance Teaching and Industrial Production: A Comparative Interpretation in Outline in Sewart, D., Keegan, D. and Hohmberg, B. (eds) *Distance Education: International Perspectives* London: Croom Helm

Peters, O. (1998) *Learning and Teaching in Distance Education* London: Kogan Page

Pratt, D. and Associates (1998) *Five Different Approaches to Teaching in Adult and Higher Education* Malabar, FL: Krieger

Rogers, C. (1983) *Freedom to Learn for the 1980s* New York: Merrill (Second Edition)

Skinner, B. F. (1968) *The Technology of Teaching* New York: Appleton Century Crofts

West, C. K., Fowler, J. A. and Wolf, P. M. (1991) *Instructional Design: Implications from Cognitive Science* Englewood Cliffs, NJ: Prentice Hall

CHAPTER 12

___

TRANSFORMING ASIAN EDUCATION THROUGH OPEN AND DISTANCE LEARNING
Through thinking

Originally presented as 'Transforming Asian Education through Open and Distance Learning: Through Thinking' (2004), unpublished paper delivered at the Chinese Distance Education and Hong Kong OU Research in Distance Education Conference, Hong Kong.

One of the most misunderstood approaches to learning by Western educationalists is that which emanates from Confucian Heritage Countries, but in addressing the subject of learning here I do not want to fall into the same trap. I want to focus on the philosophy of learning in the first instance because it points to two very important facts: to the universality of the human condition in which we do not know all the answers to the questions of our existence and, secondly, because none of us have instincts or sufficient knowledge to be able to live without learning. Human beings need to learn in order to survive. Moreover, we human beings have a paradoxical relationship with the world – we seek harmony with our life-world but because we do not have sufficient knowledge to do so, we are frequently in a disjunctural state with it and are forced to ask questions. But the way in which we all respond to our human condition is culturally-based. Only through understanding the culture can we begin to understand different approaches to learning and knowledge adopted by different countries and, traditionally, the West has not understood the East very well. As learning is a universal human process we would expect that there would be considerable similarities between the ways that all people learn but we would also expect different cultural emphases and explanations which lead to different practices. Consequently, I am not surprised to find considerable similarities between my own research into learning and the writings of Confucius and his followers. At the same time there are clearly fundamentally different cultural emphases which I hope to explore briefly in the first part of the paper.

One of the major differences between East and West is the emphasis that Confucian Heritage Countries place upon memorising and understanding the teachings of the master which has given rise wrongly to accusations that Chinese learners are rote learners. These ideas about learning occur in the rather formal Chinese society where there was respect for the elder and the master. In contrast, a lot of Western early thinking about learning has been influenced by the more romantic approach of Rousseau's (1911 [1762]) *Emile* in which he was free to live a more 'natural' life, although guided by a tutor. Consequently, the Eastern thinking is about learning in the formal context whereas a lot of Western thinking is about learning in less formal situations. At the same time, I think that the forms of learning that emerge from all forms of educational curricula, and especially in text-based distance education, can lead to an endeavour to memorise what has been written, which is both contrary to the philosophy of Confucian Heritage Countries and to Western education. This also occurs in Western education, and which I (Jarvis, 1987, 2004 *inter alia*) have referred to as non-reflective learning while Marton and Säljö (1984) call it surface learning as opposed to deep learning.

In the third part, I want to suggest that if we are going to transform Asian education through open and distance learning we must do all that we can to prevent our learners from just being rote learners by introducing them to different forms of thinking and, finally, I want to indicate a few approaches that we might utilise to broaden the learners' thinking. In this sense, I hope that this paper might be seen as a practical philosophy of learning applicable to all curricula settings and especially to open and distant learning.

Human learning

At the heart of the human condition there is the realisation that we are not born with the instincts of animals sufficient to survive our lifetime on earth. We need more knowledge and significantly the Chinese word for knowledge has two characters – one is *xue* – to learn – and the other is *wen* – to ask (Cheng, 2000, p. 441) and as Kennedy, citing Cheng (2000, p. 433) says, the 'action of enquiring and questioning is central to the quest for knowledge'. However, Schutz and Luckmann (1974, p. 7) rightly claim:

> I trust that the world as it has been known by me up until now will continue further and that consequently the stock of knowledge obtained from my fellow-men and formed from my own experiences will continue to preserve its fundamental validity . . . From this assumption follows the further one: that I can repeat my past successful acts. So long as the structure of the world can be taken as constant, as long as my previous experience is valid.

In other words, we prefer not to question but to live 'instinctively', in harmony with our environment. Moreover, when we cannot do this we tend to accept what the master has taught us, or what is generally accepted in society, which reflects the Western myth about Chinese learning. I think that this preference to accept authoritative guidance is quite universal.

Since learning has traditionally been studied within the context of teaching, it is not surprising that Confucian philosophies of learning begin with the content of teaching, and teachers should be treated with respect and their knowledge learned and understood. Whereas in my own research, I have deliberately tried to isolate learning from the context of teaching and locate it within the context of living and the life-world, so that instead of focusing upon what is taught I emphasise the learners' experience which arises from disjunctural situations – ones in which our perception of our experience is out of harmony with our biography. This leads to a need to learn in order to try to restore harmony – a never-ending quest since to achieve it would be to deny our human condition. Learning, then, is intrinsic to the human condition and cannot be separated from living. Herein lies the potential differences between East and West. Kyung (2004, p. 125), rightly to my mind, seeks to explore the differences in terms of the Western ideas of truth, transcendence and rational compared to the humanistic way, immanence and the aesthetic. He then goes on to compare the orientation of learning in relation to the self. However, these dichotomies are no longer totally valid and West and East have drawn closer in recent years. The philosophy underlying my own research into learning, and I think many who write from an experientialist or existential perspective, is closer to what he depicts as Confucian and, consequently, my own understanding of human learning is much closer to the Confucian understanding of learning – at least from the humanistic perspective. I will show this below but even more so in my forthcoming book on *Learning and Personhood*.

A great deal of recent work on Chinese learning points to the fact that Chinese learners seek to memorise what the teacher has taught, but the process is much more profound than this. While it is not a myth that many Chinese learners do actually seek to memorise, it is by no means the whole story as Lee points out. He (1996, pp. 35–36) cites Zhu (Chu, 1990, p. 135) who wrote:

> Generally speaking, in reading we must first become intimately familiar with the text so that its words seem to come from our own mouths. We should then continue to reflect on it so that its ideas come from our own minds. Only then can there be real understanding. Since, once our intimate reading of it and careful reflection on it have led to a clear understanding of it, we must continue to question. Then there might be additional progress. If we cease questioning, in the end there will be no additional progress.

Memorising, understanding, reflecting and questioning are, according to the above quotation, the four components of learning. Elsewhere, Lee (1996, p. 36) cites Wang Yangming (cited by Chiang 1924, p. 87):

> If you simply want to memorize, you will not be able to understand; if you simply want to understand, you will not be able to know the sources [of truth] in yourself.

For Wang, then, we can see that memorising, understanding and incorporation into one's own biography are the three significant components of learning. Drawing these two formulations together we see that within Confucian thinking: memory, understanding, reflecting, questioning and incorporating into the person lie at the heart of learning. It will be noted, however, that both of these quotations about learning occur within the context of teaching, in a society where the teacher had a high status and the dominant teaching method was didactic. Consequently, all of these formulations include – whether implicitly or explicitly – a dimension of power. Hence, being able to recall and understand the teaching of the master was the 'correct' approach to learning and only after having understood what the master taught was the learner in a position to reflect and question. In a sense, reflecting and questioning are a licence for the learners to go beyond the master but they are also psychological processes in learning itself.

The motivation for learning is not included in either of these statements but Confucian philosophy is replete with references to this for, as we read in *The Great Learning (IV)*: a person should 'cultivate himself, then regulate the family, then govern the state, and finally lead the world into peace' (cited from Lee 1996, p. 37). Elsewhere in the *Analects*, we also find that individuals are instructed to learn 'for the sake of the self, (so) that person has good grounding upon which to become a noble or superior person' (Kyung, 2004, p. 120). Here we see that the outcomes of the learning are incorporated into the learners' own biographies and the person is developed. It is significant that Confucian philosophy recognises that learning is an individual act and, despite the emphasis on community and family in Eastern thought, the significance of the individual self and its development is clearly recognised.

These descriptions of learning from the Confucian tradition combine a social philosophy with basic psychological truisms about learning, but they recognise that the learners are changed and developed as they go through the cognitive learning process and in this sense they locate learning in the person. My own research about human learning has always focused upon the person who grows and develops as a result of learning, although I have tried to separate learning from teaching and locate it in the wider life-world. Consequently, I do not start with memory and understanding but with experience in the life-world and with disjuncture. Disjuncture is the situation where my perception of my experience differs from the store of knowledge in my biography (my memory) to such an extent that I cannot take my situation for granted and I am forced to ask Why?, How?, What do I do?, and so on. Whether the disjuncture is self or other induced, I am forced into a position of acknowledging that I cannot act unthinkingly – the paradox of learning is that the recognition that I do not know triggers the learning process. In a sense, seeking to memorise and understand what the master has taught is also implicit recognition that the learner does not know and is in need of help. The difference lies in my focus upon the experience and, thereafter, I argue that we transform our experiences through thought, action and emotion and then integrate the outcomes into our own biographies, which is broader than the Confucian emphasis on cognition. I now regard human learning as *the combination of processes whereby the whole person – body (genetic, physical and biological) and mind (knowledge, skills, attitudes, values, emotions, beliefs and senses) – experiences a social situation, the perceived content of which is then transformed cognitively, emotively or practically (or through any combination) and integrated into the person's individual biography resulting in a changed (or more experienced) person.* But for the purpose of this paper I am focusing much more on the cognitive dimension of learning.

In the following diagram, one of two in which I depict different aspects of the learning process, I want to emphasise the cognitive route through $(1_1{\rightarrow}2{\rightarrow}3{\rightarrow}6{\rightarrow}1_2)$, but also highlight the fact that there are others that are also very important. (An earlier version of this diagram also occurred in *Distance Education in China* 2004, p. 49.)

In the following diagram, individuals are in the world and for as long as they can take their life-world for granted they act in an instinctive manner and just go with the flow of time, but once they are confronted with disjuncture – when their perception of their world and their stock of knowledge, skill, attitudes and so on are no longer in harmony – they are forced to ask questions about their situation. In a sense, they become more conscious of their life-world and they have an experience. Having an experience is being conscious of their inability to respond automatically to their situation. This experience can be induced by the learner or by the teacher, and even by repeating previous information, and so on. As a result of having that experience, I think about it – and it is here that the writers we cited earlier talk of reflecting and questioning, but I want to suggest

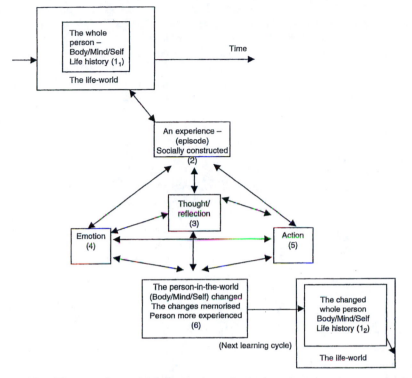

Figure 12.1 The transformation of experience in the learning process.

that this is insufficient. We also respond to our experiences emotionally and through action depending on our situation and dispositions. The outcome of our learning – both from Confucian philosophy and from my perspective – is of the learners being transformed and becoming more experienced – even more intelligent. But one of the problems with learning is that we do not all know how best to treat the information with which we are presented and so many learners just try to memorise it – this is true both East and West.

Critiques of non-reflective learning in educational settings

Any educational curriculum is a selection of knowledge, skill and so on from the culture of a society. Indeed, that selection is usually made by experts in the relevant subject and, as such, is regarded as worthy knowledge to be transmitted to the next generation. It does not matter how well-intentioned are the educators who design the curriculum or the learning programme, the very process of selecting teaching material is both an exercise in expertise and in power. It is not surprising, therefore, that those who seek to learn in an educational setting seek to grasp and memorise the content of the teaching material. This is even easier to do with text-based materials in open and distant education because the learners can go back over the material time and again seeking to memorise its contents. This is precisely what is advocated in the early stages of learning in the Confucian literature.

However, we have seen, Confucian literature does not stop at the early stages of learning but advocates further stages. For instance, Wang Yangming, cited above, was quite critical of the learners who only tried to memorise what they were taught and he rightly argued that the learners will never understand the meaning if they only try to memorise what they are taught. Memorisation is a particular problem with text-based distance education because text-based teaching materials tend to assume a didactic form.

From a Western perspective, however, Nietzsche (Cooper, 1983, p. 3) argued that if we passively accept established beliefs and traditions and learn them non-reflectively and this is, unfortunately, a normal condition of human being, we are denying our own humanity – this is inauthenticity. This is clearly what we want to avoid when we provide our students with opportunities to learn. But immediately we are forced to return to ourselves as designers of the teaching and learning material. It was this aspect of the process that concerned Foucault. He (1971, pp. 10–11 cited from Sheridan, 1980, p. 121), who was very influenced by Nietzsche's thought expanded upon it:

> . . . in any society the production of discourse is at once controlled, selected, organised and redistributed according to a number of procedures whose role is to avert its powers and dangers, to master the unpredictable event.

Education is the means by which individuals gain access to the discourse and in open and distance education we who write teaching material are the authors and even in the act of writing, we acknowledge our membership of a group which utilises and transmits the socially accepted discourses. Indeed, curriculum may be defined as a selection from culture (Lawton, 1973) and while we may now talk of a learning programme rather than curriculum, the same definition is applicable. We make that selection from culture. Now there is nothing at all wrong in this. Indeed, we cannot escape it. But it is important that we recognise that this is what we are doing and that we must also seek to help our learners move beyond the act of memorisation to those processes of understanding and reflecting. If we do not do this, then what they may memorise is what we have selected as worthwhile knowledge for them to learn – an exercise of our power as functionaries within the established discourses. Consequently, we need to move back to our understanding of learning which takes us outside of the educational setting and suggests that learning actually begins with disjuncture, when our perception of our experience and our biography (memory) are not in harmony.

It could be argued, however, that the act of memorisation itself actually deepens understanding and this is precisely what Marton and his colleagues (1996, pp. 69–83) discovered. As they recognised, deepening understanding through repetition is not new. But deepening understanding may still be merely learning at a deeper level about what others have selected as the content of the learning programme. In addition, repetition does not always lead to deeper understanding – there are occasions when the main outcome is merely remembering the same words better.

Nevertheless, Simpson (1995, p. 58) points out, the repetition also brings about self-development, which is a major element in Confucian thinking about education. However, memorisation is a process of accepting what has gone before and what we have presented to the learners. At the same time, it does help solve the paradox that whilst Chinese learners seek to memorise material, they also do extremely well in examinations and exhibit other indicators of their knowledge. One of the other reasons for this, however, might be the Confucian emphasis on effort rather than ability. Everybody is educable, as the *Analects* make clear. Lee (1996, p. 28) shows how Confucius recognised that there are differences in ability by having four categories of people: those born with knowledge, those who gain it through study, those who turn to study and those who make no effort to study. While we might want to question this categorisation, it is clear that within the *nature/nurture* debate, Confucian thinking comes down firmly on the *nurture* side. But a great deal of effort in order to deepen one's own understanding, while not a waste of time, might be an inefficient use of it. The philosophy of time, however, does not often appear in our philosophical discussions about learning – but if memorisation is merely a rehearsal of the past and we need a view of the future so that we can transform Asian education then we do need to make reference to it.

Seeking to commit to memory the words of the sage and discovering deeper meanings as we spend more time on repeating it is one approach to learning. By constant repetition, there is a sense in which in so doing, we come to terms with time (Simpson, 1995, p. 51) – for it matters not how long we spend on the exercise. Simpson refers to this as resolve (p. 51) but Confucius would see this as the necessary effort to learn. In this sense, however, we come to terms with time – what Kierkegaard (1959) called 'internal history'. But for Kierkegaard there is another approach to time – external history – when the focus is on achievement. This approach to time has become more significant in contemporary society as we have developed 'time-saving' technologies and so on, as 'time costs money'. Now, in education, the end-product is on what is learned in a specific period of time and so we design our learning in order to master time. We have modules, for instance, that are classified as 100 hours, or whatever, of learning, and so on. Herein lies a fundamental difference in approach. Confucius extolled effort, and we know that Chinese learners spend a lot of time on their learning – perhaps more than Western learners. For instance, we know that in school timetables Western children will spend less time during the curriculum on specific subjects than their Confucian Heritage Countries counterparts. Time, then, is a curriculum issue and, literally, timetables are charting passages through time.

Spending as much time as necessary through repetition is, in one sense a process of coming to terms with time – it is internal history; it is in many ways a most laudable approach to time and to learning. We are, however, confronted with a problem – since time is at a premium and the design of our education is increasingly focused on the external history of time. It is something to be mastered – it stands between us and our goal. In open and distance education, we are confronted with this approach to time: 'At the intersection of planning and technology lies the temporality of technology' (Simpson, 1995, p. 52). Perhaps by careful design we can help learners use time efficiently moving beyond the stages of repetition and memorisation to the later stages in Confucian thinking – reflecting, questioning and incorporating into the learners' biographies. Our concern is on achieving that moment of satisfaction when the learners are able to incorporate their new learning into their biographies – this, then, is Kierkegaard's external history of time.

Ways of thinking

It will be recalled from my own diagram that while there are many combinations of ways through which our episodic learning experience is transformed, I want to concentrate here on the cognitive – although we cannot actually separate it entirely from the other routes – which Zhu suggested were memorising, reflecting and questioning. Since we do not want the students to memorise the words of the master, we need to create disjuncture – a sense of not knowing – without the fear of not being able to question authoritative statements that might restore their harmony. Consequently we have to give the learners license to question even the earliest statements in the learning text. This is Socratic thinking – we have to help them to interrogate the text: we can create a sense of disjuncture by inviting them to question it. By so doing we will be creating episodic learning experiences which can be transformed through action, thought and emotion (boxes, 3, 4 and 5) so that it can be incorporated into their biographies (box 6), and this is also in accord with the teaching of Wang Yangming.

Now thinking/reflecting is rather an ill-defined process although Gilhooly (1996, p. 1) suggests that it is 'a set of processes whereby people assemble, use and revise internal symbolic models'. In this paper I want to suggest five pairs of thought processes: memorising and interpreting; creative and critical thinking; problem-solving and decision making; directed and undirected; deductive and inductive reasoning. All are important but they do not occur in a hierarchy of reflection, which I think is rather artificial. Each thought process performs different functions, all of which are significant to our learning processes – and even more so if we are going to transform Asian education through open and education. I will deal briefly with each pair in turn.

Memorising and interpreting: Memorising has a number of different meanings but in the context of the Chinese learner it refers to unreflective learning which is the process of committing to the mind the information that the learners have been presented. In contrast, hermeneutic, or interpretative, ways of thinking focus on the meaning of the communication, it is an endeavour to understand another person and the meaning of whatever is being communicated without testing it for its legitimacy, whether it is spoken or written. According to Gadamer (1978, p. 98), 'hermeneutics is the art of clarifying and mediating by our own effort of interpretation what is said by persons we encounter in tradition'. It is the art of trying to understand the meaning that the 'other' is seeking to communicate. Indeed, Gadamer (1978, p. 98) reminds us that the word is named after Hermes, the interpreter of the divine message to mankind.

Hermeneutical thought occurs in every human interaction, when we seek to understand the meaning of the person to whom we are speaking and, consequently, it demands the ability to listen and, in many cases, to read without trying to impose our own meaning upon what is being communicated. Consequently, hermeneutical thought transcends the situation of the thinker and bridges the gap between the thinker and the other – it is the other's meaning that the thinker is seeking which maybe a new understanding; this quest demands an empathy with the other and the other's life-world. While we cannot get into the mind of the other, hermeneutical thought demands that we get as close to that mind as possible. In this way we learn what the other is seeking to communicate and perhaps begin to appreciate something of the experience of the other – we try to make the other's experience our own and learn from it.

It is, I think, that this is the stage which Confucian thinkers would call understanding and it is also the beginning of Marton's deep approach to learning.

Creative and critical thought: Creative thinking poses problems since new ideas cannot be legislated for or even generated to order. 'Eureka' experiences cannot be planned. Indeed, Gilhooly (1996, p. 218) points out that many creative thinkers disclaim the ability to tell us how they think creatively or even solve problems – it just seems to come. But many years before, Wallis' (1926) suggested four stages in creative thinking: preparation, incubation, illumination/inspiration and verification and, in Koestler's (1964) *The Act of Creation,* we were introduced us to another approach through bringing together two ideas from diverse sources and showing that in synthesis they often have a novel outcome.

Critical thinking, by contrast, must be seen as thinking analytically and it is the opposite to the processes of memorising and repeating that we have already discussed. Moreover, it is also distinct from critical theory, which emerged from the Frankfurt School in the earlier part of the twentieth century, although it was from this School that the idea of emancipatory thought developed. There is a certain sense in which critical thought requires us to be emancipated from the pre-suppositions of our own thinking, and even the social powers, including those of the teacher, that influence our thought. Critical thought has an affinity with the philosophical school of scepticism. Moser *et al.* (1998, pp. 13–14) tell us that there are two major forms of scepticism – knowledge scepticism and justification scepticism. The former, taken to its logical extreme, would hold that nobody knows anything, whereas the latter asserts that no one should believe anything. While we might not want to take either of these two positions to the extreme, it is clear that critical thought demands a sceptical perspective on knowledge and belief.

Problem-solving and decision making: Problem-solving is a disjunctural situation in which there are no simple given procedures that facilitate problems to be solved, although there may be a wide variety of different possible approaches to the problem. Gilhooly (1996) suggests that experts usually concentrate on the problem itself while novices usually focus on its solution. By focusing on the problem, the expert is seeking to outline as many different options that can be examined as possible, which is the exact opposite to decision-making which is a process of closing down different possibilities and reaching specific conclusions. These are both processes of rational thought. As Gilhooly (1996, p. 191) points out, however, making the decision involves a lot of other factors such as risk-taking and the ability to take many different factors into consideration. Few people have the ability or time to take very many factors into consideration in reaching their decisions – in the game of chess, for instance, each player is given only a specified period of time in which the move must be made – and hence the issue of risk comes to the fore.

Directed and undirected: In a sense we have already dealt with directed thought above but undirected thought is a less frequently researched phenomenon. I have used the term 'undirected' to describe the types of thought that might be called 'musing' or even 'daydreaming' which is a common phenomenon (Gilhooly, 1996) and completely opposite to instrumental thought. Even so, there are times when these undirected thoughts intrude into our thought processes despite our best efforts to rid ourselves of them. There is also a sense in which we can relate this to our previous discussion on internal and external history. The more important are the external factors in our lives, the less likely we are to turn inwards and muse. It is when we have 'time on our hands' or when the external circumstances do not appear to be very pressing that we can engage in this activity. It is like the incubation stage in creative thinking. During it, we might focus on something that has recently occurred that we wish had happened differently or think about the desired outcomes of some future action or event. Gilhooly (1996), citing Singer (1975), suggests that there are three functions to this activity: anticipation and planning, reminding us of 'unfinished business' that we are trying to suppress, and maintaining arousal in dull environments. Singer suggests that both incubation and this type of thinking occur because there is continuous activity in the mind.

Deductive and inductive reasoning: Deduction is the process of inferring a particular instance from a general law; conversely induction is the process of inferring a general law from a particular instance, or also it is about the production of facts to demonstrate the validity of a general statement.

Deduction is the process that is carried out in decision making, when a number of facts, which are assumed to be true, have to be considered and a conclusion reached about them which must, therefore, be true – provided the thought processes have been logical. However, we have already highlighted how dominant discourses occupy the educational vocabulary and so we have to be prepared to question the initial facts as well as the assumptions underlying the process of reasoning. Our sub-conscious thoughts and emotions, and even our conscious ones, might well affect the process and, consequently, the logical progression of an argument has always to be carefully constructed and checked.

Induction, however, is the converse to this and is, in a sense, generating hypotheses and, perhaps, theorising from them. Theorising is similar in some ways to rational thought although it may include hunches and intuitions, but in another sense it is similar to the generalisation box in Kolb's (1984) learning cycle. I did not include in my diagram of learning because none of my respondents regarded it as a part of their learning process. Indeed, it does not occur with every learning incident but when things appear to repeat themselves, then we might seek to theorise about it. Moser *et al.* (1998, p. 183) suggest that 'human knowers are primarily *theorizers* rather than simple fact gatherers. One can find evidence for this from the earliest recorded human history – even to the extent of building theories and theologies about the cosmos. We theorise about each other, in order to try to understand what makes us tick, to explain why people behave the way that they do' (italics in original). They go on to say that we also theorise about our environment in order to try to control it. In a sense, then this also reflects the idea that every person is a scientist (Kelly, 1955) since it starts from a disjunctural experience but it seeks to postulate answers to the question 'why?' in a more general sense. It contains a mixture of some of the previous forms of thinking and yet, in the end, it becomes a distinct form in itself.

The Confucian thinkers whom we discussed earlier probably did not have sufficient understanding of the processes of thinking to be able to do justice to the learning process. However, with our additional knowledge, we should be able to help our learners move from traditional approaches to learning and transform Asian education through open and distance learning. In order to do this, in a brief final section to this paper I want to indicate some practical ways to help our learners do this, so that they do not spend so much time with endless repetition of text but go beyond it and its meaning to generate more extensive learning.

Some thoughts about teaching

As designers of the educational material we do exercise the type of power that we discussed earlier but what we do not want to do is to generate a situation where the learners feel that they need to memorise what we present to them. This calls for very imaginative design of teaching material – this is not techno-logical design like a slick PowerPoint presentation – but carefully structured thought exercises in their learning. (Incidentally, I believe that PowerPoint is of little help in this process, since PowerPoint presentations often end up being didactic, but the traditionalism of the presentation is hidden by the slickness of the technique.)

Initially then we have to create a sense of disjuncture, a sense of the need to ask Why? or, What should I do?, and so on. We have to utilise Socratic teaching notions but also to give the learners the licence not to accept what is written. In a sense, then, we have to give them opportunities to think widely but above all give them the confidence to break away from the text. Telling students that they should not memorise the material will not be sufficient to help those who have been brought up to learn in this way and so we have to build into the structure of the material deliberate techniques that are going to enable the learners to utilise the different forms of thinking discussed in the previous section.

It is possible to design exercises which require that the learners utilise different forms of thinking through using scenarios, writing exercises, directing lines of thought, and so on, through techniques such as: question setting; memory exer-cises; meaning seeking exercises; choosing from conflicting alternatives; rewarding students for the number of mistakes they find in a reading; brain-storming; choosing one 'best' answer from a number of possible solutions to a problem; practical assignments. These have to be carefully planned and appear as a natural part of the teaching and learning process. Basically we should not be looking for correct answers but asking students to exert great effort to master the various arts of thinking so that we reward the process as well as the product.

Conclusion

Through these exercises it is not only the product which is integrated into the learners' biographies, it is the process as well. Learners will become changed and more experienced – my box 6 – but then they will carry the arts of thinking to future learning situations – my box 1_2. Ultimately, it is not changing Asian education that is our end – it is transforming Asian learners so that they might travel the road to self-fulfilment and then to the service of the wider society, which is a life span quest – and then, and only then, will education begin to achieve its lofty, humanistic aims.

References

Cheng X (2000) Asian Students' Reticence Revisited *System* No. 28 pp. 435–446

Chiang M (1924) *A Study of Chinese Principles of Education* Shanghai: The Commercial Press

Chu H (1990) *Learning to Be a Sage: selections from the conversations of Master Chu, arranged topically* Berkeley: University of California Press

Cooper D (1983) *Authenticity and Learning* London: Routledge & Kegan Paul

Foucaut M (1971) *L'Ordre du discours* Paris: Gallimard

Gadamer H-G (1978) *Philosophical Hermeneutics* Berkeley: University of California Press

Gilhooly K (1996) *Thinking: directive, undirected and creative* (3rd edition) Amsterdam: Academic Press

Jarvis P (1987) *Adult Learning in the Social Context* London: Croom Helm

Jarvis P (2004) Teaching and Learning Theory in Distance Education in *Distance Education in China* No 9 pp. 47–52

Jarvis P (forthcoming) *Learning and Personhood: towards a comprehensive theory* London: Routledge

Kelly G (1955) *The Psychology of Personal Constructs* New York: Norton

Kennedy P (2002) Learning Cultures and Learning Styles; myth-understandings about adult (Hong Kong) Chinese learners. In *International Journal of Lifelong Education* Vol. 21 No 5 pp. 430–445

Kierkegaard S (1959) *Either/Or Vol 2* Princeton: Princeton University Press

Koestler A (1964) *The Act of Creation* London: Hutchinson

Kolb D (1984) *Experiential Learning* Englewood Cliffs, NJ: Prentice Hall

Kyung Hi Kim (2004) An Attempt to Elucidate Notions of Lifelong Learning: *Analects*-Based Analysis of Confucius' Ideas about Learning in *Asia Pacific Education Review* Vol.5 No 2 pp. 117–126

Lawton D (1973) *Social Change, Educational Theory and Curriculum Planning* London: Hodder & Stoughton

Lee Wing On (1996) The Cultural Context for Chinese Learners: conceptions of learning in the Confucian tradition in Watkins D and Biggs J (eds) *The Chinese Learner* Hong Kong: Comparative Education Research Centre, and Camberwell, Victoria: Australian Council for Educational Research

Liu Wu-Chi (1924) A *Short History of Confucian Philosophy* Harmondsworth: Penguin

Marton F and Säljö R (1984) Approaches to Learning in Marton F, Hounsell D and Entwistle N (eds) (1984) *The Experience of Learning* Edinburgh: Scottish Academic Press

Marton F, Dall' Alba G and Tse T L Memorizing and Understanding: the key to the Paradox in Watkins D and Biggs J (eds) *The Chinese Learner* pp. 69–83

Moser P, Mulder D and Trout J (1998) *The Theory of Knowledge* New York: Oxford University Press

Rousseau J-J (1911 [1762]) *Emile* London: Dent

Schutz A and Luckmann T (1974) *The Structures of the Life World* London: Heinemann

Sheridan A (1980) *Michael Foucault: the will to truth* London: Tavistock

Singer J (1975) *Daydreaming and Fantasy* London: George Allen & Unwin

Simpson L (1995) *Technology, Time and the Conversations of Modernity* London: Routledge

Wallis G (1926) *The Art of Thought* London: Jonathan Cape

Watkins D and Biggs J (eds) (1996) *The Chinese Learner* Hong Kong: Comparative Education Research Centre and Camberwell, Victoria: Australian Council for Educational Research

PART 5

LATE MODERNITY

CHAPTER 13

THE CHANGING EDUCATIONAL SCENE

Originally published as 'The Changing Educational Scene'
in P. Jarvis (ed.) (2001), *The Age of Learning: Education
and the Knowledge Society*, London: Routledge, pp. 27–38.
Cross-references refer to the original publication.

Education, in the West, received a significant boost to the rationale for its existence with the dawn of the Reformation. Early education was devoted to
teaching children and adults literacy so that they could read the Bible and
achieve individual salvation. Since the Bible was regarded as divinely inspired
people were expected to learn unquestionably its truths – but once people learn,
their learning cannot be controlled, so that there is another sense in which the
Reformation was the first stage in the process of secularization that has resulted
in the world that we know today. The Protestant churches, especially the more
Calvinistic ones, led the way in generating the changes that were to lead to
further major changes in society. It could be argued that without the Reformation
there would have been no Enlightenment.

While there have been many changes in society since that time, we shall
focus upon just two – the Enlightenment (the birth of modernity) and the period
since the 1970s when some scholars have claimed that we have entered a
postmodern world. The chapter contains a brief section on education in the
post-Enlightenment period; it then examines the social changes that have
occurred since the 1970s and, finally, looks at the effects of these changes on the
educational scene.

Modernity

The Enlightenment was both an historical era and a period of rapid intellectual
change. Hamilton (1992: 21–22) has suggested ten different features that char-
acterize this period, although some of them had their beginnings in the
Reformation:

1. the primacy of reason;
2. all knowledge and thought about the natural and social world are based on
   empirical facts;
3. scientific knowledge is based upon experimental method;
4. reason and science can be applied to every situation;
5. natural and social conditions can be improved as a result of reason and
   science;
6. the individual is the starting point for all knowledge;
7. all individuals are, essentially, the same despite different beliefs;

8. people are free to believe, trade, communicate, etc. without external constraint;
9. the characteristics of human nature are universal;
10. traditional religious authority should be opposed.

Many of these characteristics have become embedded in contemporary Western culture, giving it a sense that it was the apex of civilization, but, as suggested below, there are fundamental errors in these characteristics that have become problems as society continues to change. However, they were believed to be truths at that early time, and the truth discovered by science and reason had to be taught to the masses of the people. Gradually mass education emerged for children, in the UK culminating in the 1870 Education Act. There was also a wide variety of adult education movements, such as the Mechanics Institutes, all dedicated to the transmission of those discoveries that one generation thought its members should know and that the next generation should be building upon (see Chapter 1).

Teaching was a matter of transmitting a truth and learning was merely internalizing it or copying it. Education became reproductive and early learning theory, behaviourism, was a result of the same processes – based upon measurable 'scientific' data and reproduction of what was taught. Learning became identified with rote learning and training with copying the established skills and procedures.

However, as the period progressed, gradual changes occurred. The work of Piaget (1929, *inter alia*) in the West and Vygotsky (1978, 1986) in Russia focused on the way that children learnt and Dewey (1938) emphasized experience, so that education took on more of a child-centred approach and discovery learning became increasingly important. In adult education, there was a greater emphasis on the adult's experience (Lindeman, 1926) as a basis of learning, and from 1929 (Yeaxlee) the idea that education is a lifelong process grew in importance.

At the same time, new scientific discoveries were making people aware that there was a great deal of new knowledge in existence and that they might have to continue their education and training beyond school and university. Further training, in-service training, continuing education and similar concepts were emerging. In addition, it was becoming recognized that adults were actually self-directed learners (Houle, 1961). By the 1970s, knowledge was changing so fast that it became inevitable that education in all its forms also had to change. Education was obviously a recipient of the dominant social pressures for change, rather than being a major force for change in itself. Kerr *et al.* (1973) were already suggesting that education was the hand-maiden of industry.

Reason and science had been promulgating change throughout the whole of the post-Enlightenment period and new discoveries were making the speed of change faster than ever before. These changes were to alter education but more at the adult end of the educational lifespan.

Capitalism flourished in the world of modernity, but, by its very nature, it was bound to generate change and expand its market. However, the changes were not merely a matter of corporations competing within state boundaries and then reaching beyond them to purchase raw materials and sell finished commodities. Now the corporations spanned the globe, at first as multinationals and later as transnational companies. The world was becoming a global village that was also to be a highly competitive global market.

By the beginning of the 1970s Western business was threatened by the oil crisis and the growing superiority of the commodities of Japan and the other Pacific Rim countries. Businesses in the West tried a number of different strategies in order to retain their control and profitability. Manufacturing industries began locating some of their production in third-world countries; forms of protectionism were tried, but GATT operated against it. They attempted to cut costs in order to become more productive, but this was not always successful. They then embarked on company mergers and takeovers in order to reduce administrative costs and enhance their profitability. This, then, was the period when monetarist economics gained ascendancy in theory as well as in practice.

With the introduction of information technology, this was also the period when the process of globalization speeded up (see Chapter 2) and the world became a smaller place. Positive and technological knowledge were changing increasingly rapidly. The fundamentals of the Enlightenment were being questioned, if not eroded, and some scholars began to ask whether the Enlightenment project was over; late or postmodernity had appeared. But this new society was a global market with a capitalist sub-structure driven by information technology. It was a knowledge society; knowledge workers needed to keep abreast of developments and, even more significantly, they became creators of a great deal of them – for new knowledge was now being generated in the workplace and away from the laboratory. New award-bearing courses were being introduced at all levels, new ways of recognizing non-classroom learning were being introduced, and accreditation of prior experiential learning became acceptable. Indeed, learning theory itself is changing and becoming experiential, although behaviourism, like some of the other ideas of modernity, still has its disciples.

With the rapid developments in and spread of information technology, it is hardly surprising that institutions began to deliver education and training in the same manner. Otto Peters (1983: 95–113) argued, for instance, that distance education was a form of industrial production and as the means of production have changed so have distance education techniques. By the 1990s many educational institutions were using electronic means for the delivery of some, if not all, of their courses.

The educational scene has undergone tremendous change as we approach 'the learning society'; the next section of this chapter outlines some of them.

Changes in educational theory and practice

From childhood and adult to lifelong education

From both the Reformation and the birth of the Enlightenment all age groups were encouraged to learn the truths that were being discovered. After 1870, school education grew by virtue of its compulsory nature and education was seen by many as preparing children for adulthood; 'education' was generally assumed to refer to 'schooling'; anything else was 'adult education'. Perhaps the popular distinction introduced in the US by Malcolm Knowles (1980) between pedagogy and andragogy reflects this divide.

During the twentieth century considerable efforts were made in Britain to emphasize the place of adult education (see the 1919 Report preface as an example; University of Nottingham, 1980). Adult education really became accepted in the UK as a result of the 1944 Education Act, which placed certain responsibilities on local education authorities to ensure the provision of further education within their areas. As early as 1929, however, Yeaxlee began writing about lifelong education. 'Adult education' was developing strongly when it was overtaken by 'lifelong education', the latter spurred on by the adoption of the idea by the OECD and UNESCO (Lengrand, 1975).

This actually led to two different approaches to lifelong education, one favoured by OECD and adult educators generally, and the other by UNESCO. In the former, there was a popular idea that people should have an adult educational entitlement after they left school – this became known as 'recurrent education', a term used in some of its publications (see OECD, 1973, for example), In the latter, the term that gained popularity was 'continuing education', ie education might continue after schooling. This concept carried no implications of educational entitlements and, not surprisingly, it became widely accepted in the UK in the 1980s. Continuing education has no end point and so the transition to lifelong education, in the late 1980s/early 1990s, was a simple one. However, the two different philosophies of lifelong education are still apparent in the European Union.

With the ageing of society, we are now beginning to see an increase in education for older people, through the growth of Universities of the Third Age, Elderhostel and other such organizations. However, the discourse about lifelong education, especially lifelong learning, is beginning to be controlled by the discourse about work, so that its meaning is becoming limited to work-life learning, and schooling hardly enters the discourse at all.

From teacher-centred to student-centred education

Education was traditionally about teaching the truths that one generation considered valuable enough to be preserved and passed on to the next, but there are at least four reasons why there has been a greater emphasis placed on student-centred learning of late:

1. While behaviourism was the generally accepted theory of learning, education was naturally teacher-oriented. But as other theories began to emerge, such as the cognitive theories of Piaget emphasizing the developmental stages of growth and its relation to the child's learning, education became more student-centred.
2. In the 1960s some of the more progressive ideas of the American philosopher John Dewey (1916, 1938), emphasizing the children's experience, were incorporated into school education.
3. It was during the same period that Malcolm Knowles (1980, *inter alia*) in the USA popularized andragogy, which was a student-centred approach to adult education. Some adult educators rightly claimed that this was no new discovery, since adult education had always been student-centred. Be that as it may, Knowles' ideas became extremely popular; his own intellectual pedigree can be traced back to John Dewey through Lindeman – Knowles' first educational employer and a person who had a great influence on his work.
4. As the modernity era was drawing to a close, the speed of change of knowledge was such that it became much more difficult to equate knowledge with truth. The debate about the relativity of all knowledge began to emerge and

educators could no longer specify 'correct' knowledge or truth, so that they had to place greater emphasis on the learners' own beliefs about the content of their learning.

After the expressive period ended in the mid-1970s, the values of student-centred learning became much more widely recognized. Nevertheless, the extent to which it was practised, rather than being merely rhetoric, is open to question. There is no doubt that the rhetoric of learner-centred education is still very strong, not only in adult education, but in human resource development However, there are conservative forces, especially in school education, which would seek to return to more traditional teaching methods.

From classical curriculum to romantic curriculum to programme

The curriculum is a selection from culture and the classical curriculum implied that there was only one truth, or interpretation, of the material to be taught; there was only one possible way of presenting that curriculum knowledge. However, it was accepted in England in the 1960s that in a multicultural society there is more than one possible interpretation of cultural knowledge, that is there is more than one type of history, religion etc. The 1960s saw the development of curricula that recognized this; they were called 'romantic curricula', reflecting the 1960s 'romantic' period (Lawton, 1973; Griffin, 1983).

This pluralistic society led to the recognition that it was becoming increasingly difficult to prescribe precisely what should be taught in the school week, despite many efforts by the government to do just this. But by the 1990s, it was widely recognized that there is just too much knowledge to get into every curriculum, so options have been built in to the system. This recognition was even truer in higher education, where modules have been developed on a wide range of topics, resulting in students being presented with a programme of courses from which to choose. Modular programmes also form the basis of a great deal of school education in the US.

The changing status of knowledge

Knowledge was regarded as the fruit of reason and scientific method and must, therefore, be true. However, as early as 1926, the German sociologist Max Scheler (Stikkers, 1980) began to chronicle the way that different types of knowledge were changing at different speeds, with positive and technological knowledge changing much more rapidly than religious knowledge. He suggested that knowledge seemed to be changing 'hour by hour'; now it is changing minute by minute and second by second. With this rapid change, it is almost impossible to regard knowledge as a truth any more – we are now talking about something that is relative and can be changed again as soon as some new discovery is made. The way that knowledge is changing has been analysed by Lyotard (1984), who regards a great deal of it as narrative, and in this sense he has tried to retain something of the value-free nature of the concept. Foucault (1972), on the other hand, has treated knowledge as discourse which is ideological and that which becomes accepted as truth is usually the discourse of the powerful. Consequently, the knowledge taught has to be understood more critically than ever before, so that critical theory has also entered the educational vocabulary.

The world is awash with new discoveries – but this means that there is a greater need for the knowledge-based occupations to keep up with the new developments. Indeed, Lyotard (1984) argued that performativity has become the basis for knowledge to be regarded as legitimate and so knowledge is now only true for the time being. This has resulted in education having to become much more flexible in what it offers and much less authoritarian.

From rote learning to learning as experiential and reflection

When knowledge was regarded as something true, something that had been verified either by the force of rational logic or by scientific research, then it was to be learnt, that is, it had to be memorized. However, it is now recognized that learning stems from experience and that learners develop their own narratives.

Since most knowledge is either narrative or discourse, it all has to be considered, criticized and reflected upon in order to ascertain the extent to which it contains any truth. Hence rote learning has become less significant and learners are expected to reflect upon their learning experiences (Kolb, 1984; Jarvis, 1987, 1992), although authoritarianism in some forms of management and teaching still enforces rote-learning procedures.

From face-to-face to distance

Education has traditionally been conducted face-to-face. Only in extremely large and sparsely populated countries, like the Australian outback, Russia, etc, were alternatives used. With the advent of new information technology, all of this was to change.

In 1970, the birth of the British Open University was to be a catalyst in the new information society in education. It proved that educational courses could be delivered successfully at a distance, through print, radio and television. With the rapid development of information technology, distance education has been transformed yet again. Even the Open University, with its Fordist methods of production (Rumble, 1995) is having to find new markets and new modes of production – and other universities with post-Fordist techniques of production have already been exploiting a global market for education.

Educational courses are now being delivered through the World Wide Web, and adults can study when and where it is convenient for them. Time and space have been transformed in education.

With the development of distance education and the recognition of the significance of practical knowledge, it is now possible to understand how learning workstations might be introduced into the work place by corporate universities and by the University for Industry.

From the few to the many

The British system of education has always been rather elitist, training the few to assume responsible positions in government, the professions and the church. Hence, the school curriculum was narrow and selective, with a great proportion of children being condemned to blue-collar occupations early in their education. Comprehensive reforms tried to overcome this, but they were not regarded as being very successful.

By the 1980s, there was still only a small percentage of young people going on to higher education. This was regarded as a waste of people's talents and it was certainly not enough to provide new workers to fill all the knowledge-based jobs. Consequently, the education reforms of the late 1980s and early 1990s in the UK – in line with a general democratic feeling in society – expanded higher education to a mass system, with more than 30 per cent of young people being able to attend university. This reflected the form of higher education to be found in the US, but it has not yet been introduced in many other countries in the world.

However, the expansion of higher education to mass education has not really overcome the problem of widening access to those who come from the marginalized or excluded groups, so that there is still considerable concern about universities expanding their student entry to cater for the socially excluded.

From emphasis on the liberal to the vocational

While there is a sense in which the educational institution has always acted as a filter preparing the elite of the land for their work, there has been a general rhetoric that education has had a humanistic basis preparing the whole person for adulthood. Naturally these two do not have to be in opposition but the rhetoric has distracted attention for the selective and divisive functions of education. Even so the Open University began as a 'liberal arts university' since it was easy to offer these courses at a distance. This actually reflected a great deal of the debate that had gone on in school education in the 1960s and early 1970s. R Peters (1977) had argued that the aims of education were to produce a rounded person (an educated man) rather than one who was oriented just to work.

However, as society, and consequently education, became less welfare-oriented and society developed a more knowledge-based workforce, so it became more incumbent on people to learn the knowledge necessary to keep abreast of the demands of their work. Continuing education, which had subsumed adult education, almost became synonymous with continuing professional, or vocational, education. New degree courses mushroomed in universities and colleges of higher education, nearly all of which were vocational.

Employers now became the clients of educational institutions, since it was often they who were paying for their employees' continuing vocational education – the students ceased to be the clients. But employers have specific demands for their own industry and educational institutions are relatively slow to change. Many employers already had large training institutions, which became even more technical and knowledge based, and they have become much more academically acceptable. This has led to some employers seeking to establish their own universities (Eurich, 1985; Meister, 1998) – British Aerospace set up its own university in the UK in 1997. The new Labour government has also granted finance for the establishment of the University for Industry.

For a while liberal adult education was almost completely sidelined, although it is currently in receipt of some government funding. At the same time, a whole new area of non-vocational education is emerging with third-age education. Throughout the developed world, this non-formal education is expanding rapidly, as Universities of the Third Age in the UK, Europe and Australasia and as Institutes of Learning in Retirement and Elderhostel in the US.

From theoretical to practical

Until very recently, education in one form or another has had a monopoly in teaching all forms of theory, and it has been generally felt that theory had to be taught before new recruits to a profession could go into practice. The idea that practitioners applied theory to practice was widely accepted and research was conducted in order to build up the body of knowledge that could be taught to the next generation of recruits. By the 1970s, this view was being questioned in a number of ways. Stenhouse (1975), for instance, suggested that teachers should research their own practice; after all they were implementing their curriculum. At the same time, Lyotard (1984) was suggesting that the legitimation of all knowledge in the future would be through its performativity (he later modified the 'all').

Practice became more central to teaching and learning, and with the development of experiential learning theories it is hardly surprising that problem-based education, and then work-based learning, became more significant. Naturally, this was also in accord with the corporate world's own aims to educate its own workforce. Increasingly, we have seen continuing education courses, at Master's level, being totally work-based. Now, we are beginning to see practitioner doctorates emerge – and with this, there is an increasing emphasis on practical knowledge (see Jarvis, 1999).

From single discipline to multi-disciplinary to integrated knowledge

As a result of the Industrial Revolution and Enlightenment, the individual disciplines of study emerged and knowledge about society began to be categorized by discipline – philosophy, sociology, psychology, etc. Each of the disciplines developed its own array of sub-disciplines and even overlapping sub-disciplines such as social psychology.

By the 1960s this discipline division was beginning to be recognized as somewhat artificial and there emerged ideas of multi-disciplinary study. Consequently, it was possible to study the social sciences – and look at each of the social sciences and even at their different interpretations of the same phenomenon, so that we could have a philosophy of education, a sociology of education and even a social-philosophy of education. The new universities, especially Keele in the 1960s and the Open University in 1970, introduced multi-disciplinary foundation courses of study. The Open University has still retained them, even as compulsory until the mid-1990s, although pressure to drop multi-disciplinary foundation courses has been fairly strong in some quarters.

As the orientation to research and study became more practice-based, it was recognized that practice is not multi-disciplinary but demands integrated knowledge. Knowledge has become widely recognized as a seamless robe. Practical knowledge is integrated and it is knowledge about doing things, e.g. nursing knowledge, teaching knowledge, so that it is impossible to divide it into its separate elements. It might be suggested that this makes nursing, for instance, a discipline. However, it is possible to have a sociology of nursing but not a nursing of sociology. The same is true for education. Hence, there is something profoundly different about practical knowledge – it is integrated and subjective. The growth of continuing education vocational courses is to be found in this area of integrated practical knowledge.

From welfare needs to market demands (wants)

As the modular approach to the curriculum becomes more acceptable, the idea that education is part of the welfare provision of society becomes less dominant. Now the idea that we have needs-meeting curricula has become less important and the idea of needs has changed its connotations (Jarvis, 1985; Griffin, 1987). Need no longer refers to a generalized need of potential students; it refers to those special needs, perhaps those which are residual in society and even ones which can be eradicated through good governance.

Once education ceases to be welfare provision, it can only become market provision and – this is precisely what Bacon and Eltis (1976) argued – Britain had to transform its welfare provision into wealth producers. This is the economics of monetarism, introduced by the American economist Milton Freidman. Education had to be seen to be a money earner, which was much simpler after the success of the Open University and the realization that the wide choice of modules that it offered constituted a market for 'off-the-shelf' courses. Educational needs had turned into a matter of supply and demand – a market.

This process has been exacerbated since funding for higher education has been restricted and higher education institutions are having to compete with each other in order to attract students – the educative society has become a learning market.

From education and training to learning

It will be seen from this chapter that there has been a gradual move away from the traditional view of education as the means by which the older generation passes on to the next generations that knowledge it regards as worthwhile and valuable. Now, formal education is not the only way to pass on worthwhile knowledge to the next generation and, as one among many, its status has diminished.

In addition, the traditional distinction between education and training has disappeared with the need of all workers to have practical knowledge at the different levels at which they work, including postgraduate degree level. Learning is a status-free term, unlike education or training, and as training (or vocational education) became more crucial to the knowledge society, it also became status-free. Unfortunately, there is a sense in which vocational education is now taking over the educational discourse.

Conclusion

In the preceding sections we have been able to see how the amount of knowledge is growing at an exponential rate, demanding some form of continuing learning from all who work with it. At the same time the number of people needing to learn has grown immensely and the spread of the World Wide Web means it is now possible to transmit learning materials to people throughout the world. They can learn at their own pace, in their own time and in their own environment. This is clearly the start of an age of learning.

References

Bacon, R and Eltis, W (1976) *Britain's Economic Problem: Too few producers*, Macmillan, Basingstoke

Dewey, J (1916) *Democracy and Education*, Free Press, New York
Dewey, J (1938) *Experience and Education*, Macmillan, New York
Eurich, N (1985) *Corporate Classrooms*, Carnegie Foundation for the Advancement of Teaching, Princeton, NJ
Foucault, M (1972) *Archaeology of Knowledge*, Routledge, London
Griffin, C (1983) *Curriculum Theory in Adult and Lifelong Education*, Croom Helm, London
Griffin, C (1987) *Adult Education as Social Policy*, Croom Helm, London
Hamilton, P (1992) 'The enlightenment and the birth of social science', in ed S Hall and B Gieban, *Formations of Modernity*, Polity Press, Cambridge
Houle, C O (1961) *The Inquiring Mind*, University of Wisconsin Press, Madison, WI
Jarvis, P (1985) *The Sociology of Adult and Continuing Education*, Croom Helm, London
Jarvis, P (1987) *Adult Learning in the Social Context*, Croom Helm, London
Jarvis, P (1992) *Paradoxes of Learning*, Jossey-Bass, San Francisco, CA
Jarvis, P (1999) *From Practice to Theory*, Jossey-Bass, San Francisco, CA
Kerr, C, Dunlop, J T, Harbison, F and Myers, C A (1973) *Industrialism and Industrial Man*, 2nd edn, Penguin, Harmondsworth
Knowles, M (1980) *The Modern Practice of Adult Education*, 2nd edn, Association Press, Chicago, IL
Kolb, D (1984) *Experiential Learning*, Prentice Hall, Englewood Cliffs, NJ
Lawton, D (1973) *Social Change, Educational Theory and Curriculum Planning*, Hodder & Stoughton, London
Lengrand, P (1975) *An Introduction to Lifelong Education*, Croom Helm, London
Lindeman, E C (1926) *The Meaning of Adult Education*, New Republic, New York
Lyotard, J-F (1984) *The Postmodern Condition*, Manchester University Press, Manchester
Meister, J (1998) *Corporate Universities*, revised edn, McGraw-Hill, New York
OECD (1973) *Recurrent Education: A strategy for lifelong learning*, OECD, Paris
Peters, O (1983) 'Distance teaching and industrial production', in eds D Stewart, D Keegan and B Holmberg, *Distance Teaching: International perspectives*, Croom Helm, London
Peters, R (1977) *Education and the Education of Teachers*, Routledge & Kegan Paul, London
Piaget, J (1929) *The Child's Conception of the World*, Routledge & Kegan Paul, London
Rumble, G (1995) 'Labour market theories and distance education', *Open Learning*, 10, 1–3
Stenhouse, L (1975) *An Introduction to Curriculum Research and Development*, Heinemann, Oxford
Stikkers, K (1980) *Problems of a Sociology of Knowledge: Max Scheler*, Routledge & Kegan Paul, London
University of Nottingham (1980) *The 1919 Report*, Department of Adult Education, University of Nottingham
Vygotsky, L (1978) *Mind in Society*, Harvard University Press, Cambridge, MA
Vygotsky, L (1986) *Thought and Language*, revised and edited by A Kozulin, MIT, Cambridge, MA
Yeaxlee, B (1929) *Lifelong Education*, Cassell, London

CHAPTER 14

INFINITE DREAMS, INFINITE GROWTH, INFINITE LEARNING
The challenges of globalisation in a finite world

Originally published as 'Infinite Dreams, Infinite Growth, Infinite Learning: The Challenge of Globalisation in a Finite World' in P. Jarvis (2007), *Globalisation, Lifelong Learning and the Learning Society: Sociological Perspectives*, London: Routledge, pp. 203–13. Cross-references refer to the original publication.

The theme of this paper is unashamedly utopian, reaching beyond any single academic discipline and looking at the hopes and the fears generated by this rapidly changing world. But it is one that reflects some of the current concerns in global politics, partly initiated by the UK government and partly expressed as a response to the tsunami disaster. This is a world of globalisation and, perhaps, it is the effects of these global processes, especially disasters, that have made us aware that we live in a global village and that we are all one people, with all our similarities and our differences – glocalisation as well as globalisation. Beck (1992), for instance, argued that globalisation has a standardising effect on the world and I think that he is to some extent correct, but it was long before the effects of globalisation that we first became aware that we are a world of nations that should be united, and even before then religious thinkers and other idealists looked upon humankind as a whole. We are all one people, united in our humanity and, perhaps, in our ideals although certainly not always in our cultures, aspirations or practices. We live in a world in which we seek to understand and to give meaning to our lives. But, despite the efforts of science over many centuries, it is a world that we do not and cannot understand. Science examines facts and empirical evidence but no fact has intrinsic meaning. It is we who give facts meaning; it is we who have dreams and visions of a world where empirical realities may be put to different uses as we, the people, seek to discover our humanity and our unity.

Consequently, this paper has a utopian theme running through it – it looks to the future but it also challenges the present. It looks at a world that is about questions and not answers, that is about learning not education, that is transformed (or at least in a permanent state of transformation) without prescribed ends. I want to argue that we need visions of the infinite rather than an infinite number of visions and I will do this in three short sections: infinite dreams – religious, political and economic utopias; infinite growth – the challenges of globalisation in a finite world; infinite learning – but not an organised learning society, despite the fact that a utopian strain underlies some educational theory. My conclusion is that we do not need answers but a willingness to keep on learning and acting in relationship with the others who always impinge upon our freedom creating moral demands on us all and that our responses, actions, should be founded upon one universal value of concern for the Other rather than a multitude of cultural ones (Jarvis, 1997). At the same time, I have to acknowledge that since I come from one culture – Western, which is itself a combination of Judeo-Christian and Greek thought – this paper must reflect that culture and so I acknowledge from the outset that this is a fundamental weakness in my presentation.

Infinite dreams: religious, political and economic utopias

Utopia is itself difficult to define. Nozick (1974, p. 294), for instance, suggests that 'it must be, in some restricted sense, the best for all of us; the best world imaginable', while Levitas (1990, p. 1) claims that 'Utopia is about how we would live and what kind of world we would live in if we could . . . (It is the) construction of imaginary worlds, free from the difficulties that beset us in reality . .'. She suggests that it embodies form, function and content and she (1990, p. 191) indicates that utopianism 'has as a precondition a disparity between socially constructed need and socially prescribed and actually available means of satisfaction'. It is what is desired and it is 'desire for a better way of being. It involves imagining a state of being in which the problems that actually confront us are removed or resolved' (p. 191). Mannheim (1936, pp. 184–190) thought that utopianism is associated with wish-fulfilment. These hopes and aspirations have generated religious, political and economic responses in which visions of a better world, a republic, an ideal city or even a paradise from which humankind emerged and will rediscover are to be found throughout the literature.

Religious utopias: It is here that I am forced to acknowledge my cultural limitations for I can only write of those from my own religious culture. Judeo-Christian thought has always had prophets who denounced the evils of the present world and announced the coming of a better one – a kingdom that God would create. Such pronouncements often appeared at times when the Hebrew faith, in the first instance, was under attack. When Christianity was also suffering the same fate, it responded in the same manner. Indeed, during one of the early persecutions the writer of the Revelation of St John the Divine 'saw a new heaven and a new earth' (Revelation, 21, v.1) which reflects the writings of the Old Testament prophet (known by Old Testament scholars as trito-Isaiah), 'For behold, new heavens and a new earth' (Is 65, v.17). Immediately one reads these passages, there is a sense of a timeless dream – as if utopia is created and will be unchanging for ever. Time has been stopped!

Throughout the history of the Christian church there has always been a utopian, even an eschatological, future in which there would be a new heaven and a new earth – the Kingdom of God would come. In similar ways throughout that period, Christian sects have established their ideal communities seeking to establish their own perfect world in an imperfect society, and there have been many studies of these movements (see, for instance Wilson, 1967). But the ideal community seeks structures, and often languages, that are perfect and unchanging, since the ideal cannot change. Other utopian ideals to be found within religious utopias lie within the framework of millenarianism – when the present world will end with the coming of the Messiah who will establish a new reign on earth.

Without probing more deeply into these interesting religious movements, we can see that they emerge out of a sense of desire for a better world and when they are created they seek a form of perfection, stability that is unchanging, but this must lie outside of the realms of time and, therefore, beyond practicality.

Nevertheless, we find underlying these religious ideals ones which are both political and economic.

Political utopias: Kumar (1991) claimed that utopia as a political concept began with Sir Thomas More's famous study in 1516, *Utopia*. Levitas (1992) disagrees and in a sense Kumar is himself inconsistent because he recognised Plato's *Republic* as a late development in Greek utopian thought. He (1987, p. 3) suggested that:

> Utopian themes reach back to the earliest Greek writings. From Hesiod's *Works and Days,* of the early seventh century BC, came the canonical depiction of the Golden Age, the bitterly lamented age of Kronos's reign when men 'lived as if they were gods, their hearts free from sorrow, and without hard work or pain'.

In precisely the same way Plato pictured an ideal city state in *The Republic,* with a carefully thought out system of governance. In the 19th century in England two political utopian classics were produced: Marx's *The Communist Manifesto* and William Morris' *News from Nowhere.* Marx agued that the proletariat would rise up against the ruling classes and the ensuing revolution would result in a dictatorship of the proletariat who would abdicate when the time was right for a stable classless society to be introduced – perhaps a timeless one! But one of Marx's weaknesses lies at this point since his theory of change is that thesis produces its own antithesis and results in a synthesis. But unless we stop time, classlessness becomes its own thesis which produces its own antithesis, and so on. In contrast, Morris pictured himself in the twenty-second century when there is no need of government, money, or private property since everybody lived in harmony as a result of the workers' revolution. Once again, in both visions, it is necessary to step outside of time in order to realise them since they postulate an unchanging world where government and even money itself seems to be redundant.

In a sense, the right met the left in the middle of the twentieth century when the right-wing theorists postulated a world where the state was rolled back (Hayek, 1944, Norzick, 1974) and there was minimal government; private property and the free market constituted the basis of their way to a better society. Only in this situation, they argued could the people be free and achieve self-fulfilment. In one sense they were right, since people need freedom to be creative and to achieve their potential. But, in another they were wrong since the market is neither equal nor free and, as we shall argue below, it generates inequality and poverty, so that their vision is also flawed.

Economic utopias: In fourteenth century England, visions of economic utopias began to appear and these were far less sophisticated than the visions of Hayek and Norzick. For instance in the poem mocking the monasteries and their indulgent life style we read:

> There are rivers broad and fine
> Of oil, milk, honey and of wine
> (*The Land of Cokaygne*)

Kumar (1987, p. 9) also notes the Big *Rock Candy Mountain.* But, O'Neill (1993) points to another more contemporary food manifestation – McTopia, which seeks to relate fast food to some aspects of utopian thinking, although it may also be dystopian since it lowers the levels of aspiration of the 'milk and honey' for all to consuming the food that the poor, in the West at least, can afford – in this sense there is a democratisation of eating. But here time plays a significant part since fast food cannot be slow because the space occupied by the consumer must constantly be filled by another paying customer or else that occupation eats into the profits of the industry. Yet, the food and the processes are universal for wherever one goes one discovers precisely the same timeless process and taste. From the sophisticated economic analyses to the more critical and polemical, we find economic visions of a better world, but they are impracticable or even offer a distorted perfection.

Adult educators have also been fascinated with these utopian visions. In the dialogue between Myles Horton and Paulo Freire (Bell *et al.* 1990, pp. 52–53), we hear Horton saying:

> I thought maybe that's the answer, these utopian colonies, these communes, getting away from life, and kind of separating yourself and living your own life. I was attracted to it but I was very sceptical from the very beginning. It seemed to be too precious, too 'getting away' from things. I ended up visiting all the remains of the communes in the United States – Oneida, Amana, New Harmony in Ohio . . . I ended up concluding that they were just like I had already concluded – that a person shouldn't live within himself . . . And I discarded utopian communes. Finally, it just became very clear that I would never find what I was looking for. I was trying the wrong approach. The thing to do was just find a place, move in and start, and let it grow.

Grow it did – it became Highlander, a place that helped to foster the civil rights movement in the southern states of the USA. Yet neither he nor Freire regarded education as anything other than utopian. Elsewhere, Freire (1972, p. 40) actually wrote: 'When education is no longer utopian . . . when it no longer embodies the dramatic unity of denunciation and annunciation, it is either that the future has no meaning, or because men are afraid to risk living the future as creative overcoming of the present, which has become old'.

There have been many visions of utopia, religious, political and economic. We can have an infinite number of dreams but they may not be attainable. Indeed, their major function may well be to remind us that we do not live in a perfect world and to help mould our desire for a better one since there are different worlds to which we can aspire even if some of them remain unrealistic and unrealisable. In this way, utopian thought breaks the bonds of the social order, as Mannheim (1936, pp. 184–190) argued, whereas ideologies do not. But embedded in utopian thinking are ideologies. This is clearly true of Hayek's analysis in which the market and the economic system – the capitalist system that can create freedom and perhaps infinite growth. Certainly by the time of late capitalist ideas, we constantly hear politicians claiming that their policies will produce more growth – infinite growth – rather than the slowing down of economic growth, and so on.

Infinite growth and the challenges of globalisation

One of the constant claims of capitalism is that of growth – constant growth, almost unrestrained growth and so in advanced capitalism we discover a covert ideology of infinite growth that will produce a utopian world of consumption in which to live. The reference above to McTopia points to the global nature of this phenomenon of advanced capitalism, but globalisation is not really utopian.

Globalisation might best be understood as a socio-economic phenomenon that has profound political and cultural implications. From an over-simplistic perspective, it can be understood by thinking of the *world* as having a sub-structure and a super-structure, whereas the simple Marxist model of society was that each *society* had a sub-structure and a super-structure. For Marx, the sub-structure was the economic institution and the super-structure everything else in social and cultural life – including the state, culture, and so on. Those who owned the capital, and therefore the means of production, were able to exercise power throughout the whole of their society. But over the years owner-ship has changed to control, and the capital has become intellectual as well as financial. But the other major change has been that this sub-structure has become global rather than societal and comprises two main driving forces: the first is the way that those who have control of the economic and technological sub-structure in the countries of the dominant West have been enabled to extend their control over the sub-structures of all the other countries in the world; the second is the standardising effects that these sub-structural changes are having on the super-structures of each society since the common sub-structure means that similar forces are being exerted on each people and society despite each having different histories, cultures, languages, and so on. Consequently we can see why the forces of globalisation exercise standardising pressures while a variety of peoples and societies resist this by endeavouring, to differing extents, to retain their own cultures and values – the glocal.

The process of globalisation, as we know it today, began in the West (USA followed by Western Europe) in the early 1970s. There were a number of contributory factors at this time that exacerbated this process, such as:

- the oil crisis, which dented the confidence of the West;
- the demise of the Bretton Woods Agreement, that eventually enabled both free trade and the flow of financial capital to develop throughout the world;
- the development of sophisticated information technology through the star wars programme, through which the information technology revolution took off, with one development leading to another, as Castells (1996, p. 51f.) demonstrates. He (1996, p. 52) makes the point that 'to some extent, the availability of new technologies constituted as a system in the 1970s was a fundamental basis for the process of socio-economic restruc-turing in the 1980s';
- the economic competition from Japan, that challenged the West;
- using scientific knowledge in the production of commodities in the global market;
- the fall of the Berlin Wall – the democratisation of the Eastern Bloc – for, from the time it occurred, there has literally been 'no alternative' (Bauman, 1992) to global capitalism and so it reinforced the process.

While this is a brief outline of the globalisation process, we want to focus on three aspects here in order to develop our argument: power, inequality and social exclusion and natural resources [see Held *et al.* (1999) for a full discussion of global transformations].

Power: The driving force of advanced capitalism is the transnational corporations and their law is the law of the global market, whereas the laws of the states are still apparently controlled by the democratic (or not so democratic) governments, although the extent to which the national governments are sovereign is much more questionable (see Korten, 1995, Monbiot, 2000). Certainly the laws of the market have simply by-passed the laws of the states and the corporations are now able to exert tremendous pressures on national and local governments in order to pursue their own policies. These processes have made the nation states far less powerful than ever before in their history, so that politicians now call for partnerships between the public and private sector. But they are only willing to do this and to cooperate with these powerful institutions because they are realists and recognise where the power lies – it is at least shared, if not lost! But as Bauman (1999, p. 156) noted:

> Once the state recognizes the priority and superiority of the laws of the market over the laws of the *polis*, the citizen is transmuted into the consumer, and a 'consumer demands more and more protection while accepting less and less the need to participate' in the running of the state.
>
> (italics in original)

In other words, the consumer becomes a less active citizen and the political dimension of citizenship becomes little more than electing those who will manage the state, political power is subsumed within economic power and democracy suffers.

Inequality and social exclusion: The global market always favours the rich – since the market is never free. Very few people who have had power have not used it in some way to become rich – even very rich (fat cats). Those countries that have developed a knowledge economy have continued in their growth, others like much of sub-Saharan Africa are virtually excluded from the market. Bauman (1999, pp. 175–176) summarises a United Nations' Development report which illustrates these points:

- consumption has multiplied by a factor of six since 1950, but one billion people cannot even satisfy their most elementary needs;
- 60% of residents in developing countries have no basic social infrastructures, 33% no access to drinking water, 25% no accommodation worthy of the name and 20% no sanitary or medical services;
- the average income of 120 million people is less than $1 per day;
- in the world's richest country (USA), 16.5% live in poverty, 20% of the adult population are illiterate; 13% have a life expectancy of shorter than 60 years;
- the world's three richest men have private assets greater than the combined national products of the 48 poorest countries;
- the fortunes of the 15 richest men exceeds the total produce of the whole of sub-Saharan Africa;
- 4% of the wealth of the world's richest 225 men would offer the poor of the world access to elementary medical and educational amenities as well as adequate nutrition.

This is the other side of Hayek's vision of economic utopia – the creation of a new serfdom and what is being described here is a situation within which there is no global welfare and the poor of the world have no social rights as such by virtue of their humanity – but need care and concern. Moreover, while the lack of welfare provision is not a pre-condition of globalisation, it certainly helps global capitalism expand its profitability with greater ease since the people are merely human resources and the greater their need the easier it is to exploit them.

Natural resources: But it is not only human resources who are used and impoverished in the process, it is natural resources. We constantly hear that the world's oil stocks are running out, the forests are being destroyed in Brazil, the 'greenhouse gases' are destroying the ozone layer, and so on. The global market has made infinite demands on the globe and its people in order to produce finite growth – let alone infinite growth. The vision of infinite growth is an ecological nightmare. This is a world which exploits the many and their environments in order to satisfy the demands and wants of the minority.

The vision of economic growth has produced corporate power, the decline of democracy, impoverishment of people and potential ecological disaster. The challenge is to halt the destructive processes of globalisation and to facilitate and equal distribution of the world's resources. Religious visions are idealistic and unrealisable; political and economic ones are not only not universal, they are unrealistic, wrong and even dystopian. And so we turn to learning – to infinite learning.

Infinite learning

The present age has made people realise the reality and potentiality of lifelong learning – now this is being taken for granted as we recognise that schooling is not the end of education nor of learning and that some forms of intelligence still continue to expand with learning experiences throughout the life time. Adult educators have always recognised this and there has always been an emphasis on self-directed learning in adulthood (Houle, 1961; Tough, 1979). Learning, then, has always been recognised as something that individuals undertake and, to some extent, it is something that they choose to do. But more recently, the focus has been on the actual learning experience. This has produced a very wide variety of theories of experiential learning (Kolb, 1984; Jarvis, 1987 *inter alia*). Over the past twenty years the writing on experiential learning has been volu-minous, but that on existential learning less so. Yet it is important to recognise that by virtue of our existence, we learn. Learning is the driving force of our human-ness itself. It is the foundation of the process of our being and our becoming throughout the duration of our finitude (Jarvis, 1992).

But globalisation has brought another challenge to learning, since this rapidly changing economic system of production is demanding a more knowledgeable workforce. So lifelong learning has gained prominence – not because of the efforts or writings of adult educators but because of the needs of the economic system. This has also produced theories of the learning organisation, learning society, and so on. Everyone learning! Infinite learning! And so, Ranson (1994, pp. 101–129) conceived of this learning society as a new order – one which would, or should, produce a more democratic way of living.

> The challenge for the time is to create a new moral and political order that responds to the needs of a society undergoing historic transition.
>
> (Ranson, 1994, p. 105)

Here then, once again, we look forward to that utopian society – in this case a political democracy created by rational thought and debate and a clear understanding of education. Three conditions for the learning society are suggested: pre-suppositions – learning is valued and with it openness to new ideas; principles – active citizenship and practical reason; purposes, values and conditions – at the levels of self, society and polity. Ranson goes on to map these out in considerable detail, which includes a discussion on reforming government at national and local level and locating education within it. He recognises that this is a vision, one which will not be realised, if society does not change to enable this to happen. He concludes with the rather lame plea that teachers and educational managers can help spread this vision throughout society. In other words, this utopian vision merely fulfils the functions of other utopian thought – to remind us that our present system is not perfect and to educate our desire for a better world.

A wider educational vision is adopted by O'Sullivan (1999) whose utopian vision of learning embeds 'the human community within the earth community and ultimately within the universe' (p. 30). His vision is not of the learning society that Ranson sees, it is far less prosaic for his is a vision of learning, transformative learning. Of course his vision is attractive, of course his vision of the universe kindles within us that desire for a better world and in this sense he is both educating our desire and pointing to the fact that all the apparent advances in the world have not produced that perfect world. And so, we need to keep on learning, to keep on being transformed and yet the paradox of this transformative learning is that even when we produce transformations in the world, the vision still seems as far away as it is ever was – and so we just have to keep on learning. Infinite learning, infinite transformations, but like the mirage in the desert that utopia still lies in front of us and beyond us – beyond time itself. But then so it should do for these dreams of different worlds serve both to show us that we have not yet travelled far along the road to the perfect society and also educate our thinking so that we too can desire that which lies beyond – beyond time, even beyond our dreams. Herein lies one of the greatest paradoxes of human existence – we who are (finite being in time) desire a world that can only lie beyond time – in infinitude itself.

Utopianism is more than just a motivating factor however significant it has been in the lives of many great thinkers. E.P. Thompson (1977, pp. 790–791) wrote:

> And in such an adventure two things happen: our habitual values (the 'commonsense' of bourgeois society) are thrown into disarray. As we enter Utopia's proper and new found space: *the education of desire*. This is not the same as 'a moral education' towards a given end: it is rather, to open a way of aspiration, to 'teach desire to desire better, to desire more, and above all to desire in a different way'.
>
> (italics in original)

But, as we shall argue, perhaps teaching and learning does not lie in the realms of education itself – but in relationship with the Other. Indeed, it is not infinite learning to which we point now but learning the infinite.

Conclusion

So then, it is not only transformation that we desire but transcendence. We have to transcend that which is – transcend the boundaries, even those of visionary worlds. For many of these who draw boundaries limit freedom and offer a world of control; they are totalizers (Levinas, 1991[1969]). And so these have to be transcended but what more is there to transcend? Perhaps we need to learn to transcend even ourselves without destroying our own integrity. It was Emmanuel Levinas (1991[1969]) who pointed us in this direction. For him, there is a clear distinction between 'need' and 'desire': the former seeks to fill something that is lacking, which is like many of the visions that we have described above, where a desire is what transcends the self – the me and myself self-centred categories, as John Wild puts it in his Introduction (Levinas, 1991 [1969] p. 16). For him this desire is never satisfied – it is infinite – and Being is a journey into the infinite. A perfectly disinterested desire is goodness. But it is not a journey undertaken alone but with the Other, with whom I might establish a bond without seeking control. This is what Levinas (1991, p. 40) calls religion. It is in the endeavour to discover perfect relationship that points to infinity – it is people not place. For it is the society of the I with the Other, when freedom itself is maintained and when it is recognised that when my spontaneity (freedom) is impinged upon, there is the beginning of ethics. Herein, concern for the Other, within impinging upon that freedom, lies at the heart of the infinite – it is seeking a quality of life.

> To approach the other in conversation is to welcome his expression, in which at each instance he overflows the idea a thought would carry away with it. It is therefore to *receive* from the Other beyond the capacity of the I which means exactly: to have the idea of infinity. But this also means: to be taught. The relation with the Other, or Conversation, is a non allergic relation; but in as much as it is welcomed this conversation is teaching (enseignment). Teaching is not reducible to maieutics; it comes from the exterior and brings me more than I contain. In its non-violent transitivity the very epiphany of the face is produced.
>
> (Levinas, 1991, p. 51 – italics in original)

So then in relationship itself lies the idea of infinitude. In a world of perfect relationship we can begin to explore infinity and so in exploring the face to face, the vision of the infinite is caught and learned and offers us something that lies beyond time in Being itself. So then, it is not infinite visions, even of the learning society that we need but the vision of the infinite that produces different worlds – and the others interact with us as we seek to transcend the finitude of our being in this journey of life.

References

Bauman Z (1992) *Intimations of Post-Modernity* London: Routledge
Bauman Z (1999) *In Search of Politics* Cambridge: Polity Press
Beck U (1992) *Risk Society* London: Sage
Bell B, Gaventa, J and Peters, J (eds) (1990) *We Make the Road by* Philadelphia: Temple University Press
Castells M (1996) *The Rise of the Network Society* Oxford: Blackwell (Vol. 1 *of The Information Age: Economy, Society and Culture*)
Freire P (1972) *Cultural Action for Freedom* Harmondsworth: Penguin
Hayek F (1986[1984]) *The Road to Serfdom* London, ARK Paperbacks
Held D and McGrew A, Goldblatt D and Perraton J (1999) *Global Transformations* Cambridge: Polity Press

Houle C (1961) *The Inquiring Mind* Madison: University of Wisconsin Press
Jarvis P (1987) *Adult Learning in the Social Context* London: Croom Helm
Jarvis P (1992) *Paradoxes of Learning* San Francisco: Jossey-Bass
Jarvis P (1993) *Adult Education and the State* London: Routledge
Jarvis P (1997) *Ethics and the Education of Adults in a Late-Modern World* Leicester: NIACE
Kolb D (1984) *Experiential Learning* Englewood Cliffs, NJ: Prentice Hall
Korten D C (1995) *When Corporations Rule the World* London: Earthscan
Kumar K (1987) *Utopia and Anti-Utopia in Modern Times* Oxford: Blackwell
Kumar K (1991) *Utopianism* Milton Keynes: Open University Press
Kumar K and Bann S (eds) (1993) *Utopias and the Millennium* London: Reaktion Books
Levinas E (1991[1969]) *Totality and Infinity* AH Dordrecht: Kluwer
Levitas R (1990) *The Concept of Utopia* New York: Philip Allan
Levitas R (1992) Review of *Utopia* by K Kumar *Sociology* Vol 26 No 2 pp. 355–356
Mannheim K (1936) *Ideology and Utopia* London: Routledge & Kegan Paul
Monbiot G (2000) *The Captive State* London: Macmillan
Nozick R (1974) *Anarchy, State and Utopia* Oxford: Blackwell
O'Neill J (1991) McTopia: Eating Time in *Utopias and the Millennium* (ed) Kumar and Bann (1991)
O'Sullivan E (1999) *Transformative Learning* Toronto: OISE in association with Zed Books (London)
Ranson S (1994) *Towards the Learning Society* London: Cassell
Thompson E P (1977) *William Morris: Romantic Revolutionary* London: Merlin Press
Tough A (1979) *The Adult's Learning Projects* Toronto: OISE (Second edition)
Wilson B (1967) *Patterns of Sectarianism* London: Heinemann

CHAPTER 15

BEYOND THE LEARNING SOCIETY

Globalisation and the moral imperative for reflective social change

Originally published as 'Beyond the Learning Society' in the *International Journal of Lifelong Learning* (2006), Vol. 25 Nos 3–4, pp. 201–11. Cross-references refer to the original publication.

In the 1970s and early 1980s there was a clear sense in which we were moving towards lifelong education and a learning society and away from traditional adult education. Books on the learning society, such as Hutchins (1968) and Husen (1974), were flagging up the change and so the International Journal was founded with the expectation that we would soon be encountering lifelong education on an international scale. But social change seems to occur in epochs and now we are moving towards the end of a brief era, in my opinion, and reaching beyond the learning society. Hence we need to ask in what ways, if any, are we able to predict this 'beyond'.

The nature of the concept of the 'beyond' is complex: it can point to a future caused by evolutionary or more conflict situations; it can point to a 'beyond the parameters of the learning society; or even point to something underlying the learning society, and these foundations might also be moving the super-structure in a new direction. Nothing lies beyond learning, except death, but the future depends on the way we, as people, learn and respond to the out-workings of the sub-structures of society. In a sense, what occurred, as a result of neo-liberalism, has produced unfortunate conditions in our society from which we learn, through reflection amongst other patterns of thought, and seek to change what has occurred since they now appear unacceptable. A pragmatist ethical argument suggests that we continue to learn and change our understanding of the good society as we reflect upon the global conditions that have arisen as a result of the global knowledge economy. In a sense, a neglected form of knowledge is reasserting itself – moral knowledge – and with it a form of idealism. This argument is presented here in four brief sections: the nature of the learning society; the nature of learning; what the learning society neglected; beyond the learning society?

The nature of the learning society

There has, of course, been a vast volume of literature on the learning society and it is beyond the scope of this paper to review it here. However, five features of the learning society that are important for this argument are discussed here: the growth of the open society; globalisation; types of knowledge; instrumentalism/pragmatism; learning. Naturally, they are all inter-linked and there is a logic in the way that they are inter-related.

Growth of the open society: Both Toennies (1957) and Durkheim (1933) have documented how communitarian, or even tribal, society has gradually loosened its structures and by the 1960s and 1970s the logic of industrialisation thesis (Kerr, 1973) suggested we had moved towards an open, individualised society. Individualism has gradually assumed a dominant place in our thinking although some of it has probably been much too simple and, I think, misleading. There is a major difference between openness and individualism. Society is not a mere agglomeration of individuals but it is an open network of relationships. Individuals have their freedom but they still need to relate and, indeed, without relationship there could be no society. We are born in relationship, brought up in relationship, live in relationship and only die alone. This over-emphasis on individualism has had important consequences for our emphases on morality since it focuses our thought on the significance of the self rather than on the self's relationship with the Other – a point to which we shall return below.

The extremes of globalisation: Fundamentally globalisation is about a world which has a sub-structure and a super-structure. The sub-structure of society is the control of capital, both economic and intellectual, and the control of information technology. It is not an upper class that has this control but a number of competing companies in a global market. The super-structure is everything else and, initially, I found studies like Monbiot's (2000) *The Captive State* to be very convincing. Now I do not feel that the sub-structure is quite so powerful as I once did since there is still some life left in the political. But I also feel that the concept of glocalisation might be seen as more significant, leading to a recognition that the inter-relationship between the global and the local is both political and combative. Hence I now see the local fighting for its place within a global framework and while it is losing out in some ways and standardisation is occurring, as Beck (1992) suggested, there are local states and cultures that are surviving, albeit having been greatly affected by the forces of globalisation. The other dominant sub-structural force is information technology and it is this that enables different local sites and the global and the local to interact almost instantaneously, creating a global village; this is important as we consider the extremes of the world in which we live.

The second extreme that I want to highlight is that of the rich and the poor which is a direct result of capitalism and exacerbated by its global dimension. We have all become aware of the plight of Africa in recent months but in global society there are vast numbers of people who appear to have no social rights. Bauman (1999, pp. 175–6) summarises a United Nations' Development Report thus:

- consumption has multiplied by a factor of six since 1950, but one billion people cannot even satisfy their most elementary needs;
- 60% of residents in developing countries have no basic social infrastructures, 33% no access to drinking water, 25% no accommodation worthy of the name and 20% no sanitary or medical services;
- the average income of 120 million people is less than $1 per day;
- in the world's richest country (USA), 16.5% live in poverty, 20% of the adult population are illiterate; 13% have a life expectancy of shorter than 60 years;
- the world's three richest men have private assets greater than the combined national products of the 48 poorest countries;
- the fortunes of the 15 richest men exceeds the total produce of the whole of sub-Saharan Africa;

- 4% of the wealth of the world's richest 225 men would offer the poor of the world access to elementary medical and educational amenities as well as adequate nutrition.

What is being described here is a situation within which there are no global social rights and no global form of government which could protect these rights, if they ever actually existed. However, we have been made increasingly aware of this social situation by globalisation itself; the power of information technology at the sub-structure of global society has brought these terrible conditions to our television screens. In other words, we have become increasingly dissatisfied with the outcomes of neo-liberalism and, perhaps, our vision of the ideal world is undergoing change.

Types of knowledge: It is the societies, however, that are at the centre of economic globalisation that Daniel Bell (1973) first called the post-industrial societies. For him, knowledge was their fundamental resource, especially theoretical knowledge (Bell, 1973, p. 14) and, as Stehr (1994, p. 10) later pointed out, these societies signal a fundamental shift in the structure of the economy, since the primacy of manufacturing is replaced by knowledge. It is not knowledge *per se*, however, that is significant to the knowledge society but scientific – including social scientific – knowledge (Stehr, 1994, pp. 99–103) since this underlies the efficient production and marketing of new commodities and services and, consequently, it has economic value. Knowledge, as such, has no intrinsic value; it is only its use-value as a scarce resource which is significant. Hence, research and development are at the heart of the productive processes and knowledge has to be practical.

But as early as 1926 the German sociologist Max Scheler (1980, p. 76) began to classify knowledge into seven types based upon their speed of change:

- myth and legend – undifferentiated religious, metaphysical, natural and historical;
- knowledge implicit in everyday language – as opposed to learned, poetic or technical;
- religious – from pious to dogmatic;
- mystical;
- philosophic-metaphysical;
- positive knowledge – mathematics, the natural sciences and the humanities;
- technological.

Scheler regarded his final two forms of knowledge as the most artificial because they changed so rapidly, whereas the other five are more embedded in culture. Whilst his analysis was a little over-simple, he does make the point clearly that many forms of positive and technological knowledge change rapidly – he suggested 'hour by hour' – but that was in 1926! Not all scientific knowledge changes rapidly – the speed of light, for instance, has not changed, whereas our understanding of the nature of light has changed. Hence, Scheler's typology, whilst useful for our discussion, only represents some aspects of our understanding of the complex nature of knowledge itself. We might also dispute with Scheler that the humanities should be coupled with mathematics and the natural sciences – I would place them in the same category as philosophical and metaphysical knowledge. While Scheler was not totally correct, his artificial forms of knowledge are related to the dominant forms of knowledge in the knowledge economy.

Four other points we need to make about the nature of knowledge: first artificial scientific knowledge is presented as value-free but this is disputable since it is used by those who have power. Even if the knowledge itself is value-free, factual knowledge has no meaning until it is ascribed meaning by those who use it. Secondly, we have lived in a society which has been dominated by the use of only a portion of the spectrum of knowledge and from within Scheler's typology, philosophical-metaphysical and religious knowledge, amongst others, have been downplayed, even though we actually learn them. Thirdly, our scientific knowledge no longer deals with certainties but as Beck (1992) pointed out it deals at best with approximations and policies are being implemented before we can be certain of outcomes – we live in a risk society. Consequently, we are in a reflexive society in which we are constantly assessing the outcomes of the policies which have been implemented. Fourthly, we have had a tendency to confuse the concept of information with that of objective knowledge. What used to be called objective knowledge might best be understood as data and information but until these are learned subjectively they are not knowledge, or beliefs or values, and so on. Knowledge, beliefs and values, are always subjective and have to be learned – as do emotions. It is these that form the basis of our motivation to act as well as the knowledge itself, although the actions are also still learning situations.

Instrumentalism/pragmatism: The practical outcomes of knowledge use have dominated our thinking. Lyotard (1984) argued that knowledge will be legitimated by its performativity in this age, and so instrumentalism has reigned supreme. It is almost as if instrumentalism has itself become regarded as value-free, rational common sense. Indeed, it can be argued that the idea of rationality underlies the nature of instrumental thought. Contemporary society has always been regarded as a rational society, whereas this is empirically untrue. Many years ago I researched the subject of superstition in contemporary British society and I discovered that almost every person whom we interviewed (n >170) was in one way or another superstitious (Jarvis, 1980) which negates any idea that people during this period were rational.

Fundamentally, instrumentalism is a teleological ethical form in which the end might be regarded as the good but we have also seen during this period that the rich get richer and the poor poorer so that it could be argued that this is an end which we assess to be less than good in this reflexive society. Yet pragmatism has another side, as James and Dewey, amongst others, have emphasised – there is an ethical dimension. Joas (2000, p. 170) highlights two features of pragmatist ethics that are important for this argument:

> Pragmatist ethics . . . stands opposed to culturistic moral relativism and stresses the universal need for the normative regulation of human co-operation.
> . . . pragmatist ethics consists in the fact that it is an ethics based on the perspective of the actor.

In a reflexive society we become 'wiser after the event' (Joas, 2000, p. 171) and so we can reflect on and even re-appraise our ethical position.

The use of the term 'learning': Since our society is a knowledge economy and that rapidly changing scientific knowledge dominates it, it demands that certain people in specific occupations, such as the professions, people-orientated occupations and in the crafts and trades, keep abreast of and even generate new occupational knowledge. It is not surprising, therefore, that learning throughout the occupational life should in some way come to the fore and two terms have come to dominate that vocabulary: lifelong learning and the learning society. Both of which are used rather loosely and imprecisely. Learning throughout the work life has come to be known as lifelong learning although we are all well aware that work life and life itself are not the same and neither are they co-terminus, so that work-life learning is actually different from lifelong learning. And secondly, society does not and cannot learn since it is an abstract concept, but its members do.

In the learning society, 'learning' is a gerundive to describe the type of society in which we live. In this sense, it is being used to describe this flexible, open society that can respond to the changes driven by the knowledge economy and the market rather than about the process of human learning. At the same time since learning carries with it a connotation that it is good and desirable and something that leads to human growth and development, discourse about the learning society has acquired a misleading value orientation – that the learning society is intrinsically a good thing (see, for instance, the almost evangelistic tone adopted by Longworth and Davies, 1996). Two conclusions might be drawn from this: that the term 'learning' in this context has given contemporary society an appearance of goodness that is misleading and that the term has itself been inappropriately used, and so it is now necessary to briefly examine the process of learning to compare it with this conclusion.

The nature of human learning

My own understanding of learning has been undergoing considerable development since I first started to study it twenty years ago and it would be unwise to try to review this development here (see Jarvis and Parker, 2005: Jarvis, 2006). However, in the latter book I argue that since learning is a universal human phenomenon, all the different theories of learning should fit into a comprehensive model and that each different theory only emphasises some elements of the process. As a result of this investigation, I suggest that human learning is the combination of processes whereby the whole person – body (genetic, physical and biological) and mind (knowledge, skills, attitudes, values, emotions, beliefs and senses) – experiences a social situation, the perceived content of which is then transformed cognitively, emotively or practically (or through any combination) and integrated into the person's individual biography resulting in a changed (or more experienced) person.

There are four important points to make about learning as a result of the above discussion: the learner; the breadth of learning; the experience; reflection and the nature of pragmatism.

The learner: Many definitions of learning concentrate on what is learned, e.g., knowledge or skill, but they neglect the learner. This is most commonly demonstrated when we hear teachers and lecturers describing their work – one might say I teach sociology or another I lecture in education, but this is actually imprecise language. What they are actually saying is that they teach students sociology, or education, and so on. It is the person, the whole person, who learns and who also learns more than the subject being taught all the time! While we might concentrate on the sociology or the education, other learning has happened during the process even though we do not acknowledge it and it is the person who is changed as a result of the learning.

Consequently, the instrumental ends of learning, that is learning a specific knowledge or skill, actually deflects our thinking from the fact that it is the person who learns – the whole person – since this is less obvious in the first instance and if there is an end to learning it lies in the learners and in their living rather than in the specific knowledge and skill that they might display, which is only a penultimate end. It is essential that the person is put back into the centre of the learning process and the breadth of learning recognised.

Breadth of learning: The learners learn knowledge, skill, attitudes, emotions, beliefs, values and senses in every learning experience, even though they are not all specified nor assessed as outcomes of learning. Consequently, individuals have been experiencing and learning, but not necessarily articulating, a far wider spectrum of knowledge and beliefs than they might even have been aware, and this has been recognised by a number of thinkers, such as Polanyi (1967) with his tacit dimension, and I have adopted the concept of pre-conscious learning since 1987 (Jarvis, 1987). Beliefs and values have not been treated as very important so that we have not been given as much opportunity to reflect upon them or to articulate them as we have on other forms of knowledge and skill; after all, they are not assessed and carry no certification.

Experience: One of the major implications of lifelong learning is that we can potentially learn from every experience in life, which means that our learning is not controlled by what we are taught. We learn from the experiences that we have of the world. Experience lies at the intersection of objective reality and the self and we learn from our experience – our own construction of that reality. We turn sensations, feelings, data and information into knowledge, beliefs, values and emotions. Even more significantly, in the contemporary world in which information technology dominates, we are exposed to many more secondary experiences of the world through the media than ever before, including the horrendous conditions of extreme poverty exacerbated by the globalised knowledge economy in which we live. Every situation in daily living is a potential site for learning so that we can learn from our experience of the reality that we have depicted as the outcome of the global knowledge economy.

Reflection and the nature of pragmatism: We learn through reflection on subjective experience and we are constantly exposed to (experience) the ends of advanced capitalism through travel, pictures in the media and so on. We are aware of poverty, AIDS and all the needs of the under-developed world and, more recently, especially Africa. We reflect on these experiences and we feel or realise that advanced capitalism is not producing ends that are in accord with our understanding of the good society. Feeling is a fundamental sensation from which we learn. And so we can change our means to achieve those ends – this is perfectly in accord with pragmatism.

Omissions from the learning society discourse

It is clear that from the above discussion that the learning society discourse included only those features that have supported the position of the dominant

West and advanced capitalism; it has emphasised certain elements and, naturally enough, it has excluded others. Some of those omitted factors, however, are quite crucial when we begin to ask what lies beyond the present type of society and in this very brief section, four of these will be highlighted: the forms of knowledge; the instrumentalism of pragmatism; the capital rather than the people; rational thought and action rather than the emotions.

The forms of knowledge: As I have pointed out the learning society has emphasised technological and scientific knowledge, those which Scheler regarded as the most artificial. Since they form the foundations of the capitalist market their speed of change has been increased as the competition to sell the products produced as a result of this new knowledge has continued. This has also helped generate an open society with a more individualistic orientation – indeed, we have emphasised individual rights and downplayed the significance of personal relationships. People have become strangers but when the stranger becomes a face then my individualism has to be reappraised since I am no longer free to act spontaneously, as Levinas (1991, p. 43) writes:

> We name this calling into question of my spontaneity by the presence of the Other ethics. The strangeness of the Other, his irreducibility to the I, to my thoughts and my possessions, is precisely accomplished as a calling into question of my spontaneity, as ethics.

Once the Other impinges upon us the potentiality of the relationship demands an ethical response. Our society has enabled us to downplay the existence of the Other but the information technology sub-structure of our global society, the media, has ensured that we are confronted with this moral condition. There has been a neglect of moral knowledge amongst the dominant forms of knowledge and yet we are constantly confronted with the impoverished stranger demanding to become a face – to an imperative to allow moral knowledge a place in the dominant discourse and to recognise that value rationality is just as rational as other forms of rationality. We also recognise that we learn beliefs and values as well in our experience of lifelong learning.

The instrumentalism of pragmatism: Part of the dominant discourse has been than we live in a pragmatic society in which things have to be practical and, as Lyotard (1984) reminded us we legitimate contemporary knowledge by its performativity. Everything is about practical ends – it is instrumental. Yet this is quite a crude understanding of pragmatism. Some of the leading pragmatist thinkers, e.g., James (1902) and Dewey, both explored religious and ethical ideas within a pragmatist framework. Dewey (1934, pp. 49–50), for instance, discussed the way in which human ideals are generated through creative imagination and are adapted as we reflect upon them:

> Moreover the process of creation is experimental and continuous. The artist, scientific man, or good citizen depends upon what others have done before him. The sense of new values that become ends to be realized arises first in dim and uncertain form. As the values are dwelt upon and carried forward in action they grow in definiteness and coherence. Interaction between aim and existent conditions improves and tests the ideal; and conditions are at the same time modified. Ideals change as they are applied to existent conditions. The process endures and advances with the life of humanity.

It may not be new values that are learned but what has been gradually dawning has been the realisation that the means to the end might not be the most value rational.

Globalisation has not only generated new conditions in which means and ends change as they are applied to existing conditions, it has broken down the social situation in which we have been able to limit our thinking to our own society and exclude all those situations that do not fit into our mind-set. As Joas (2000, p. 174) argues:

> . . . every culture fences in the potentially universal morality by defining its areas and conditions of application. Which people (or organisms) and which situations are 'set free' for this morality is a matter of interpretation, and consequently varies across cultures and history. In each case a justification is produced for excluding people of different nationalities, ethnic groups, races and religions, of another sex or age, or other mentalities and moralities. Without such a justification, the right would become a cultural dynamic.

But this is just the point – globalisation has now prevented us from excluding these different groups from our moral discourse and so in global society a universal right has become a cultural dynamic. Pragmatist ethics allows us to change the means to obtain the good society. We can be perfectly pragmatic about it – and so we can have means of achieving the good whilst remaining perfectly consistent to the pragmatism of the age.

Capital and people: It was Kant who taught us the people are ends and never means but we have for long forgotten this fundamental tenet of his ethics. People of the third world have been a means to enriching those who control the sub-structure of global society but once it is people who are the end and not capital, once the stranger has become a face, then the means to the end must change.

Rationality and the emotions: In our research for an EU Framework fifth framework project (Etgace – Education and Training for Governance and Active Citizenship in Europe), co-ordinated from the University of Surrey, we found that many people who became active citizens in their own localities did so because they 'just felt' that something was wrong – others had a religious belief, and so on. People just felt that they had to respond to the social situation within which they found themselves. They did not sit down and rationally work it out – they felt and they acted and this was rational – value rational. Perhaps what we discovered points us to the larger picture; it is not just a matter of rational thought that has led people to question the ends of contemporary society – it is the emotions as well.

But Taylor (1989, pp. 32–40) has drawn our attention to the relationship between our sense of self and moral good which Joas (2000, p. 134) depicts as a hermeneutic cycle in which we move between our feelings, our interpretations of them and our articulation of them. In articulating our feelings we can also modify our values and produce new ones. In other words, this hermeneutic cycle is the reflexive process that we have already discussed but now it is related to our sense of self-identity.

Yet it must also be emphasised that the present learning society has also prepared the way for this pragmatic re-assessment of the end of society. In Beck's

(1992) formulation of the risk society, he recognised that policy makers implement policies long before the outcomes of the policies can be known. Consequently, he called this a reflexive society – one that is always looking back on itself and re-assessing the implementation of its policies. It is this reflexive society that is now re-assessing the outcomes of advanced capitalism and the knowledge society in terms of a vision of a more desirable society in which all people are regarded as important. It is a pragmatism that demands that members of the learning society take themselves seriously, keep on learning and have a broader vision of global life, when strangers become faces and the moral imperative is changed it enables us all to become ends rather than means.

Beyond the learning society?

It is very clear that we cannot go beyond learning and, in this sense, a society in which people continue to learn remains – but we are beginning to see fundamental changes occurring that might be seen a change in the knowledge discourse. However, the change might be cultural and this might be described, in the language used by Sorokin (see Timasheff, 1965, Merton, 1968 *inter alia* for discussions on Sorokin) in his theory of social change over a half century ago, as a swing between sensate and ideational cultures. A sensate culture is one in which ultimate validity is attested by the senses whereas the ideational suggests that reality has a deeper meaning. Sorokin actually suggested that when the two combine we have an ideological culture but if they merely co-exist we have a mixed culture. Sorokin's sociological theories lie beyond the scope of this paper and will not be discussed here; suffice to note that we may be witnessing a movement away from a sensate culture in the direction of a more ideational form. In this we are seeing a reappraisal of values in a number of different ways. In the first place, the anti-globalisation movement may merely be reflecting a traditional radical anti-capitalist position. But there is more to the change than this: we are seeing capitalism itself begin to take notice of these concerns; politicians and 'celebrities' are aware that there is a popular movement away from the extremes of global capitalism with which they feel it wise to be associated; there is a focus on Africa where the extremes of poverty have been experienced and most vividly portrayed to the affluent West by the media; the idea that the good society is a wealthy one is beginning to be questioned; people are beginning to become the ends rather than the means; a broader spectrum of knowledge in beginning to be recognised; there is an increasing emphasis on citizenship and citizenship education. But learning is not being replaced; only the focus and content of learning is being adjusted.

Conclusion

If there were no learning, there would be no life. The significance of lifelong learning has not been questioned during this argument and the need for social change has been emphasised but the direction that the learning society is taking is now being called into question. The ends of contemporary society are now open to question, as are the means through which we attain them. We cannot prescribe the ends in the way that Ranson (1994) tried to, when he mapped out what a learning society should be like, because it is constantly being re-appraised and we cannot even point to a model of the good society but perhaps we can suggest that the possibility of a better society is beginning to appear on the horizon, or as Levinas would put it – perhaps there is a movement away from totality towards infinity. In this period of social change we are not beyond the learning society. We are not beyond anything but we are in it and we might be travelling in a different direction in a society whose members are continuing to learn – even to learn to be, do, know and learn to live together – to echo the sentiments of the UNESCO report (Delors, 1996).

References

Bauman Z (1999) *In Search of Politics* Cambridge: Polity Press
Beck U (1992) *Risk Society* London: Sage
Bell D (1973) *The Coming of Post-Industrial Society* New York: Basic Books
Delors J (chair) (1996) *Learning: The Treasure Within* Paris: UNESCO
Dewey J (1934) *A Common Faith* New Haven: Yale University Press
Durkheim E (1933) *The Division of Labor in Society* (trans G Simpson) New York: Free Press
Husen T (1974) *The Learning Society* London: Methuen
Hutchins R (1968) *The Learning Society* Harmondsworth: Penguin
James W (1902) *Varieties of Religious Experience*, Cambridge, Mass.: Harvard University Press
Jarvis P (1980) Towards a Sociological Understanding of Superstition *Social Compass* Vol XXVII pp. 285–95
Jarvis P (1987) *Adult Learning in the Social Context* London: Croom Helm
Jarvis P (2006) *Towards a Comprehensive Theory of Human Learning* London: Routledge (Vol 1 of *Lifelong Learning and the Learning Society*)
Jarvis P and Parker S (2005) (eds) *Human Learning: A Holistic Perspective* London: Routledge
Joas H (2000) *The Genesis of Values* (trans G Moore) Cambridge: Polity Press
Kerr C, Dunlop J, Harbison F and Myers C (1973) *Industrialism and Industrial Man* Harmondsworth: Penguin (2nd edition)
Levinas E (1991) trans. A Lingis *Totality and Infinity* Dordrecht: Klewer
Longworth N and Davies W K (1996) *Lifelong Learning* London: Kogan Page
Lyotard J-F (1984) *The Post-Modern Condition* Manchester: University of Manchester Press
Merton R (1968) *Social Theory and Social Structure* New York: Free Press (Enlarged edition)
Monbiot G (2000) *Captive State* London: Macmillan
Polanyi M (1967) *The Tacit Dimension* London: Routledge
Ranson S (1994) *Towards the Learning Society* London: Cassell
Scheler M ([1926] 1980) *Problems of a Sociology of Knowledge* London: Routledge & Kegan Paul
Stehr N (1994) *Knowledge Societies* London: Sage
Taylor C (1989) *Sources of the Self* Cambridge: Cambridge University Press
Timasheff N (1965) *Sociological Theory* New York: Random House (Revised edition)
Toennies F (1957) trans C Loomis *Community and Society* Michigan: University of Michigan Press – published in Britain as *Community and Association* London: Routledge & Kegan Paul

CHAPTER 16

THE END OF A SENSATE AGE – WHAT NEXT?

Originally presented as 'The End of a Sensate Age – What Next?' (2009), unpublished paper delivered as the 40th Sorokin Lecture at the University of Saskatchewan.

In a world of rapid social change, even social crisis, the work of Sorokin takes on a new relevance. He was a prolific author whose work fell into disrepute at the time when Parson's theories prevailed and the USA was beginning to enjoy the fruits both capitalism and the Enlightenment. But it was this that led Sorokin, who himself was of peasant stock but strove become both a revolutionary and an international scholar, to question what was occurring. For him, the wealth and inequality of the world was a sign of the end of the age and that it would soon change from a sensate to an ideational age. His was a cyclical theory of change which is not a strong theory, but it provides the starting point for what I want to discuss in this paper. At the same time, I will turn to another book written nearly twenty years later that explores much of the same ground as Sorokin – Martin's (1981) *A Sociology of Contemporary Cultural Change* – and reaches a different set of conclusions.

In the Introduction to this paper, I want just to recapitulate Sorokin's theory of change. In the first part of the presentation I then want us to look at the end of the Sensate Age; secondly, we will look at the late developments in globalisation culminating in the present economic crisis and in the third part I will relate this to flaws in the modernity project which might eventually result in a major cultural change although I think that even this crisis is probably not sufficiently large to make people rethink the dominant values of the modern age.

Sorokin's theory of change: Basically, Sorokin posed a theory of change that was rather like a huge pendulum swinging between two ideal types of cultural mentality: the sensate and the ideational. In the process of change he postulated two other types – the idealistic and the mixed – through which the pendulum passed. For Sorokin, the sensate society is one where truth and reality are experienced through the senses – that is empirically – which are validated by the same methods. In his terminology, it is a super-system (language, religion, arts, ethics and science) since it permeates the fabric of a society and its culture. Empiricism is exemplified in the super-system by science and once we specify it in this way, it is easy to see that in order for his formulation to be acceptable the concept of truth has to be redefined in terms of empirical existence. But as truth is more than empirical existence and knowledge itself is more than the empirical we can already begin to understand some of the flaws in the Age, as Sorokin would have seen them.

The opposite pole to the sensate is the ideational cultural mentality, the potentialities of which are contained in the sensate system without being overt and about which Timasheff (1965, p. 239) says, 'If men generally accept the truth of faith, believing that behind these sense impressions lies another, deeper, reality, the super-system is *ideational*'. The verb *to ideate* means to imagine or to form an idea and for Sorokin the underlying value of the ideational age is the spiritual. The ideational is, according to Coser (1977, pp. 465–466), a form of Platonic idealism. Plato's theory of forms runs something like this: a form is an idea that must be true, an abstract idea that must be true without qualification but such a form cannot exist in reality – it transcends the world of the senses and is, in this way, spiritual. Two types of ideational culture can be detected – the ascetic and the active. When the pendulum swings away from the sensate, it begins to uncover what lies beneath it and what always exists, even within the sensate – the spiritual, non-empirical reality of life itself. Sorokin thought that when he was writing this material at the end of the 1950s and early 1960s that we were reaching the end of the Sensate Age and at this point the pendulum must begin to swing in the opposite direction. He calls this point the limit and the swing must continue because we cannot have stasis. As the pendulum swings it either gives rise to a third form – the idealistic characterised by reason simply because it is reasonable to expect a fusion of the empirical and the spiritual (1962, vol. 1 p. 75). However, the form might not be characterised in quite such a reasonable manner and then it can be seen as a mixed cultural mentality. For Sorokin, this is a historical process and it is this that he argues in *Social and Cultural Dynamics* and so for Sorokin, the Sensate Age must soon begin to change.

The end of a Sensate Age

Had Sorokin's theory of change just been a cyclical theory, then he could have written about change in a fairly rational manner, but because of his own background he felt that the manifestations of the end of the Age were most unacceptable and he condemned what he saw and experienced vehemently in his writing and especially in his autobiography. Quoting from Coser (1977, pp. 476–477), with Coser's own comments:

> All of Sorokin's tracts for the times that deal with his philosophy are imbued with a pervasive distaste, one may even say hatred, for modern urban culture and all it stands for. The *Sensate* world of the city jungle and the world of modernity as a whole are, to Sorokin, compounds of utter depravity, which he castigates in the accents of Old Testament prophets or Russian itinerant preachers. Consider the following lines from the final chapter of his autobiography: 'In the human world around me the deadliest storm is raging. The very destiny of mankind is being weighed in the balance of life and death. The forces of the Sensate order are furiously destroying everything that stands in their way. In the name of "God," "progress," "civilization," "communism," "democracy," "freedom," "capitalism," "the dignity of man," and other shibboleths they are uprooting these very values, murdering millions of human beings, threatening man's very survival and tending to turn this beautiful planet into an "abomination of desolation".'

This really contains the same type of condemnation that we find in the Old Testament. As Coser says, it is 'fire and brimstone' next! And so what did the Old Testament prophets have to say in their own condemnation of their age that was so similar? We will look at just one, Amos – from the very first completed book in the bible: having condemned the transgressions of all the surrounding peoples, Amos turned upon Israel:

> 'Hear and testify against the house of Jacob', says the Lord God of hosts, 'that on the day that I punish Israel for his transgressions, I will punish the altars of Bethel and the horns of the altar will be cut off and fall to the ground. I will smite the winter house with the summer house; and the houses of ivory shall perish and the great houses shall come to an end,' says the Lord.
>
> (Amos, 3 vv. 13–15)

These are similar sentiments to Sorokin's – the age is coming to a close – but the parallel is probably even greater than that which appears on the surface. Amos was condemning the vast wealth – 'houses of ivory' – that was made possible by mercantile capitalism: for this book was written at the time when the trade routes from Macau, then a major trading port out of southern China, came to and passed through the Middle-East and those who lived there made vast fortunes from trade. In the Old Testament we see the condemnation of one age as a result of mercantile capitalism and in Sorokin we find similar sentiments about the Sensate Age as a result of industrial capitalism. That we can find such illustrations gives some credibility for the idea of cyclical change in history although this is something that we can, and will, still debate, especially in the light of Max Weber's (1930, p. 57) comment that, 'At all periods of history, wherever it was possible, there has been ruthless acquisition bound to no ethical norms whatsoever', which opens the debate about the extent to which there is a cyclical system of change – but which in crude religious terms points us to the idea that humankind has fallen from the paradise of creation – or at least begins to ask the question as to why we do not live in a perfect world.

Sorokin (1962, vol. 4 pp. 775ff) actually sought to describe the last days (the twilight) of the sensate culture and much of what he wrote bears repetition here:

- Sensate values will become more relative and atomistic;
- Atomised Sensate values will become more debased, sensual and material – stripped of anything divine, sacred and absolute – 'a museum of socio-cultural pathology rather than the imperishable values of the Kingdom of God' (p. 775);
- The disappearance of public opinion – the world's conscience and we find in its stead a market of pressure groups;
- Contracts and covenants will lose their binding power;
- Rude force and cynical fraud will become the only arbiters of all values – might will become right;
- Freedom will be a myth for the majority and it will be turned into unbridled licentiousness by the dominant minority;
- Government will become tyrannical – giving bombs not bread and death instead of freedom;
- The family will disintegrate;
- The Sensate super-system will become increasingly shapeless, divorced from unity;
  - Creativeness will continue to wane
  - Thought will be replaced by information

- ○   Sages by smart Alecs
- ○   Best by biggest
- ○   Classic by best-seller
- ○   Inner value by glittering externality
- ○   Genius by technique
- ○   Lasting value by sensual bit
- ○   Enlightened intuitionism by operational manipulation
- ○   Real criteria by counterfeit criteria
- ○   Great leaders by frauds;
- •   In the increasing moral, mental and social anarchy and decreasing creativeness of Sensate neutrality, the production of material value will decline, depressions will grow worse, and the material standards of living go down;
- •   Populations will be split. . . .

In a sense, we have the prophet of doom looking not far into the future and suggesting that this is how the Sensate Age will terminate. While we might not use his words and our sentiments might differ slightly from his, and remember that he was writing in the 1950s and early 1960s, much of what he wrote has clearly happened. Sorokin believed in the theory of immanent change by which he meant that every cultural mentality had a career and as it came to an end so it would change. '*Immanent change* is a kind of destiny or life career of any technical system; it is an unfolding of the immanent potentialities of the system' (Timasheff, 1965, p. 283). Timasheff goes on, in the same page to explain how it operates:

> When cultural development approaches its theoretical limit, the trend is reversed (although cultural stagnation is a possibility). However, culture as such never dies; some parts may be rejected, but others are absorbed into different cultures and survive. Hence Sorokin shows himself much more optimistic than Spengler or Toynbee.

Sorokin's theory of change appears to be rather like a sine wave, or even the swing of the pendulum: from one cultural mentality to another, allowing for a mid-way position. And so as we approach the end of the Sensate Age – what comes next?

Bernice Martin (1981), writing about the cultural change in precisely this period, was influenced by two leading anthropologists – Mary Douglas (1966, 1970) and Victor Turner (1969) – and she suggests that there was not a swing of the pendulum in the way that Sorokin claimed but that there was a profound change in the 1960s because the structures of society were weakened – counterculture became a reality as changes occurred – both at a national and at a global level – which Mary Douglas saw as grid and group. The 1960s were an expressive period and the end of the period was when the social structures at the national level were re-established in slightly different places than before. For Martin, the 1960s was a period of liminality which could not last for long because when the structures of society were lowered many forms of social and cultural experimentation occurred – many of which were religious or spiritual in nature and in this sense we might begin to see it as a movement towards the ideational – but these social experiments led to some social unease and much of what Sorokin condemned remained unchanged. But there was another process of lowering of structures at global level and a new form of globalisation began to emerge with the implementation of the logic of industrialism and the growth of the information society which were in turn to lead to a period of neo-liberalism.

Kerr *et al.* (1960, 1973) argued for a logic of industrialism and, significantly, the topic of ethics does not occur in the index and is not discussed in the book – although there is a brief reference on pages 108f and recognised elsewhere is passing: Kerr and his colleagues (1973, p. 56) summarise the thesis thus:

- Work-force: increased skills, more mobile, more highly educated and structured.
- Scale of society: urban with a larger role for government.
- Social consensus: increasing ideological consensus in a pluralistic society.
- World-wide industrialisation: spreading from centres of advanced technology.

Of course they were to prove to be wrong in some of their predictions, especially in the role of government and ideological consensus, but they were right when it came to a world-wide industrialisation and a more highly educated work-force.

Globalisation and the emergence of the neo-liberal economic society

The swing of the pendulum did not occur in the 1960s and as the expressive period was soon replaced, but the lowering of structures at a global level were soon to lead to major social changes at both international and national levels that were going to affect the life styles of many people around the world and exacerbate the social conditions that Sorokin condemned. The speed of change increased dramatically and with it new priorities and life styles emerged and ushered in the period of late or post-modernity. There were a number of contributory factors at this time which speeded up this process, such as:

- the nature of capitalism itself and the need to make an increased profit on commodities produced and sold in an enlarged market;
- the technological innovations of post-Fordism that enabled commodity production to be faster and cheaper in the 1970s. Castells (1996, p. 52) makes the point that 'to some extent, the availability of new technologies constituted as a system in the 1970s was a fundamental basis for the process of socio-economic restructuring in the 1980s';
- the development of sophisticated information technology through the star wars programme, through which the information technology revolution took off, with one development leading to another, as Castells (1996, p. 51f.) demonstrates;
- the demise of the Bretton Woods Agreement, that eventually led to the GATT Agreement, enabling both free trade and the flow of financial capital to spread throughout the world;
- the oil crisis in the 1970s and the economic competition from Japan, both of which dented the confidence of and challenged Western domination, which led to corporations merging and the creation of multi-national and then transnational organisations;

- the prevalence of the idea of the minimal state and of neo-liberal economics allowed for power to pass from the State to the capitalist institution;
- the fall of the Berlin Wall – the 'democratisation' of the Eastern Bloc – for, from the time it occurred, there has literally been 'no alternative' (Bauman, 1992) to global capitalism or comparable political opposition to the USA.

I do not want to spend time here expounding each of these because that would detract us from the primary purpose of this paper. However, we can see that during the immediate decades after the Second World War, especially after the demise of the Bretton Woods Agreement, corporations began to relocate manufacturing and to transfer capital around the world, seeking the cheapest places and the most efficient means to manufacture, and the best markets in which to sell their products. They were being forced to do this because of the loss of Western confidence, when the oil crisis demonstrated that the West was vulnerable to those who controlled oil production and because, as the Japanese economy took off, the West realised that it would be forced to compete with another very efficient economic enterprise. This process was exacerbated in the Thatcher-Reagan era by the belief in a minimal state (Nozick, 1974) and through the process of privatisation not only of companies but of public assets, such as water. It was perhaps not recognised by many who supported this process that it was not just a transfer of economic processes 'for the sake of efficiency' but it was also providing a power base for those corporations who were given ownership of public assets. Corporations were able to use the functions that the State had specified to build up their own power-base and as they have expanded so they have become the transnational corporations that form the sub-structure of the global world. With the fall of the Berlin Wall, the United States of America remained the only superpower and as its government has been inextricably intertwined with the large multi-national corporations, it has lent it political and military might that support the capitalist system, which in turned furthered its own imperialist aspirations.

And so the limit that Sorokin suggested that would start the pendulum to swing in the other direction did not occur in the 1960s and 1970s – despite the emergence briefly of a counter-culture – and there was no swing backwards at all. Global capitalism endeavoured to conquer the world without the restrictions of state or government and the direction of change was the same. Indeed, Habermas (2006) made the point that the politicians were left behind powerless and they could either seek to catch up or endeavour to protect their people from the ravages of global capitalism – at that time neither appeared possible although the strong welfare states did play a stronger role during the period of neo-liberal economics. We have seen how global bankers and many other global corporations have pursued vast wealth, profits for their corporations: viewed from one perspective 'profit' is seen as good to those who benefit from it, but viewed from another perspective, 'profit' is the exploitation of the masses: in both cases it is the excess of income over expenditure but we do not use this more factual statement because it is cumbersome. The corporations and the bankers have pursued this end, as Weber suggested, whatever the cost and the cost has been great – as Sorokin argued. Indeed, profit, not people, has become the end of the process and the means to achieve that end have often been very dubious – often immoral, as Sorokin claimed. This is an expression of instrumental rationality.

What we have been doing to achieve these ends claimed Sorokin, we have done 'in the name of God, progress, civilisation, communism, democracy, freedom, capitalism and the dignity of man'. The paradox that he notes is that these are the very phenomena that contain the values of the better world that we seek and so in order to attain these conditions we murder millions and human-kind and the planet are put at risk. The paradox is that we destroy these values that we seek in the process – but we do so by employing other valued aspects of modern thought for at the heart of modernity lies an instrumental rationality that is a form of a rule-bound teleological approach to thought that imprisons people within its rationale: we seek to act in a rational fashion to achieve our desired ends irrespective of the cost of the process. And one of the fundamental weakness of nearly all teleological arguments is that it is the ends that count and not the means. Bauman (1993, p. 69) summarises this position thus:

> Desubstantiation of the moral agent in favour of proceduralism does a lot for the subordination of the moral agent to the external legislating agency, yet little or nothing at all for the increase of the sum total of good; in the final count it disarms the forces of moral resistance to immoral commands – very nearly the only protection the moral self might have against being a part of inhumanity.

The pursuit of profit has been taken for granted – it has been part of the cultural mentality of this period. It seems rational and common sense that this is what we do – and it is a form of rationality that has itself grown up with the money economy and science. Simmel ([1903] 1971, p. 85) recognised this problem many years ago when he wrote of modern urban society: 'Modern mind has become more and more calculating. The calculative exactness of practical life which the money economy has brought about corresponds to the idea of natural science . . .': urban society and money economy generate a greater degree of instrumental rationality which is associated with natural science and people act with their heads and not their hearts. Empiricism, science and rationality have been joined together and are seen as being the most logical and efficient way of producing goods and of apparently making the world a better place. Almost all politicians have talked of development and growth and relied on the global capitalism to realise it. Science has become a symbol of instrumental rationalism and then, by default, everything else is less than rational. But the rationality that has developed from the Enlightenment is a less than a complete understanding of rationality *per se* and it is this incomplete picture that has been linked to pragmatism (instrumentality) and science, so that it now seems almost common sense that we should have aims and endeavour to achieve these ends. But instru-mental rationality is not the only form of rational thought: indeed, morality is not irrational for as Max Weber reminded us that there is more than one form of rationality: he distinguished between at least two forms: *zweckrational* action and *vertrational* action: the former is purposive or instrumental action and the latter is evaluatively rational action (Wilson, 1970, p. xiv) but he recognised in *The Protestant Ethic and the Spirit of Capitalism* that the former was driving out the latter. This has led us to further mistakes in our use of the term rational – it has been linked to pragmatic practical, measurable, outcomes (or in Lyotard's [1984] understanding of post-modernity all legitimate knowledge has to be performative) and this is also associated with science and technology. Herein lies another of the irrationalities of this age – we know that there is no conceptual relationship between a fact and a value but scientific facts are frequently treated as if they are intrinsically good and will naturally lead to progress, which is a way in which the hegemony of the system functions.

But before we conclude this second part of the paper we need to ask further questions about this instrumental (teleological) view of rationality: we need to question the ends of the process – wealth/profit – and ask at least three questions all of which have moral overtones: has the end been pursued in a moral manner?; is it a legitimate end?; and if so, is the profit fairly distributed? The first of these questions, Sorokin clearly answers when he writes about murdering millions and putting the future of the planet at risk – and it would be easy to adduce many more examples of this that have occurred since he wrote. The second reflects, I think, another of the values of modernity – society, apart from those who control the system, has been depersonalised and we now have the celebrity culture who make their wealth out of exposing themselves as persons, which deflects us from recognising the depersonalisation of the whole society and now people are servants of the system: this, in its turn, demonstrates something more of the inconsistency of modern thought since it was Kant, the great thinker of the Enlightenment, who insisted that people should always be ends and never means. Finally, has the profit been fairly distributed? People are underpaid, exploited and their resources stolen for the sake of profit: the system is managed by those who have power and it is they – in their banks and boardrooms – who have displayed this ruthless quest for acquisition and a great number of us in the West who have benefited have been happy to concur – we are the silent majority. What we are seeing is a process that is defined as progress by those who define social reality and this is one way in which the hegemony of the powerful is retained. The difference between the financial returns of the most wealthy and their employees has become greater in recent years and the vast remuneration for the few has been justified by the rational argument that they receive the market rate for their work and no other evidence is produced about the extent to which the market is making a just return for the work rendered in relation to all the other working people who receive many times less returns. In a televised broadcast of one of the Hearings by a Parliamentary Select Committee in February 2009 following the credit crash it was pointed out to one of the bankers giving evidence that his monthly salary could have paid the wages of 36 members of his staff – and that was without the bonuses and other perks that he had received, and we know of far more excessive salaries than this so that it would be easy to go into all the facts and figures to demonstrate that this is no isolated case – but that is not my purpose in this presentation; the purpose is merely to show that Sorokin's condemnation of the Sensate Age is not without foundation. Indeed, we can see that this Enlightenment view of rationality is itself flawed by its very incompleteness and immorality.

We could look at other aspects of the Enlightenment and treat them in a similar critical manner but that would needlessly prolong this argument (see, however, Bauman, 1993; Gray, 1995; Jarvis, 2008, *inter alia*). But this instrumentalism has now been built into our culture and our way of thinking despite the fact that we know that teleological arguments are flawed because they rarely consider the means to the end. It is the means that Sorokin was concerned about – murdering millions, putting humankind and the planet to risk and we have sought to justify by the type of rational argument to which he refers but it is here that we need to introduce a concept that is rarely mentioned in the terms of neo-liberal economics – power – the power to do these things operates because we have accepted the instrumental rationality that puts profit first but slowly we are beginning to recognise that this appeal to the market is flawed and that it is being very costly. Indeed, the present economic crisis is demonstrating that the means are wrong and failing and that the ends achieved are less than good – it is but another nail in the coffin of the Sensate Age of modernity. But what comes next? Will the pendulum now begin to move backwards?

What next?

Presenting this paper at a time of global economic crisis brings to the fore Sorokin's concerns yet again – have we reached the end of the Sensate Age? If so, what next? Can we now consider Sorokin's ideas of change? Coser suggests, in Sorokin's thinking, rather like the Hegelian dialectic, we see a new form of cultural mentality arising from the excesses and natural decline of the past age and now we might be moving towards the ideational. But the major problem here lies in the fact that cyclic theories of change are no longer accepted and most social theorists no longer accept Sorokin's historical research for a number of reasons, including the point that he over-simplifies the facts of history (Timashaff, 1965, p. 283). And so, is he a utopian thinker? Significantly Kumar (1978, p. 178) views him as a philosopher of history rather than a utopian thinker – probably because he did not see the ideational period as the end of time but as a phase in the development of history; none of the utopian writers that I can find mention his work although the idea of the ideational certainly points in the utopian direction without being utopian since it recognises that even if it is obtainable the ideational state is not the end of the age. But he was certainly a critic of the age: Coser claims that he was a social prophet and he (1977, p. 477) suggests that

> Sorokin saw himself as another Moses who, even though he could not enter the promised land, was still able, owing to his cultural estrangement, to forecast its main features in his Integralist philosophy. Let him who has never dreamt of a redemptive Utopia of the future cast the first stone.

Throughout this paper I have argued that Sorokin's critique of the Age is an early critique of modernity, one which reflects his own background and struggles and so it is hardly surprising that it was not viewed very kindly at the time when he was writing by those in the USA who were enjoying the fruits of the age. At the heart of his work he condemns the means-ends ethical philosophy of the Age because it downplays the means and foregrounds the ends: it is instrumental. It is the classical teleological ethical position with all its well-known weaknesses – four fundamental ones being: What are the means? When does the end of an act occur since time does not stand still? What were the intentions of the act? Can we assess the morality of an act by its unspecified and unknown consequences? It is, for instance, hard to determine what the ends of any action are because what happens one day may be reversed the next and, secondly, can the means to those amorphous ends be justified morally? Let me illustrate how these criticisms work in practice – in two very simple examples. Firstly, if the better life is the good – the end-product of an action or policy – then the global capitalist neo-liberal economics structural adjustment policies espoused by the World Bank should result in the greater good for the people. But the means to implement these policies required governments to cut back on their spending on education and welfare and Torres and Puiggros (2009, p. 67) make the point that the implementation of these policies – forced upon national governments by the World Bank – has resulted in a tremendous step backward in the standard of living of the people of Latin America. A second example that occurred in UK as I was writing this paper: government targets – in order to meet government targets on cost and waiting list times for hospitals, hospitals actually cut the number of staff, left patients in terrible conditions which probably resulted in some deaths and considerable excessive hardship. The target is the end and the means to the end are very subsidiary. These are examples, and many others could be found, but in neither instance do the means justify the ends? But what about the ends themselves? In the first instance, we might never know if these policies would have achieved a better standard of living in the longer term since the present economic crisis has just added to the woes of the people who have already suffered as a result of the means to achieve the World Bank's ends. In the second, fewer people would have suffered had the patients been put before the targets. I think that we can say that the neo-liberal economic policies have not worked because ends have been put before people – neo-liberalism has a limited perspective on rationality and no strong ethic – amongst other reasons. Instrumental rationality itself is a flawed concept, as Sorokin recognised. But, those in power have pursued, and still pursue, ends – their own or those set by governments – at the expense of others but does this crisis mean that we will detect that movement towards the ideational for which Sorokin hoped? I am not sure since the financial markets have turned to the politicians for help – as Habermas (2006) observed, some of the politicians who were running to catch up with the global market are now – at the end of March and the beginning of April – seeking to create a global political platform which will allow them to regulate the market. But, they are also trying to patch-up the failing system with the values of the modern age – values that have already failed! Only one politician, just a few days before the G20 Conference, called for a new form of capitalism with ethics.

Amongst academic debate about the Enlightenment, MacIntyre (1981, p. 52) argues that the project had to fail because ethics was not a major factor in the project:

> Within that teleological scheme there is a fundamental contrast between man-as-he-happens-to-be and man-as-he-could-be-if-he–realized-his-essential-nature. Ethics is the science which is to enable men to understand how they make the transition from the former state to the latter. Ethics in this view therefore presupposes some account of potentiality and act, some account of the essence of man as a rational animal and above all some account of the human *telos*.
>
> (italics in original)

While I am not happy with his solution of virtue since he seems to be trying to resurrect the past, we can see that his criticism lies at the heart of this argument that teleological arguments omit the ethics of the means to the end. More recently, Gray (1995) also postulated that modernity is dead, and he takes his argument much further than MacIntyre (and he also argues against Rorty whom he sees as a modernist) since he (1995, p. 259) argues that Western rationality and religion has resulted in our present Western cultures being a 'nihilist expression of the will to power'. He (1995, p. 267) goes on to suggest that 'the Westernizing project of Enlightenment humanism has desolated cultures in every part of the globe and visited devastation upon their natural environments'. Such a comment comes close to the sentiments that Sorokin expressed a genera- tion earlier. Clearly the sensate society still exists but now the weaknesses of the Enlightenment are more clearly exposed and more generally accepted. With the current economic crisis and with global warming we see that Sorokin's criti- cisms were not without foundation but they were ahead of his time and that they were made at a time when change was occurring but before Sorokin's limit had actually been reached. However they were also made with the voice of an ideologue – not with the dispassion of a social scientist.

Conclusion

We have argued here that the rationality of the Enlightenment is impoverished because it is incomplete: we do need instrumental action – but we also need the rationality of ethical action: this latter has been forgotten in the relentless search for profit and in the process we have done precisely what Sorokin said we were doing – we have uprooted the values of humanity, we have murdered millions, we had made whole peoples and nations redundant and we have put the planet at risk. This process has been exacerbated by the forces of globalisation – which removed the boundaries between societies and created a global core of finance and information technology – and thus, we are seeing collapse around us at the present time and the politicians are trying desperately to patch up the system with the very values that has caused it. But in the process, we have also seen a brief experiment in social living when the social structures were lowered at national level – the 1960s. It was at this time that personal relationships, peace, flower-power, and so on came to the fore – but the promised land was a mirage that soon disappeared and yet I think that in that mirage we can see the under- lying values about which Sorokin was concerned and these are something that we have probably all experienced many times and which we actually experience for even shorter periods – like the period of a festival, or a party or even just a few magic moments with friends – it is what Turner called *communitas* – when the structures are lowered and we experience people, as people, and the prevailing ethical value is concern for the other, *agape*. Christ actually taught that the Kingdom of God is in the midst of you – perhaps Sorokin was looking in the wrong place for the Kingdom of God, for the ideational! Businesses see these times as times of team-building, and so they make them possible with 'away-days' and other forms of activity but they are artificial compared to the reality of the *communitas* that emerges naturally in the process of daily living (I have discussed this further in Jarvis, 2008).

But society needs structures to function and so in everyday life they are soon re-erected and the structured society re-appears with perhaps a few slightly different features. The same process occurred at the end of the 1960s: the new global structures were being put in place and global capitalism emerged and many of us in the West enjoyed unprecedented wealth and luxury while others were to live in dire poverty and many die of malnutrition and illness at a very young age. But we might well ask now – with the near collapse of the global system of capitalism – have we yet reached the end of the Sensate Age – or will we ever reach it? What does lie beyond it? Will we discover that ideational society that Sorokin believed underlies the sensate? Or was Max Weber correct when he said people will always endeavour to acquire and were the elite theories right when they claimed that there is an iron law of oligarchy? Is the classless society – is the new Jerusalem or the City of Man even a remote possibility? Perhaps, as Gray suggests, we need an even bigger catastrophe to change our values – perhaps we do need an apocalypse (Bull, 1995) of global warming to force us to move from this Sensate Age – because of the prevalence of this debate currently, it is almost as if we are waiting for the end and yet not believing that it can or will really happen. But even if it does, we might still well ask 'What next?' since it will not be the end of time nor the end of the human project – and humankind will still look forward towards a world in which we would like to live as we continue to strive to acquire – herein lies the paradox of human hope and existence that is captured by Sorokin's unrealistic cyclical theory of social change.

References

Bauman Z (1993) *Postmodern Ethics* Cambridge: Polity Press
Bull M (ed) (1995) *Apocalypse Theory and the Ends of the World* Oxford: Blackwell
Castells M (1996) *The Rise of the Network Society* Oxford: Blackwell (Vol. 1 of *The Information Age: Economy, Society and Culture*)
Coser L (1977) *The Masters of Sociological Thought* New York: Harcourt Brace Jovanovich (2nd edition) (downloaded from www.bolender.com 1/12/08)
Douglas M (1966) *Purity and Danger* London: Routledge & Kegan Paul
Douglas M (1970) *Natural Symbols* London: Barrie & Rockliffe
Gray J (1995) *Enlightenment's Wake* London: Routledge
Habermas J (2006) *Time of Transitions* Cambridge: Polity Press (edited translated by C Cronin and M Pensky)
Holy Bible
Jarvis P (2008) *Democracy, Lifelong Learning and the Learning Society: Active Citizenship in a Late Modern Age* London: Routledge
Kerr C, Dunlop J, Harbison F and Myers C (1960 [1973]) *Industrial and Man* Harmondsworth: Penguin
Kumar K (1978) *Prophecy and Progress* Harmondsworth: Penguin
Lyotard F-F (1984) *The Postmodern Condition: A Report on Knowledge* Manchester: Manchester University Press
MacIntyre A (1981) *After Virtue* London: Duckworth
Mannheim K (1936) *Ideology and Utopia* London: Routledge & Kegan Paul
Martin B (1981) *A Sociology of Contemporary Cultural Change* Oxford: Blackwell
Simmel G ([1903] 1971) The Metropolis and Mental Life reprinted in Thompson K and Tunstall J (eds) *Sociological Perspectives* Harmondsworth: Penguin
Sorokin P (1958) *Fads and Foibles in Modern Sociology and Related Sciences* London: Mayflower Publishing Co and Vision Press Ltd
Sorokin P (1962) *Social and Cultural Dynamics* New York: Bedminster Press (4 vols)
Sorokin P (1966) *Sociological Theories of Today* New York: Harper & Row
Timasheff N (1965) *Sociological Theory: Its Nature and Growth* New York: Random House (Revised edition)
Torres C (2009) *Globalizations and Education* New York: Teachers College, Columbia University
Torres C and Puiggros A (2009) The State and Public Education in Latin America in Torres C *op cit.*
Turner V (1969) *The Ritual Process* Harmondsworth: Penguin
Weber M (1930) *The Protestant Ethic and the Spirit of Capitalism* London: George Unwin Translated by Talcott Parsons
Wilson B (ed) (1970) *Rationality* Oxford: Basil Blackwell

CHAPTER 17

GLOBALISATION, KNOWLEDGE AND THE NEED FOR A REVOLUTION IN LEARNING

Can we really build a City of Man?

Originally presented as 'Globalisation, Knowledge and the Need for a Revolution in Learning' (2007), unpublished paper revised from *Democracy, Lifelong Learning and the Learning Society: Active Citizenship in a Late Modern Age* (2008), London: Routledge, and delivered at the Danish Pedagogical University.

The world has reached a crucial stage in its development and there are many reasons why it is time for us as educators to stop and take stock of precisely what place we are playing in it. I think that the credit crunch has made us all aware of this for we have seen something of the weakness of the capitalist system – but I think that the credit crunch is itself a symbol of something far deeper and more problematic. As a result of the European Enlightenment we have viewed things far too simply and from a skewed position and I want to suggest that we can see it in many areas of our work as well. But the world has also become a complex place and even simple things no longer appear simple. I want to illustrate this from my own definition of learning which is much more complex than many that we see in other text-books because it tries to take the whole person into consideration – our conceptualisation is itself far too narrow. Elsewhere I (Jarvis, 2009) have defined it as

> the combination of processes throughout a lifetime whereby the whole person – body (genetic, physical and biological) and mind (knowledge, skills, attitudes, values, emotions, beliefs, meaning and senses) – experiences social situations, the content of which is then transformed cognitively, emotively or practically (or through any combination) and integrated into the individual person's biography resulting in a continually changing (or more experienced) person.

This definition is existential rather than being merely behaviouristic or about information processed – both theories being extremely weak philosophically – as we learn in every situation and so learning must also be defined experientially. However, the narrowness of these two other approaches reflects in part our need for a revolution in learning but the argument is even more profound than this and I want to demonstrate this sociologically as well as educationally.

The complexity of our world has been created by many factors although for heuristic purposes I want to outline two here – modernity and global capitalism

– the latter being an outcome of the former. The presentation itself falls into four parts and has a brief concluding discussion: modernity and the City of Man; globalisation; the knowledge economy and the realisation that utopia must be deferred indefinitely; restricted learning and the need for a revolution in learning. Finally, we look for a way forward in trying to create that better world, or as many thinkers considered it – an alternative ethical society, whether it should be religious or political and, at this point, I see little difference between the New Jerusalem and the classless society. Fundamentally, my thesis falls into four parts:

- Global capitalism is a major player in creating a world which is: first segregated into the rich and the poor, the powerful and the powerless – although I would not say that had it not existed there would not have been this division; secondly, stretched of its resources through consumerism so that its future is threatened.
- Global capitalism has produced a world whose emphases are on a very restricted understanding of knowledge and, therefore, of learning which also restricts the growth and development of individuals.
- The need for a revolution in our understanding of learning and the learning society.
- Finally, I want to suggest that vision is kept alive by certain of our daily experiences of what a better world could be like – in Victor Turner's (1969) terms – *communitas*.

The thesis is unashamedly utopian and reflects my own recent book (Jarvis, 2008) which deals with these topics in much more detail.

Modernity and the City of Man

Just over two hundred years ago the Enlightenment ushered in this modern world and through the process of historical change a new world was born. Hamilton (1992, pp. 21–2) tried to capture these differences when he suggested that modernity has ten features: reason; empiricism, science, universalism, progress, individualism, toleration, freedom, uniformity of human nature and secularism. Such a classification is difficult because many of the categories overlap. Other scholars have made similar classifications. Nevertheless, the division between the pre-modern and the modern is not as clear cut as some commentators might have us believe and we will show in this chapter how the problems of pre-modern society prevail even today. But since we now talk of late modern, or post-modern, we can begin to see that the process is not only on-going but still undergoing considerable change.

It was with the hopes and aspirations of the birth of modernity and upon these values that the idea that we could build the perfect society – utopia or the City of Man. It was no accident of history that More's (1516) *Utopia* appeared when it did, seeking that perfect world and re-echoing Plato's *Republic* (see Cornford, 1941). In a sense it was pointing to what was to come and there have been many studies of utopia since but they are beyond the scope of this paper (see Mannheim (1936); Levitas (1990); Kumar (1978, 1987; Gorz (1985); Marin (1984): Baudrillard, 2006, *inter alia*). In many ways Kant's ethical thinking was based upon the fact that now the religious justification had been demolished we could build pour own kingdom of man and more recently,

Manent (1998) has traced how the ideas of the City of Man evolved through the great thinkers of the period.

And so it was that over the years economic growth and wealth have grown together as the heart of a rational, scientific world – based upon work and technology. But given the almost five hundred years since More's utopia was written, it might have been expected that we have got a lot closer to achieving the state that he envisaged had the Enlightenment been successful. Living in the West with our high materialistic standard we might claim to be on the 'path to paradise' (Gorz, 1985) but then we look at the poor and homeless in our own countries and we do not need the statistics to show how the gap between the rich and the poor have grown when we hear of the million pounds a year bonuses of bankers and footballers being paid £4–5million per annum and we hear of the many who live below the poverty line. But then we might also ask if we (the wealthy) are any happier – perhaps the answer is in the negative – and this is something I have heard time and again when I have been travelling throughout the world. We can consume until our bodies and minds are satiated and yet we are still unsatisfied – we still desire more. And as we look beyond the West, we find a billion people living on less than one Euro a day. Poverty in the third world! Poverty in the first – material and psychological! It is no wonder that Baudrillard (2006) can write a book *Utopia Deferred*, and as I put in my new book *deferred indefinitely*. But if those values were right about modernity why should the City of Man still remain a dream? But perhaps all those values were not right and we have been trying to build the city on very shaky foundations. And so to those ten values: reason, empiricism, science, universalism, progress, individualism, toleration, freedom, uniformity of human nature and secularism. Of course, they are not all right – and certainly not all right all the time, and I do not have time here to do more than offer pointers while I also accept many of the positive aspects of these values I want to illustrate some weaknesses:

- Reason – my own research (Jarvis, 1980) into superstition found that everybody we interviewed had superstitions – we are not always reasonable and neither should we be.
- Empiricism – we know so many scientific facts that are not empirical and so what about values and meaning? The whole of culture and cultural appreciation defines so much of empirical measurement.
- Progress – to what and where? We have a process through time but nothing we can measure as universal progress, although in health care etc. for the wealthy it might be claimed to exist.
- Individualism – I was not born an individual but at the end of a cord in a loving relationship – ethical values must be based upon relationship and not on individualism. I have to learn as I grow. Many anthropologists call this into question.
- Universalism of human nature – there may well be a common humanity – genetically over 99% – but what of the different cultural values?

We could write books about this – some have (see Gray, 1995, 2007 *inter alia*).

We have been trying to build the City of Man of very shaky foundations and so what are these foundations?

Globalisation

Globalisation is a much used word with a variety of meanings but which I want to use here in a specific socio-economic manner. It is inappropriate to explore the various theories of globalisation in any depth here, but Weede (1990) has isolated three other approaches: Galtung's (1971) 'structural theory of imperialism; Wallenstein's (1974) 'world system approach' and Bornschier's (1980) idea of 'investment dependence'. In a way all of these relate to the power of those who control the sub-structure of society – both the financial and intellectual capital and who employ technology, especially information technology, to produce desired outcomes. I want to introduce you to my own understanding of globalisation (Jarvis, 2007) which, to some extent, incorporates each of the above ones. It is neo-Marxian in some ways, although it is also in line with other forms of critical theory.

The significance of this model is that there is a global sub-structure represented here by the core running through all the different countries – it exercises a centralised power over each of the countries and, in this sense, it is force for convergence between the different countries of the world. It consists, first, of the economic system but also of the technological one, especially information technology. Those who control it exercise global power and that control rests with large transnational corporations whose directors are un-elected and very powerful throughout the world through the power they exercise in controlling their countries. But these forces are supported by the one super-power, the USA, and so it would be possible to place the USA at the top of the hierarchy of countries, represented by the hierarchical discs or as part of the sub-structure. I

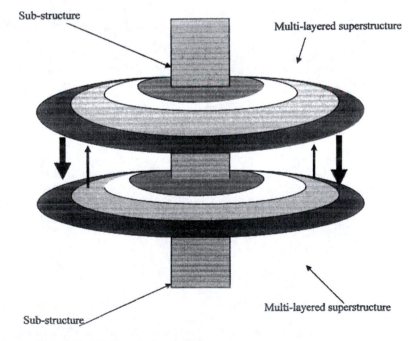

Figure 17.1 A global model of societies.

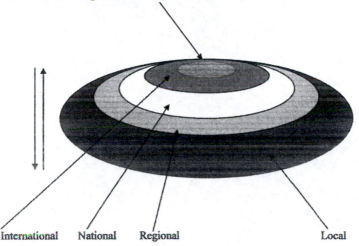

Economic/technological/American political sub-structure

International   National   Regional   Local

Figure 17.2 Multi-layered model of society.

personally regard the USA as part of the global sub-structure, at this moment in history, although its position could change. A great deal of power resides in the global sub-structure but it can also be exercised between countries through political, trade, aid and other inter-national mechanisms and within the political process of each country.

The large downward-pointing arrows illustrate that there is a relationship of power between the 203 countries of the world (this is the number recorded by UNESCO 2006), while the two small black upward-pointing arrows depict the resistance to the forces of globalisation. However, it would be true to say that there are probably blocks of countries at different levels of the global power structure, with the G8 countries (except the USA which is so powerful that I see it as part of the sub-structure) being the most powerful stratum. However, the global meeting point for these economic and technological forces is 'The World Economic Forum' held in Davos, in Switzerland, in the winter (ski season!) each year. In the above diagram each layer represents a country which is penetrated through the centre by the sub-structure, and each country can now be repre-sented in the following manner.

We have depicted the layers hierarchically in order to illustrate that it is not merely a geographical matter but that there is also a hierarchy of power stem-ming from the core to the periphery, although it has to be recognised that power is not a one-way process since, by the nature of democracy, the 'lower orders' can and should be proactive as well, but we are also aware of passive resistance amongst individuals to the pressures coming from the hierarchy. Hence we have illustrated this democratic process by the two vertical arrows pointing in oppo-site directions. Naturally, individuals can exercise more power but only within an organisational context in one of the other layers of society so that individuals and organisations are not located in any hierarchical layer in this diagram.

There are a number of points that we want to highlight from these two diagrams:

- The sub-structure is united and runs through all the different countries, and we must recognise that there are over two hundred countries, and so the two layers here depict only a few of the many, that have to negotiate between themselves in order to cooperate. Now this core is united in a manner that the individual countries are not – it runs through each making similar demands on each – as Beck (2000) puts it, it criss-crosses national boundaries. While there is an apparent unity of the core, there is also internal competition since each transnational company that makes up the core is competing with every other one in order to produce products that can be marketed in nearly all the countries of the world. The fact that there is internal competition means that the speed of change within the core is fast, driven by the demands of the market which it is both creating and to which it is seeking to respond. It is, therefore, changing faster than those aspects of the global system that are not so market-driven. Additionally, it is necessary to recognise that change is neither gradual nor even, since new discoveries tend to generate change in fits and starts. At the same time, change itself has profound effects on lifelong learning, as we shall see below.
- These companies, and the technological-economic core, are protected by the political and military might of America and the institutions over which it exercises hegemonic control – such as the World Bank and the International Monetary Fund. There is considerable confusion within America itself between the core and the political – this confusion has been exacerbated during the presidency of George W. Bush whose government does not always seem entirely divorced from the corporate sector and which seems always to act in favour of the economic system of the core.
- Since the core controls information technology, as well as technology for production, and so on, it has the power to advertise its products globally and generate both a huge market for its products but also to produce a considerable degree of standardisation across the globe.
- Each society is a separate entity and, consequently, co-operation between countries/states is a matter of political negotiation and agreement, something that takes time – as the working of the United Nations and the European Union show. However, I have shown a separate international layer since it is not only governments which act internationally but also non-governmental organisations. Nevertheless, it is clear that countries are less able to change as rapidly as the global core and so there is almost an international global situation of 'divide and rule', with the global core exercising a degree of dominance. This means that law, democracy and civil society are all exposed to another source of power, other than the State – that of the global market; a transnational civil society is still a long way from a reality, even though we live in a world society (Beck, 2000). Habermas (2001, p. 61) suggests that:

  > There is a crippling sense that national politics have dwindled to more or less intelligent management of a process of forced adaptation to the pressure to shore up purely local positional advantages.

- Some societies are more accessible to this process than others, so that social change does not spread completely evenly across the globe, with countries like those of sub-Saharan Africa and Nepal not able to respond to the changes at the same speed as does the United Kingdom, and so on. These poorer countries get poorer whilst the richer ones prosper – indeed, enticing them with international trade agreements may not be altogether beneficial to them in the long run since they lose their own protection against the might of the global powers. However, it should also be noted that even in the first world, the poor continue to be excluded and get poorer. In the USA, for instance, 16.5% live in poverty, 20% of the adult population are illiterate and 13% have a life expectancy of shorter than 60 years, according to Bauman (1999) citing a United Nations development report.

In a sense, then, we can see that the capitalist core is the driving force of each society – to some degree or other, but we have to recognise that within the national and local cultures there are both wider interests and concerns than those to be found in the core and also some instances a degree of resistance to the changes that are occurring and these are to be found at every level, including the international. But what is clear is that not only has this approach to society not eradicated poverty in the West – it has certainly done little to eradicate it in the remainder of the world – and so the City of Man is not being built very successfully.

The knowledge economy and the end of the modernist dream

If we look back at those ten features of modernity, we find not only are they flawed – as we have already showed, there are major aspects of our humanity completely missing from them. Let me illustrate from knowledge itself. The problem of what precisely is knowledge is an issue that is reflected in our definition of learning where we refer to attitudes, beliefs and values – all of which may be regarded as cognitive, but for the purposes of this part of the discussion I want to focus on knowledge from a slightly tangential position and we can locate that within the idea of the knowledge economy: it is those societies that are at the centre of economic globalisation that Daniel Bell (1973) first called the post-industrial societies. For him, knowledge was the fundamental resource for such societies, especially theoretical knowledge (Bell, 1973, p. 14) and, as Stehr (1994, p. 10) later pointed, out when these societies emerge they signal a fundamental shift in the structure of the economy, since the primacy of manufacturing is replaced by knowledge. It is not knowledge *per se*, however, that is significant to the knowledge society but scientific – including social scientific – and technological knowledge (Stehr, 1994, pp. 99–103) since this underlies the production of new commodities and services and, consequently, has economic value. Knowledge, as such, has no intrinsic value which is part of the problem in a globally capitalist world; it is only its use-value as a scarce resource which is significant, or as Lyotard (1984) called performative knowledge. Indeed, new knowledge is a scarce resource valuable for what might be produced through using it. Hence, research and development are at the heart of the productive processes. Every marginal addition to the body of scientific knowledge is potentially valuable in the knowledge economy. Not all societies, however, are knowledge societies; some are agricultural and others manufacturing, which has produced an international division of labour, whilst others – such as sub-Saharan Africa – are to be located in the realms of social exclusion. But the fact that the knowledge economy only uses restricted forms of knowledge is significant for legitimated knowledge is rational, empirical or pragmatic. Basically, this reflects the values of modernity but not all knowledge can be verified by these approaches nor is all knowledge immediately and verifiably useful, a point that Scheler (1980[1960], p. 76) raised as early as the mid-1920s when he tried to classify knowledge into seven types:

- myth and legend;
- everyday knowledge, implicit in everyday language;
- religious knowledge;
- mystical knowledge;
- philosophical, metaphysical knowledge;
- positive knowledge of mathematics and the sciences;
- technological knowledge.

Scheler was also concerned to demonstrate that each of these types of knowledge changed at different speeds which he suggested constituted different degrees of artificiality – by this, he meant, their speeds of change in relationship to the natural world-views which changes most slowly. Now we can certainly argue with Scheler's classification in many different ways. For instance, the social sciences hardly feature at all in it, but it would be possible to include them within positive knowledge, except that not all social science knowledge is positive! In the same way, we can say that certain empirically based scientific knowledge is far from artificial: for instance, the speed of light does not change but our understanding of the nature of light might. In addition, we could argue that some forms of indige-nous knowledge are pragmatic and do change as the social conditions change. Scheler differentiated between the first five forms of knowledge and the bottom two – which he regarded as the most artificial. He suggested that even in the mid-1920s, as a result of research, and we could also say as a result of the intense competition to produce new useful knowledge to produce consumer goods, posi-tive knowledge changes hour by hour – perhaps we might now say that it changes minute by minute, or even second by second.

Scheler's classification is not correct when we consider our contemporary understanding of knowledge, neither can knowledge be so simply classified, but he does raise a number of significant issues for our discussion of the knowledge society: that there are different forms of knowledge; that not all knowledge changes at the same speed; that certain forms of scientific and technological knowledge change exceedingly rapidly; that knowledge in the arts and human sciences change more slowly; that relativity is much more complex than is usually understood. Indeed, it could well be argued that some values do not change at all over time (Jarvis, 1997). However, the dominant forms of knowl-edge do fall within Sender's later categories and, by and large, are those which are assumed to be knowledge in today's society. It is perhaps significant here to recognise that although power lies at the heart of the global society, the capi-talist market is, to some extent, open for new forms of knowledge. It is not only the large transnational companies that are producing this new knowledge, it many cases it is small and medium sized companies – even university companies – that seek to market their new commodities. Change in knowledge and commodity production does not alter the power structures of society but, in a sense, it actually reinforces them.

Fundamentally, then, we can see that only a small part of the spectrum of knowledge, however we categorise it, underlies the foundations of the knowledge economy. Ethics and morality, democratic processes and community living are all amongst those aspects of knowledge missing from the scene. A great deal of knowledge and practice that underlie social living is omitted and so we are not only building a City of Man on shaky foundations we are building it with an incomplete understanding of what we are building – indeed, because of the prevalence of individualism some of the most profound paradoxes of human living such as the relationship between the individual and the group are not even considered. Not only is utopia deferred – it is deferred indefinitely.

A revolution in learning

But this knowledge economy has forced us to think about lifelong learning – ever since the first European Commission policy document (EC, 1995) we have been confronted with this policy of lifelong learning which has been defined erroneously and rather simplistically (EC, 2001, p. 9) as:

> All learning activity undertaken throughout life, with the aim of improving knowledge, skills, and competences within a personal, civic, social and/or employment-related perspective.

There are many flaws in this definition, such as learning does not have to have 'aims', but comparison with the definition with which this paper opens shows others which I do not need to explore here. A significant feature of this definition is that employment plays such a small part in the definition which it has played such a major role in so many of the policy documents. Indeed, lifelong learning has effectively been work-life learning, which has been as narrow and as restricted as has the use of the full spectrum of knowledge. Education has always been controlled by the needs and the power of the sub-structures of society, or in this case – the globe. Education, in its widest sense, has been seen as a preparation for work rather than a preparation for life and adult education has been reduced to work-life learning – as far as policy and funding have gone.

And so, lifelong learning has become focused on work-life learning – learning to produce, but there is another side to this picture. From our earliest years until our departure from this life, most of us are exposed to the media and its advertising – young children know brand names of many products, even hundreds, and we are all exposed to advertising. I know about the sociological theories of advertising, but they are based upon these weak definitions of learning – we all learn not only to consume but, as children, we learn the desire to consume. This cannot be measured by empirical research but we live in a society as totalitarian as any Eastern Bloc country ever was in as much as we are indoctrinated into consumption. Lifelong learning has also become learning throughout our lives to consume. Here we have the flip side of lifelong learning: *we learn to work to produce the goods that we learn to desire to consume.* The question arises: how can we get off this merry-go-round of learning? We certainly need a revolution in learning. We need to re-discover what learning itself is – as an existential phenomenon it is the driving force for human growth and development, and so we need to redefine the learning society – a society that exists for people and their development.

But as modernity is flawed, we need to re-start the major debates about life itself and what it is all about. These debates are not only philosophical but they are political and it is thinkers like John Rawls (1999) with his understanding of public reason and Jurgen Habermas (1998, 2006) with deliberative politics that point the way. These approaches to political debate are genuine endeavours to discover a political way forward, even though in their different ways they reflect the flawed values of modernity. There is a sense in which democracy is itself a part of the indefinite referral of utopia – you see we have to keep learning, not only for individual human living and development but learning how to live together, as Delors (1996) put it. This requires a new understanding of ethics, which I have called agapistic ethics, in which we seek to realise love in relationship between people rather than power in a way that Levinas (1985, 1991 [1969]) points us. But significantly, we see that we have moved into those realms of knowledge that have been relegated to the periphery in the learning society of the knowledge economy.

And so we do not really know where we are going and so at least three sets of people are needed: first, we need the prophet who, in Freire's (1972) words, both denounces and announces; secondly, we need teachers who will help us achieve a better way of life but not by teaching us an autocratic manner but by facilitating us to pursue those things which interest and concern us rather than our political and economic masters (Daloz, 1986; Palmer, 1998); thirdly, we need the leaders who can be individuals and stand out from the group and who can lead us forward – but the questions remain – to where? and, why? These then are the questions confronting today's learning society.

Conclusion

These are the unanswerable questions that modernity failed to answer but we know that the economic growth promised us by the politicians of every party will not lead to a utopia, only the destruction of our planet. And so if we have no City of Man and if the City of God, as per the New Testament, appears too unrealistic – do we have a picture of what we would really like the world to be like? In a strange way I do not think we have to look too far forward but perhaps look to what we already know and fail to recognise for what it is. It was Turner (1969, p. 127) who pointed me towards it:

> Once more we come back to the necessity of seeing man's social life as process, or rather a multiplicity of processes, in which the character of one type of phase – where communitas is paramount – differs deeply, even abysmally, from that of all others. The great human temptation, found most prominently among utopians, is to resist giving up the good and pleasurable qualities of that one phase to make way for what may be the necessary hardships and dangers of the next. Spontaneous communitas is richly charged with affects, mainly pleasurable ones. Life in 'structure' is filled with objective difficulties: decisions have to be made, inclinations sacrificed to the wishes and needs of the group, and physical and social obstacles overcome at some personal cost. Spontaneous communitas has something 'magical' about it. Subjectively there is in it the feeling of endless power. But this power untransformed cannot readily be applied to the organizational details of social existence. It is no substitute for lucid thought and sustained will. On the other hand, structural action swiftly becomes arid and mechanical if those involved in it are not periodically immersed in the regenerative

abyss of communitas. Wisdom is always to find the appropriate relationship between structure and communitas under the *given* circumstances of time and place . . .

Here then is the learning society – spontaneous communitas is a fleeting moment – a picture of utopia that is with us all the time. A future utopia and a permanent condition is referred indefinitely – but we do have to learn to live together in the present, building a city not built on shaky foundations but on a mirage that continues to appear in the midst of us fleetingly if only we have the wisdom to see it and the understanding to keep learning from it.

References

Baudrillard J (2006) *Utopia Deferred* New York: Semiotext
Bauman Z (1999) *In Search of Politics* Cambridge: Polity Press
Beck U (2000) *What is Globalization?* Cambridge: Polity Press
Bell D (1973) *The Coming of Post-Industrial Society* New York: Basic Books
Bornschier V (1980) Multinational Corporations and Economic Growth *Journal of Development Economics*, Vol.7 pp. 191–210
Cornford F (1941) *The Republic of Plato* Oxford: Clarendon Press
Daloz L (1986) *Effective Teaching and Mentoring* San Francisco: Jossey-Bass
Delors J (Chair) (1996) *Learning: the treasure within* Paris: UNESCO
European Commission (1995) *White Paper on Teaching and Learning: Towards to Learning Society* Brussels: European Commission
European Commission (2001) *Making a European Area of Lifelong Learning a Reality* Brussels: European Commission COM(2001) 678final
Freire P (1972) *Cultural Action for Freedom* Harmondsworth, Penguin
Galtung I (1971) A Structural Theory of Imperialism *Journal of Peace Studies* Vol. 8 pp. 81–117
Gorz A (1985) *Paths to Paradise* London: Pluto Press
Gray J (1995) *Enlightenment's Wake* London: Routledge
Gray J (2007) *Black Mass* London: Allen Lane
Habermas J (1998) *The Inclusion of the Other* Cambridge: Polity Press
Habermas J (2001) *The Postnational Constellation* (trans M Pensky) Cambridge: Polity Press
Habermas J (2006) *Time of Transitions* Cambridge: Polity Press (ed. and trans. C Cronin and M Pensky)
Hamilton P (1992) The Enlightenment and the Birth of Social Science in Hall S and Gieben B (eds) *Formations of Modernity* Cambridge: Polity Press in association with the Open University
Jarvis P (1980) Towards a Sociological Understanding of Superstition *Social Compass* Vol. XXVII pp. 285–295
Jarvis P (1997) *Ethics and the Education of Adults in Late Modern Society* Leicester: NIACE
Jarvis P (2006) *Towards a Comprehensive Theory of Human Learning* London: Routledge
Jarvis P (2007) *Globalisation, Lifelong Learning and the Learning Society: sociological perspectives* London: Routledge
Jarvis P (2008) *Democracy, Lifelong Learning and the Learning Society: active citizenship in a late modern age.* London: Routledge
Jarvis P (2009) *Learning to Be a Person in Society* London: Routledge
Kumar K (1978) *Prophecy and Progress* Harmondsworth: Penguin
Kumar K (1987) *Utopia and Anti-Utopia in Modern Times* Oxford: Blackwell
Levinas E (1985) *Ethics and Infinity* Pittsburg: Duquesne University Press (trans. R Cohen)
Levinas E (1991[1969]) *Totality and Infinity* AH Dordrecht: Kluwer
Levitas R (1990) *The Concept of Utopia* New York: Philip Allan
Lyotard J-F (1984) *The State of Knowledge* Manchester: Manchester University Press

Manent P (1998) *The City of Man* Princeton NJ: Princeton University Press

Mannheim K (1936) *Ideology and Utopia* London: Routledge & Kegan Paul

Marin L (1984) *Utopics: the semiological play of textual spaces* New York: Humanity Books

More T (1516[2003]) *Utopia* Harmondsworth: Penguin

Palmer P (1998) *The Courage to Teach* San Francisco: Jossey-Bass

Rawls J (1999) *The Law of Peoples* Cambridge: Harvard University Press

Scheler M (1980[1926] *Problems of a Sociology of Knowledge* London: Routledge & Kegan Paul

Stehr N (1994) *Knowledge Societies* London: Sage

Turner V (1969) *The Ritual Process* Harmondsworth: Penguin

Wallenstein I (1974) *The Modern World System* New York: Academic Press

Weede E (1990) Rent Seeking or Dependency as Explanations of Why Poor People Stay Poor in Albrow M and King E (eds) *Globalization, Knowledge and Society* London: Sage

PART 6

LEARNING IN LATER LIFE

CHAPTER 18

LEARNING MEANING AND WISDOM

Originally published as 'Learning Meaning and Wisdom' in P. Jarvis (2001), *Learning in Later Life*, London: Kogan Page, pp. 97–110. Cross-references refer to the original publication.

In the next two chapters we are going to deal with three interrelated ideas – meaning, wisdom and spirituality. All three of these terms have religious connotations, as we shall show below, and they clearly overlap with each other so that any division can only be for heuristic purposes. Meaning here refers to answers to ontological questions of the human condition and so it is a metaphysical, philosophical or theological term. Wisdom relates to understanding everyday life, although it is often seen as a religious term, since the concept occurs frequently in the Bible (Young, 1999). Spirituality, which will be discussed in the next chapter, refers to a specifically non-material domain of human being that in some ways transcends the cognitive.

Definition of meaning

The problem of meaning has been central to the human quest. It has hovered around the edges of learning theory without having been fully incorporated into it. Not all scholars have neglected this topic. For example, Mezirow (1988, p. 233) tautologously defines meaning as 'a process of construing or appropriating a new or revised interpretation of the meaning of one's experience as a guide to decision and action' (also see Mezirow, 1991, pp. 12–13). Likewise, according to Dahlgren (1984, pp. 23–24) to 'learn is to strive for meaning, to have learned something is to have grasped its meaning.' Dahlgren seems to imply that experience has a meaning, while Mezirow suggests that we give meaning to experience – a constructivist position that is also taken in this book.

We have examined the idea of learning as a process of constructing experience in situations in which we find ourselves and reaching outcomes earlier, and we will not repeat this discussion here. However, the problem of meaning has not been fully incorporated into those earlier chapters and so we must first explore briefly the concept, and then we shall link it to understanding and truth. A much more extended discussion of this can be found in Jarvis (1992). What, then, is the meaning of meaning? The term has many definitions, including a metaphysical meaning and a socio-cultural one. It may be used as a noun and when it is used as a verb it conveys individual understanding or intention.

Metaphysical meaning: The quest to understand human existence has been with us since the beginning of recorded history. It is part of the human condition which we all experience. Fromm (1949, pp. 44–45; original italics) summarizes this nicely:

> Man can react to historical contradictions by annulling them through his own action; but he cannot annul existential dichotomies, although he can react to them in different ways. He can appease his mind by soothing and harmonizing ideologies. He can try to escape from his inner restlessness by ceaseless activity in pleasure or in business. He can try to abrogate his freedom and to turn himself into an instrument of powers outside himself, submerging his self in them. But he remains dissatisfied, anxious, and restless. There is only one solution to his problem: to face the truth, to acknowledge his fundamental aloneness and solitude in a universe indifferent to his fate, to recognize that there is no power transcending him which can solve his problem for him. Man must accept responsibility for himself and the fact that only by using his own powers can he give meaning to life. But meaning does not imply certainty. Uncertainty is the very condition to impel man to unfold his powers. If he faces the truth without panic he will recognize that *there is no meaning to life except the meaning that man gives his life by the unfolding of his powers, by living productively*; and that only constant vigilance, activity, and effort can keep us from failing in the one task that matters – the full development of our powers within the limitations set by the laws of our existence. Man will never cease to be perplexed, to wonder, and to raise new questions. Only if he recognizes the human situation, the dichotomies inherent in his existence, and his capacity to unfold his powers will he be able to succeed in his task: to be himself and for himself and to achieve happiness by the full realization of those faculties which are peculiarly his of reason, love, and productive work.

Not everyone would accept this position since some sets of beliefs suggest that there is meaning to human existence (Hanfling, 1987a, 1987b), and that these are found through revelation. The endless quest for meaning to make sense of existence, however, is something that everyone understands, and which might well become more important to some of us as we age.

Socio-cultural meaning: Sometimes belief systems about human existence get embedded into our culture and we acquire them as young children. Luckmann, for instance, writes of a universe of meaning into which individuals are born and they acquire beliefs through the socialization process. He emphasizes (1967, p. 44) the connections between the metaphysical and the non-transcendental and regards them as a total system: 'Symbolic universes are objectivated-meaning systems that relate the experiences of everyday life to a "transcendental" layer of reality. Other systems of meaning do not point beyond the world of everyday life; that is, they do not contain a "transcendental" reference.' These meaning systems reflect the sub-cultures into which we were born, and which we learn unreflectively and memorize. It is these early experiences that give rise to the birth of the conscious self, which helps us find our place in a specific social structure and social situation.

Meaning as a noun: Though we have been talking about systems of meaning, it is possible to use the term meaning much more specifically: words have meanings, situations have meanings, experiences have meanings, and so on. But words do not have meanings in themselves, nor do situations. Language is a system of arbitrary symbols. Nothing has intrinsic meaning; things only appear meaningful later in life because individuals grow up to take their universes of meaning for granted.

Meaning systems are socially constructed, but they are also situation-specific. Individuals have their own socially constructed and yet individualistic universes of meaning, and these are contained within their individual biographies. Hence different people may have different interpretations of a situation, and interpretations reflect something of both the interpreters and their social situation. Indeed, it follows from Bernstein's (1971) work that language might be used differently by different social groups. A simple example is that in American English the word elevator means the same as the word lift in British English. In British English an elevator is a mechanical hoist. Understanding how others use language and the meaning that they are trying to convey is part of the hermeneutic exercise. Achieving understanding is an outcome of the learning process. This understanding enables people to place their own meaning on a word, a situation, and so on. Meaning is, therefore, an outcome of learning and has to be linked conceptually to knowledge. People's individuality is reflected in the different meaning they attach to objects, events, and so forth, for understanding is being.

To mean: When people say that they mean something, they are trying to convey an understanding or express an opinion to other people. It is here in the verb to mean that the subjectivity of meaning is to be found. Communicating means seeking to share understandings, opinions, and attitudes with other people. Even when the word is used in the sense 'They meant to add it but they forgot,' the speaker's intention is still to make others understand the experience.

Meaning, then, is a complex concept, and it is difficult to provide a single definition. It contains elements of interpretation and of understanding – both aspects of the learning process. Initially, however, meaning refers to interpretations of human experience, and this is how we shall treat it here.

Luckmann (1967, p. 50) suggests that the child becomes a 'self' by constructing with others an 'objective and moral universe of meaning.' As such a universe of meaning is constructed, many questions of meaning are posed. This process of focusing on the 'unknowns' of human experience begins in early childhood (Piaget, 1929) and appears to be fundamental to humanity. As the child's universe expands, its questions of meaning change. For most people, trying to understand the meaning of our existence is an intermittent but lifelong quest, as we saw in the third chapter when we looked at Fowler's stages of faith. Mezirow (1988, p. 104) also argues that people move through a maturity gradient during adulthood that involves a sequential restructuring of frames of reference that enable them to construct meanings, and change occurs as the meaning perspectives of others are adopted. Mezirow may not be correct when he suggests that there is a maturity sequence, as though people are moving in a linear manner through time, since, ultimately, it almost pre-supposes some form of pre-destination. Neither is he correct when he implies that people acquire new perspectives through adopting those held by others, although this clearly happens very often but ultimately it is an implicit denial of creativity.

This brief analysis demonstrates that, even though we are born into a universe of meaning, we are still faced with questions, for which there are no ready answers. We learn answers, but these are less definitive than they might have been in an earlier period of history. Consequently, the quest that began in child-hood continues throughout life and, living in a multi-cultural society, we are increasingly aware that there are many systems of religious meaning and that no one might offer the absolute truth. However, as institutionalized religious answers to these questions of meaning have declined in significance, the human quest itself has not disappeared but, if anything, gained a new importance in the contemporary world.

The mechanism of this quest is significant for our understanding of learning throughout life. When people are in harmony with the world, when our meaning system is sufficient to cope with the daily process of living, we are not faced with the 'unknown' and so we can presume upon the world and need not learn. But if we are suddenly confronted with a situation with which our meaning system cannot cope – a disjunctural situation – we are forced to ask questions and learn. It does not matter whether the unknown demands a major theological exposi-tion or merely a brief explanation from everyday experience. This desire to discover meaning is fundamental to humanity, but is there a discoverable truth at the end of this quest?

Truluck and Courtenay (1999, p. 184) suggest that as adults age their quest might not actually be for an ultimate truth but to identify and examine their basic assumptions about life. It is a quest for a new world view as they need to refocus their lives as a result of major changes in it, such as retiring, losing one's independence, and so on. This might be achieved though contemplative learning or through discussion with others, deliberately or incidentally.

However, the question still remains for some: does objective truth exist, and are there phenomena that have unchanging and self-evident meaning? If objec-tive truth exists, can people break through the cultural relativity to discover what is true beyond the confines of culture? If not, is everything relative? This seems to be one of the paradoxes of human existence'. Children's 'why?' for every experience that they do not understand (Piaget, 1929) reveals the origin of this quest, and adults' 'why?' indicates that it continues throughout life. But are the answers that are discovered true? Can they be regarded as indisputable? Can they be verified? People want to treat their interpretations as if they are true; they want to regard the meanings that they impose on words and actions as if they are unchangeable. People appear to be conservative and seek security in meaningful answers and unchanging truths. Lifelong learning is a symbol of the way meaning unfolds with new experiences throughout life; it shows that people can keep seeking and finding meaning, but always there is new or deeper meaning that lies beyond it.

Meaning systems are relative, but they are often presented as if they were objective and unchanging; sometimes it is as if people collude in a delusion to feel secure. As Luckmann (1967) points out, everybody is born into a universe of meaning, and so it appears objective because this is their experience of it and it reflects the traditions of the culture into which they were born. But in order to fit into society, it is almost a pre-requisite that people accept some of its pre-existing universe of meaning, even though this universe is socially constructed and might not always function in their own best interest. Sceptics are sometimes treated as outcasts because they throw doubt on what is generally accepted. But there is more than a good chance that in many situations the cultural answer will satisfy the questioners, and they may believe that they have acquired a meaningful answer. The apparent objectivity of the answer becomes a criterion for accepting it as true, or its functionality in the everyday world reinforces the idea that it is valid.

People hold beliefs, ideologies, an understanding of the world, a familiarity with culture and language that enable them to function meaningfully in their world. These beliefs and understandings become part of their biographies. Sometimes people recognize them as being relative and subjective, but others may regard them as objective and true. Within their experience, individuals have degrees of certainty about elements of their understanding: in some instances they are highly certain, but in others less so. They sometimes know something to be true, in other cases they believe it to be so, and at other times they think that it might be. In some situations, they are open to having their understanding changed, but in others, they may be less prepared to have their perspectives transformed. Such is the complexity of the human biography; its very structure reflects both the social background and the past experiences of every individual.

People are their biography, and as they enter potential learning situations throughout their lives, they seek to interpret them and respond to them, so that it might be claimed that all meaningful knowledge results from interpretation of experience, or that learning is the process of transforming experience into knowing or understanding. Through this process, individuals acquire understanding that they may regard as objective knowledge that is 'true'. This is what guides their actions, although they might realize that their beliefs are only relative and that they can learn and change their minds if they discover anything more satisfying. Some people are convinced that they have actually discovered truth, and nothing will change their minds but others rely on the fact that they are in agreement with other people and this sense of agreement reinforces their own position and legitimates it. If these support systems are removed, people may begin to doubt and this might be dispiriting in old age.

Indeed, there is a sense in which the structures of the world of work function as support systems. The very 'busyness' of life itself means that individuals continue to function, often without considering the questions of meaning since they have more immediate problems. However, after retirement, the meaning-giving function of work disappears; people might have more time on their hands and they are forced to ask these existential questions of meaning. This can be an exciting adventure as people seek to make sense of their lives, whereas for others it can be a time of uncertainty – as we saw earlier.

The process of discovering meaning usually teaches those who learn that more meaning exists beyond it. The very fact that still more meanings can be discovered indicates that the quest for meaning might not be meaningless. Meanings, however, are only relative and may in some way point to yet more sophisticated questions being asked and more sophisticated answers being given in this human quest that Fromm (1949) suggests has no ultimate answer. Bohm (1985, p. 75) writes that:

> . . . in physics, reflection on the meanings of a wide range of experimental facts and theoretical problems and paradoxes eventually led Einstein to new insights concerning the meaning of space, time, and matter, which are at the foundation of the theory of relativity. Meanings are thus seen to be capable of being organized into ever more subtle and comprehensive overall structures that imply, contain, and enfold each other in ways that are

capable of indefinite extension – that is, one meaning enfolds another, and so on.

Consequently, the quest for ultimate meaning, truth, is like being on a journey that has no end and knowing this might well be one stage in the growth of wisdom. For others, wisdom might be the acceptance that there is no meaning to it.

The concept of wisdom

Wisdom is understandably a problematic concept at the present time – especially in its religious form – and the wisdom of the elders is almost generally regarded as defunct. The concept has also rarely been used in educational or learning literature. It is something that was relevant in traditional society when things did not change so fast and were not so technological as they are now. Consequently, the term has fallen into disfavour, but there have been a few attempts to return to it (Cochrane, 1995; Young, 1999). Cochrane (1995, pp. 8–9) suggests that there are three different meanings of the term: individualistic, civic and cosmological. His cosmological definition has been briefly touched upon in the previous section of this chapter. His civic definition is utopian and reflected in the utopian idea of the learning society discussed briefly earlier in this book in which ideas of the good society, justice, fairness and the citizens' rights to participate in a democratic society, are central. However, our concern is more individualistic, since wisdom is no longer a generalizable concept; we are going to analyse it afresh and relate it to learning in everyday life. We are going to argue that wisdom is something learnt from experience rather than something that can be taught to others as a truth and utilized in their lives.

Wisdom is not an educational concept, nor is it something taught, but it occurs as the result of learning. *Collins Dictionary of the English Language* defines it as 'the ability or result of an ability to think and act utilizing knowledge, experience, understanding, common sense, and insight' and as 'accumulated knowledge, erudition, or enlightenment'. Wisdom is in some way the biographical store of knowledge, opinions, and insights gained, often through long years of life. Wisdom often implies being able to provide reasons for why things are the way they are, and in this sense it is metaphysical and cultural.

In this section we are going to explore the relationship between everyday experience and learning and then knowledge, everyday practical knowledge and wisdom and, finally, the value of the wisdom of elders in contemporary technological society.

Everyday experience and learning: Throughout our lives, many of these experiences are encountered, incorporated into our biographies. Or, as Schutz (1967, p. 51), citing Husserl, claims, 'I live *in* my Acts' and by reflecting upon them – which is outside the process of pure duration and a part of discontinuous time – we acquire meaning.

Everyday knowledge: We do not only learn knowledge but, as our definition has suggested, we also learn skills, attitudes, values, beliefs, emotions and the senses from our experiences. A great deal of the literature on learning has concentrated on knowledge but not all of it has analysed the different forms of knowledge. Scheler (1980, p. 76), however, has suggested that there are seven types of knowledge:

- myth and legend – undifferentiated religious, metaphysical, natural and historical;
- knowledge implicit in everyday language – as opposed to learnt, poetic or technical;
- religious – from pious to dogmatic;
- mystical;
- philosophic-metaphysical;
- positive knowledge – mathematics, the natural sciences and the humanities;
- technological.

Scheler called his final two forms artificial because they change before they can become embedded in society's culture, although they are amongst the driving forces for global change. They are amongst the forces that help create the social conditions to which we are forced to adapt all the time, discussed earlier in the section on the learning society. Scheler's artificial forms reflect the knowledge of the knowledge society – a rapidly changing phenomenon, becoming so complex and differentiated, that it is hardly surprising that older people do not always manage to keep abreast with it all the time – but then neither do younger people!

The other five types of knowledge are part of everyday knowledge and are slower to change. Scheler formulated this list in the 1920s and clearly it is limited because in this knowledge society, knowledge itself has changed quite drastically. He did not discuss that type of everyday knowledge that we learn in order to cope with the exigencies of everyday – practical knowledge. As we age, so we learn a great deal of everyday knowledge from everyday experiences of our society and culture, and slowly older people gain a great deal of practical knowledge of the everyday.

However, this technological knowledge society is also generating another new form of everyday knowledge. For instance, the ability to use a personal computer and to keep on learning the program updates is still distinct from being able to understand how a computer works. There is a new everyday technical knowledge emerging which is distinct from the everyday practical knowledge. We are now in a position to elaborate on the seven forms of everyday knowledge, which exclude those two artificial forms that underlie and drive much of our advanced capitalist and global society:

- myth and legend – undifferentiated religious, metaphysical, natural and historical;
- religious – from pious to dogmatic;
- mystical;
- knowledge implicit in everyday language – as opposed to learnt, poetic or technical;
- practical/functional knowledge of daily living;
- philosophic-metaphysical knowledge, including values;
- everyday technological knowledge.

Nevertheless, it is easy to see how older people can become alienated from some aspects of everyday life in this knowledge-based society if they do not feel at home with these new types of practical and technical knowledge and the skills required to utilize everyday appliances. Older people can, therefore, appear to be out-dated and unable to cope with contemporary society, so that the idea that older people are wise seems harder for some younger people to grasp. Since some older people, as do some middle-aged people, find it difficult to cope with this technical knowledge, and even more with the artificial positive and techno-logical knowledge, they are consigned to the scrap heap and their accumulated learning treated as obsolete – like so many other things in this 'throwaway' world, where obsolescence is now designed into the system.

However, there is an active intent of many older people to keep up with this everyday functional knowledge in this society in which the rapidly changing positive and technological knowledge is emphasized. Although most formal adult learning is vocationally orientated, a greater percentage of older adults than any other age group who undertake adult education classes, do not have such an orientation in their learning (Beinhart and Smith, 1997, p. 176). Learning to use the computer and the World Wide Web are among the most popular subjects studied by the elderly. Their other interests tend to be in cultural subjects and the humanities – non-vocationally orientated – since learning is for learn-ing's sake. Yet it is through the study and research, such as local history research groups, that third age learning can help to preserve and articulate the cultural values of society.

Despite not always being able to cope with positive and technical knowledge (artificial knowledge), many do have the knowledge learnt from their experi-ences of everyday life, knowledge that they know works for them. As we pointed out above, everyday knowledge is pragmatic knowledge – it is practical and functional. Heller (1984) actually suggests that everyday knowledge is always opinion and never scientific knowledge, but that depends on how scientific is defined and here the definition seems to be too narrow. Science is a matter of exploration and experiment – this we all do throughout our lives and it is through the process of trial and error in everyday living that we have acquired the practical knowledge and skills that we have. In this sense living is itself an experiment and as we age so we reach certain conclusions about living. Many of these we constantly test in the process of daily life and they are found to work, or else we are in situations of disjuncture and discontinuity when we realize that we are forced to learn new things – which most of us are doing much of the time.

People develop and mature from all of these experiences – for learning is fundamental to the process of human development. However, not all pragmatic learning produces the 'correct' solution. Consider the following illustration. Through a self-directed learning exercise, a person acquires the skills to repair a problem in an old car. However, the fault recurs, and the second time it is easier to repair the fault, because the lessons learnt on the previous occasion are put to use. Experience is a useful reservoir for future learning. The next time the fault occurs, it seems even easier to repair than the previous time, because of the expe-riences gained on the previous two occasions. A pattern for the repair emerges, a form of habitualization, and each time the fault occurs it gets easier to repair it. The only trouble is that the fault keeps recurring because the self-directed learning exercise did not completely solve the problem in the first place, and the pattern that evolved to repair the fault became habitualized. Yet, there is always the possibility of learning to repair the fault another way and becoming more proficient in car repair, and so on.

The knowledge we have of everyday life is pragmatic – we know that it works for us. Even the metaphysical knowledge that relates to ethics and values is pragmatic – we know that this value system works for us – we can live with it and with ourselves for having adopted it. Much of our everyday knowledge is actually embedded in culture, but we go on creating new knowledge for ourselves as we live through the experiences of everyday life, and what makes our society a learning society is that a greater proportion of the knowledge that we use everyday has to be learnt from these experiences rather than from the culture into which we are born. Yet those forms of knowledge that Scheler referred to as positive and technological knowledge still lie beyond the everyday and, in this sense, they are still artificial and are changing even more rapidly.

We shall return to some of these aspects of everyday knowledge in the next chapter, but for the present we can see that there are a number of dimensions, or forms of knowledge, included in everyday knowledge. The older we are and the more experiences we have had, the greater the foundation of everyday knowledge that we have to guide the way we act. It is this that constitutes the basis of wisdom.

Wisdom: This is a synthesis of all of these seven forms of knowledge learnt from experiences of everyday life and incorporated into our own maturing biography. But the wisdom gained is each person's own theory about living and reality. It is subjective, whereas wisdom has traditionally been regarded as objective and possessed by all older people. 'In the later years, the imposed expectations for changes in work/retirement and the innate drive to refocus induces reintegration of cognitive and social repertoires. Havighurst . . . described this as a refocusing of one's past into the present in order to derive *meaning of life* for the present: the act of reviewing one's "biography" and, potentially, the emergence of wisdom' (Thornton, 1986, p. 74).

Moody (1986, p. 127) also highlights this process: 'Those older people commonly judged "wise" are those who respond to genuinely novel situations by applying the lessons of experience in an entirely new context. They do not abandon past experience, but they apply their learning analogically.' He notes that there is a return to story-telling to assist people in their search for meaning in this rapidly changing, technological world. As we have already discussed, he also recognizes that there are some older people whose learning and actions have become habitualized, so that their reactions to new experiences are rigid. They are unable to respond to change, and so they take refuge in not learning.

However, older people are able to use their past learning, their biography, to understand and cope with many contemporary situations. Whilst this does not apply to every situation or to every form of knowledge, it does apply to those forms of knowledge that are embedded in society's culture and learnt from everyday life. They have acquired a practical understanding of the world – practical knowledge, skills, attitudes, beliefs, values, emotions and senses – and we examined this process of maturation in the third chapter. Older, mature people have learnt pragmatically what works for them, and also some of the things that do not. It is their learning and it might, or might not be useful, to others. And it is their own wisdom – something that is subjective – but it may not be recognized by others, especially those of younger generations; neither might it be useful to them. Heller (1984, pp. 165–215) examines the relationship between knowledge and everyday life. She (1984, p. 166) acknowledges this when she writes that 'the best example of . . . adopting a theoretical attitude toward the world in relation to the world of things is provided by cases of failure, lack of success; when a method I have used over and over again fails to work, the pragmatic attitude itself, the desire for efficiency, makes me stop and ask "Why?", "What has gone wrong?" and at once I am thinking along theoretical lines.'

The significance of this claim is at least threefold. First, we see that, as we have argued throughout this book, learning begins when there is a disjuncture between biography and experience that leads to a questioning attitude. Second, everyday knowledge is pragmatic in nature. Learning from primary experience results in pragmatic knowledge, and this is also true whether the situation involves professional practice or everyday experience. The learning gained makes us even more experienced. This is the way that everyday knowledge is learnt and everyday beliefs are acquired. Third, we develop a theoretical orientation toward the world which we shall suggest is precisely the nature of wisdom – it is, as it were, a theory of life. Elsewhere it has been argued (Jarvis, 1999a) that in the workplace, individuals have to generate their own theory from practice and that they have to take what they learn from other sources and try it out for themselves. What was traditionally called theory has become information that practitioners can use and try out in their professional practice to see if it works for them. When it works, they incorporate their learning into their own theory of practice. This is also true of all people's learning about everyday life – it is everyday wisdom and as we mature so it develops.

Elders do have a great deal more experience of the everyday that is useful to them but it cannot be assumed to be valid or useful to others. It will also be recalled from the fourth chapter that Cattell (1963), and Cattell and Horn in subsequent work, developed a theory of fluid and crystallized intelligence, in which they argued that crystallized intelligence increased with experience. Older people do have more crystallized intelligence, they have had more emotional experiences, and they have learnt to live with ambiguity and contradiction, and so on.

Consequently, it is suggested here that those elders who have learnt from their life's experiences have developed a theory of life that works for them. It is subjective and individual and whatever the advice or guidance that elders give to others, it can be no more than information that has to be tried out in the recipient's life. Many elders will have developed their own wisdom but its possession is not their automatic right and neither is it an objective phenomenon.

The value of the wisdom of the elders: To know that we have accumulated knowledge and skill gives individuals a sense of personal worth which is important in itself. In this sense, understanding one's own wisdom is of value in itself – it provides a sense of integrity to our personhood. To have reached the stage in life where we value life itself and the world in which we live for no other reason than that we are alive and live in the world, where we can treasure being itself and appreciate the wonder of existence, is of great value. Perhaps, above all, this is where wisdom lies. No longer do we have to conquer the world, only to recognize that we have a part to play within it. But once we have achieved this state we are, paradoxically, in a position to demonstrate our wisdom to others – to show precisely why the wisdom of the elders is still valuable.

Older people have memories of the culture of a society and can, perhaps, see better the implications for some of the things happening in society than some younger people still caught up in the process of pursuing their careers and being responsible for their families. For younger people, living is still about finding their way through the journey of life. The adventure is by no means over as we age, but perhaps we have learnt to treat it a little differently and even to tread the path a little more judiciously, even though we are only too well aware that we are closer to the journey's end. But it is because we are where we are that we can play our part in society. We can help it preserve the heritage that has been vested in us through our learning and living our lives.

We can pass on to others the fruits of our learning, but now we have to recognize its status. It is personal, subjective knowledge that may, or may not, be applicable to other people. Older people are, as we showed earlier, potential mentors (Daloz, 1986) for any who wish to seek advice and support. But, mentoring is not teaching but a process of using one's wisdom to support another. However, it is unfortunate that, unlike the experts in the world of work, they are often not called on to share their expertise – even in that industrial world in which many of them worked for so long. The society in which the elders have functioned has changed beyond recognition so that their biographical experience may be discounted by some. When this occurs, individuals who have gained a great understanding of the practical wisdom that is still embedded in society's culture are denied the opportunity to demonstrate their usefulness.

Older people can also volunteer to undertake jobs in those sectors of society which governments and other bodies do not fund adequately, thereby demonstrating the inappropriateness of such priorities. However, there is an important caveat to be made here – older people should not be seen as a substitute for governmental and civic involvement in such activities, but as a symbol of the priorities of human society and of social living. In addition, they can undertake research and put on the national agenda, those local and national problems that older people regard as important but that neither government nor industry will fund and prefer to sweep under the table. In a sense, the freedom of older people gives them the power to influence the public agenda in a variety of ways.

There are a number of areas in which older adults can demonstrate and use their wisdom but four have been emphasized throughout this book. We can, for instance:

- help preserve society's culture through what we continue to value;
- pass on to others what we have learnt and value through acting as mentors;
- help to create a better society and the good life through our own social activities – through both volunteering and social activism;
- emphasize those dimensions of human life, such as the spiritual and aesthetic, that tend to get under-emphasized by the demands and values of contemporary society.

Conclusion

We have argued in this chapter that wisdom is personal and subjective, learnt throughout life but not necessarily applicable to other's lives, so that it cannot just be taught to them as if it were truth. Clearly wisdom incorporates the quest for meaning; it often implies being able to provide reasons for why things are the way they are, and in this sense it is metaphysical and pre-sociological. It explains the 'thus-ness' (Heller, 1984, p. 214) of this world. Heller (1984,

p. 212) suggests that it stems from a form of contemplative learning that could occur only after humankind had conquered the physical hardships of survival: 'The emergence of contemplation as an independent mental attitude depends on man's having attained a state of existence beyond the struggle for mere survival . . . The world in which he lives and moves awakens man's interest and curiosity. And whenever there is neither need for, nor possibility of a pragmatic attitude, man's [interest and] curiosity become ends in themselves. Anything that is of pragmatic interest in one coordinate system can become an object of contemplation in another.'

Perhaps it was not only in the early world that humankind was able to contemplate the meaning of existence only when it had overcome the basic struggles to exist. Even today, it is only in the later stages of life, when people are freed from many of the constraints of contemporary society and when they own their own space, that they are able to stop and contemplate and to come to terms with life. Certainly there is something metaphysical in this idea, although it is as much a psychological process as it is a metaphysical one. It might be a manifestation of spirituality or religiosity, but it is not necessarily something that could be called Christian or Muslim or Buddhist. Having the ability to provide an explanation for the way that the world works and also to explain its 'thus-ness' lies at the heart of wisdom. Indeed, this is the basis of philosophy – the love of wisdom. The possession of wisdom was much treasured in the ancient world, because the sages had contemplated the nature of existence and then they taught others who learned from them. Wise people were nearly always old, since they had accumulated the experiences and learned knowledge which was then incorporated into their own lives. Bot this was, of course, probably less true of the Greek philosophers who developed the art of philosophical contemplation and made it a way of life.

Nevertheless, having contemplated the everyday for many years does result in the acquisition of a body of knowledge, a theory, that is more orientated to life itself than to the technical and positive knowledge that Scheler called artificial. It is this endeavour to understand life itself that also lies at the heart of religion. Despite the apparently secular society in which we live, it is crucial that we recognize that religion, defined in this broader sense, is still almost universal. It is only Christianity in the West that appears to be declining. This universal quest to understand life manifests itself in most people, especially as we age.

Wisdom itself, however, is no longer seen as something universally applicable just because it has been learnt throughout the life of the elderly. It has to be tested by others to whom it is offered and found to be useful before it can be claimed to be valid. Its status has changed and it is no longer truth, merely information that might be useful. The status of the elderly has, therefore, changed from something that is ascribed to something that is achieved. Older people gain the respect of others if they and their wisdom are seen to be valuable to society and this they have to demonstrate through the advice and support they are able to render, in their priorities in social living and through their integrity with themselves.

There is the danger in this changing situation, especially if some of the learning of the elderly is rejected, that the elderly themselves will be rejected; that their personhood will no longer be respected, merely because they are old. Society has to learn to differentiate between the person and the person's usefulness to society. There might be some grounds for rewarding people with higher status who contribute more than others to the good of society, but the humanity and person-hood of everybody in society needs to be equally respected and enhanced, whatever their age.

References

Beinhart S and Smith P (1997) *National Adult Learning Survey 1997* London: Department of Education and Employment

Bernstein B (1967) *Class, Codes and Control* London: Paladin

Bohm D (1985) *Unfolding Meaning* London: ARK Paperbacks

Cattell R (1963) Theory of fluid and crystallized intelligence in *Journal of Educational Psychology* Vol 54, pp. 1–23

Cochrane D (1985) *Wisdom* (Unpublished Essay) University of Saskatchewan

Collins English Dictionary Glasgow: Collins

Dahlgren L-O (1984) Outcomes of learning in Marton F *et al. op cit*

Daloz L (1986) *Effective Teaching and Mentoring* San Francisco: Jossey-Bass

Fowler J (1981) *Stages of Faith* San Francisco: Harper & Row

Fromm E (1949) *Man for Himself* London: Routledge

Hanfling O (1987a) *The Quest for Meaning* Oxford: Blackwell in association with the Open University Press

Hanfling O (1987b) *Life and Meaning* Oxford: Blackwell in association with the Open University Press

Heller A (1984) *Everyday Life* London: Routledge & Kegan Paul

Horn J and Cattell R (1967) Age differences in fluid and crystallized intelligence *Acta Psychologica* Vol 26 No 107–129

Jarvis P (1992) *Paradoxes of Learning* San Francisco: Jossey-Bass

Jarvis P (1999) *The Practitioner-Researcher* San Francisco: Jossey-Bass

Luckmann T (1967) *Invisible Religion* London: Macmillan

Marton F, Hounsell D and Entwistle N (eds) *The Experience of Learning* Edinburgh: Scottish University Press

Mezirow J (1988) Transformation theory in *Proceedings of the 29th Annual Conference of the Adult Education Research Conference* University of Calgary

Mezirow J (1991) *Transformative Dimensions of Adult Learning* San Francisco: Jossey-Bass

Moody H (1986) Education and the life cycle in Peterson *et al. op cit*

Peterson D, Thornton J, and Birren J (eds) (1986) *Education and Aging* Englewood Cliffs, NJ: Prentice Hall

Piaget J (1929) *The Child's Conception of the World* London: Routledge & Kegan Paul

Scheler M (1980) *Problems of the Sociology of Knowledge* London: Routledge & Kegan Paul

Schutz A (1967) *The Phenomenology of the Social World* London: Heinemann

Truluck J and Courtenay B (1999) Learning style preferences amongst older adults *Educational Gerontology* Vol 25 No 3 pp 221–236

Young F (1999) *Recovering the Wisdom of the Past for the 21st Century* Hugh Price Hughes Lecture, London: Hinde Street Methodist Church

CHAPTER 19

LEARNING TO RETIRE

Originally published as 'Learning to Retire' in P. Jarvis (2001), *Learning in Later Life*, London: Kogan Page, pp. 60–9. Cross-references refer to the original publication.

Life may be viewed as a passage through time, but the world in which that journey takes place is undergoing very rapid change. In years past, people could expect to live in a world that changed hardly at all from the time that they were born until the time that they died. They changed and gained more knowledge about it, but the world apparently did not change and so the wisdom of the elders was useful and influential. Elders had lived longer and had learnt the answers to some of the problems that younger people faced. Now things are different. Modernity has brought with it tremendous changes. Whether this is a post-modern phase is debatable, but certainly the world is still undergoing tremendously rapid change and elders are not so highly regarded any more because the knowledge of the modern world is not necessarily *their* knowledge. Apparently it is the knowledge of younger people. This is a period of late modernity.

Living in such a world has implications for older individuals, for their sense of identity and the security that they experience in a world that appears to be constantly changing and unstable. A world of risk, potential chaos and chance. A world where people have to rely on abstract systems and one that seems to be getting smaller as the communication systems alter people's comprehension of space and time. Giddens (1990) talks about space–time distanciation and Harvey (1990) about the compression of space and time. It is a world from which it is easy to feel alienated, especially as we age. We have examined the maturation process in earlier chapters; in this chapter we will explore the process of ageing in terms of stages of life. Thereafter we shall look at one specific transition period – retirement.

The stages of a person's life

Erikson (1965, pp. 239–266) was one of the first scholars to discuss life stages and he did so by elaborating on Shakespeare's seven ages of man from *As You Like It*. This he did in his well-known Eight Ages of Man:

- basic trust v basic mistrust;
- autonomy v shame and doubt;
- initiative v guilt;
- industry v inferiority;

- identity v role confusion;
- intimacy v isolation;
- generativity v stagnation;
- ego integrity v despair.

It is only in the final two stages that Erikson focuses upon adulthood, but many of the values discussed by Hudson (1999) in Chapter 3 are developed in the earlier stages of Erikson's typology. We build these into our biographies through learning from experiences in earlier life and carry them with us towards integrity or despair.

Other scholars have looked at the idea that human beings pass through life stages. Perhaps the best known is Daniel Levinson's work on the seasons of life. Initially (1978) he looked at the seasons in a man's life but much later (1996) he looked at the seasons of a woman's life. His idea of seasons was much inspired by the work of van Gennep (1908) on *rites de passage,* but van Gennep's study took place against an entirely different social situation than the one in which we now live. Nevertheless, Levinson's stages and periods of transition can be seen in terms of learning to cope and adapt as we age. I will not recall here the whole of Levinson's typology (1966, p. 18) but it can be summarized as:

- pre-adulthood (0–22 years);
- early adulthood (17–45 years);
- middle adulthood (40–65 years);
- late adulthood (60+ years).

It will be noted that between each season Levinson sees a period of transition. This transition period is one in which an individual learns to let go of one set of roles and role behaviours and learns new ones. Perhaps the most obvious area of transition is the midlife transition – that period when we all realize our own mortality and confront the fact, perhaps for the first time. Transitions are periods which anthropologists call liminality, when individuals are learning how to play the new roles attached to their new status in society. However, lifestyles and roles are not really quite so fixed and age-related in late modern society, so that some recent writers have not regarded ageing as a stage developmental process but have merely used biological age as a point in the lifespan to stereotype role behaviour. Both Sheehy (1995) and Hudson (1999), for instance, discuss ageing by 10-year periods, rather than by any more sophisticated theoretical framework. But these are really no more than broad brushstrokes. Giddens (1991, p. 148) comments that the lifespan becomes structured around 'open experience thresholds' rather than a ritualized passage. We learn from the experiences we have during life and we develop as we age – but in no particular idealized direction – although there are sets of values and characteristics at which individuals regard it desirable to aim.

One ritual in this process of ageing still remains, but even this is being reconceptualized – retirement. Society still ritualizes retirement and many individuals still undergo such a ritual only once, but some people in this late modern world retire two or three times during their lives. In addition, it used to be something that occurred at a fixed time, e.g. 65 years, but even this has become variable now. In some careers, e.g. the military services, individuals retire a lot earlier, but other people are beginning to suggest that 65 years of age is too young to retire since individuals will spend a quarter or even a third of their adult life in retirement. This is costly to the State, in terms of loss of knowledge and expertise and in economic terms too, since the State pays a retirement pension to all who have reached retirement age. Consequently, the State is now beginning to advocate private pension arrangements. Flexi-retirement is being mooted by some as a way of overcoming this situation, with people gradually decreasing the length of their working week. Moody (1998, p. 69) notes that there are now the young-old, the old-old and the oldest-old. This latter group is becoming more numerous as the average life span has gradually increased.

We shall examine the retirement ritual here as part of the process of learning to grow old since it is suggested here that when we first undergo this ritual, it does have an effect on our understanding of ourselves as human beings. In addition, it is the first time in some people's lives that they have actually found themselves in this position.

Retirement

It is difficult to determine when later life actually begins. Many apparently older persons will say that they feel quite young and sprightly, whereas some not so old will exclaim that 'they are beginning to feel quite old!' Some people might say that they are old when they reach a specific age, but it is hard to say that people who are 65 years of age are automatically old, if they do not feel old, are still actively employed and still have many activities and hobbies in their private lives. Consequently Moody (1998) asks whether retirement is an obsolete concept now.

So what constitutes later life? Governments might claim that this begins at retirement age, but not all countries have a compulsory retirement age! Indeed, the pensionable age for women has been altered in recent years to create some form of conformity across Europe, and in the United States there is now no compulsory retirement age. These changes have prompted theorists to regard retirement as a way of managing the labour force (Moody, 1998, p. 324). Going through the ritual, however, does serve to locate an individual at the edge of the social structure as far as work is concerned. We learn that we have reached a stage in our development and our expectations about what lies beyond may well be mixed. Four dominant modes of experiencing retirement seem to be most prevalent (Gee and Baillie, 1999, p. 110, cited from Hornstein and Wapner, 1985):

- transition to old age/rest – relax, slow down and prepare for ageing;
- new beginning – free to tackle long-awaited goals and live life to the full;
- continuity – the basic pattern of life continues;
- imposed disruption – job is irreplaceable and retirement is meaningless and frustrating.

Indeed, Gee and Baillie's (1999, p. 126) own research into retirement expectations confirm that there are 'complexities and individual differences in retirement expectations' that present challenges and opportunities. The retirement process is, however, a ritual and so we will now briefly look at the ritual process and then at retirement itself.

In moving from one place to another people often ritualize their moves. They have leaving parties to symbolize that they are about to depart from their present home and after they have moved into a new one they have a house-warming party to celebrate the fact that they have 'put down their roots' in a new abode. (For a full analysis of this, see van Gennep, 1908; Turner, 1974.) This is quite a significant process and has three major parts to it:

- The leaving party is a symbol of departure, which signifies the idea of leaving a place and of breaking the social relationships. It might well be described as a ritual of separation.
- Although there may not be a long period before moving into the new home, there is a short period when a person is in a stage of transition. In the United Kingdom, this might be no more than a day but if a person migrates from one country to another a considerable period of time may elapse before the new home is reached.
- The house-warming party is a symbol of arrival, of putting down new roots and of establishing new relationships. This might be described as an incorporation ritual.

In contemporary society, these parties may hardly appear to be deeply significant rituals, but in primitive societies and in close-knit communities, they had more overtly significant social occasions. Among the functions of the ceremonies are those that signify movement, those that break and create relationships and, above all, that sustain social stability and normality during a transition period.

Because geographical migration in contemporary secular society is such a common phenomenon, its ritualistic significance is not recognized as frequently as it might have been in more primitive societies. Indeed, it might not even be practised. Similarly the rituals that occur as people cross time are less frequently recognized and yet they are still there and new ones are emerging. Travelling through time is a journey upon which everybody embarks from birth. During this journey people occupy different positions in society and different statuses, some of which occur naturally as a result of the ageing process and others because of the level of achievement that individuals reach within the hierarchical structures of society. For example, a person may be a husband and father within the former type of status and managing director within the latter. Each of these statuses is relatively clearly defined and has its own associated roles, and people play those in accordance with their interpretation of the way in which they should be performed.

A much more recent status change has been that of worker to non–worker. In primitive society work was not formalized, nor was it practised far away from the tribe, the village or the family. Work was an integrated part of daily living in the community and something everybody did so that retirement, as such, would not have been understood. It is hardly surprising, therefore, that this status change is not ritualized and enshrined in the religious rites of passage of such societies. It is a new ritual that has developed in our more secular society and so it has not been incorporated into the religious rituals of late modern society. Even so, a secular ritual of retirement has appeared and the process can be examined in precisely the same way as other rituals:

- The ritual of separation might begin at the moment when the company welfare, or training, officer approaches an older person with an invitation to attend a pre-retirement course. Of course, retirement might be a long way off, one or two years in some companies and very occasionally even further. Naturally, this seems important for the company representatives, because it is giving the future retiree the opportunity to consider aspects of life beyond work. But for some employees the invitation comes too early; for them work still has a few years to run and they are not yet ready to think about a future without work. The debate about how long before retirement the company should offer the first day(s) of pre-retirement education is important, but it is not the purpose of this analysis, and therefore it is not pursued here any further. The point is, that this first invitation to attend pre-retirement education might mark the first day in the ritual process of retirement.

- During the following days the potential retirees might well begin to turn their minds to the future, thinking perhaps about some of the issues that have been raised on the pre-retirement course or, even, of others that have been pushed aside in the 'busyness' of everyday life and lain dormant. Additionally, the company might begin to provide cover for these older workers so that their successors can begin to learn the job that they will eventually inherit. This is a period of transition – it might be relatively short or a few years in length depending upon different companies' policies. This period might well end with a last day party, when the company representatives make nice sounds, present gifts and send the retirees on their way with a good feeling about the company.
- The retirees leave their company and the next stage of the ritual is that of completion of liminality and reincorporation into the wider society.

But this is the problem! Unlike other rituals there is no structural ritual of incorporation. Status change has occurred but in this instance there is no structural or ritual way back into society in order to mark the change and initiate the retirees into their new status and the roles attached to it. Retirement, then, is an incomplete ritual and the incompleteness symbolizes the fact that society has not evolved ways of dealing with retirees in a structural manner, so that they are apparently condemned to always being in liminality. This is what Rosow (1967) called a 'roleless role'. Turner (1974, p. 81) describes this period of liminality as a time that is 'neither here nor there ... betwixt and between'. At this stage, individuals have a new experience: they are free. Phillipson (1998, p. 64), following Atchley (1993) refers to this as emancipation. Provided that the retired have appropriate resources to learn how to be retired people, they are free to create and explore their role how they wish, and to learn from the experiences that they create. They have to devise their own way back into society. However, there is still an expectation that people will 'just wind down and disintegrate' (Goodman, 1999, p. 66) after retirement. Our expectations may be one of the problems with which we have to learn to cope when we have retired and are free.

Sheehy (1995, p. 260) describes some of the problems experienced by those who have been forced to take early retirement, rather than those who were able to complete their anticipated working life. She notes their tremendous needs – especially the need to learn how to cope – and how many turn to counselling for help. They have to learn, not only to be, but also to learn new skills so that they can relocate themselves in the world.

If we think back to that model of learning in Chapter 2, people are now free to practise and experiment, free to learn new knowledge and skills, and so on. Retired people have become free agents within society since there are no prescribed structural roles to be played. However, Giddens (1991, p. 156) highlights one of the major problems with retirement when he suggests that 'the ontological security which modernity has purchased, on the level of day-to-day routines, depends on the institutional exclusion of social life from fundamental existential issues which raise central moral dilemmas for human beings'. The process of becoming individuated is one that also increases the likelihood of feeling alone. This is an element of the fear of freedom that Fromm (1942) discusses and with which many, including those early-retired people, cannot cope. Now the structures of society do not prescribe role performance and do not shield us from the issues of humanity. Older people are relatively free, perhaps for the first time, to structure their lives in the manner that they wish and to respond to these existential issues in precisely the manner they wish. Herein lies the need to achieve balance – between work and leisure, between self and others, and so on. There are both advantages and disadvantages to freedom – a paradox of human living to which we shall return.

However, being a part of the social structure carries certain privileges as well, and the ritual of separation also removes the retirees from these. Being part of the social structure and having employment provides:

- a sense of personal identity for many people, e.g. I am a factory manager;
- social identity, e.g. she is a doctor;
- personal and social worth, e.g. his work gives him a sense of usefulness to society;
- status and self-respect, e.g. she has a good position in society;
- a sense of purpose and meaning, e.g. I can contribute something to society through my work;
- a structure to time, e.g. for many people the passage of time is structured by the demands of work, etc.

It would be possible to continue with these points and to show that for many people some, or all, of these aspects of their lives are the direct consequence of being within the social structure of society. They also relate to the core values of human development that we discussed earlier in the chapter. When individuals are freed from the structures, they are also parted from all the consequences of being integrated into society. Therefore, at retirement, society ritualizes people out of some, or all, of the consequences of being part of it, but it does not ritualize them back into new structures and consequences, so that it becomes easy for people to be 'lost', and to feel alone in their freedom. We have to learn to be in new roles. Pre-retirement education needs to focus a little more on these key issues.

Pre-retirement education

The first day of a pre-retirement course clearly marks the first day of a ritual that is incomplete and can lead to individuals being ritualized out of society. This is not, therefore, a necessarily desirable state, nor a function of pre-retirement education intended by those who offer this service. Nevertheless, the fact that it is the start of such a process should be recognized by those who are involved in pre-retirement education and they need to be aware of the implications of the freedom.

Mary Davies (1993, p. 68) pointed out that traditionally pre-retirement courses were constructed around Heron's formulation that in order to have a good retirement, six factors are necessary:

- good health;
- congenial amicable companions;
- adequate housing;
- adequate incomes;
- something satisfying to do;
- having an adequate personal philosophy.

She suggested that the last of these six receives scant attention – a factor that is quite basic to this book. When I (1980) researched pre-retirement education, I also noted the significance placed on the instrumental aspects of life – health, finance and leisure. Significantly, Gee and Baillie (1999, p. 121) note that for both British and Australian retirees, these are still the most dominant topics, although the Australian respondents did specify 'educational courses' as being one of the areas about which they would like more information.

However, this does raise quite significant questions about the design of the learning experiences that should be given to participants in pre-retirement education. Clearly, all participants should be given information and reassurance about these areas of social life in which they are interested. Indeed, early research on pre-retirement education (Phillipson and Strang, 1983, p. 202) suggests that reassurance was a major function of the courses that they studied, but the authors also warned educators that some courses actually create more concern in the retirees, and that this is something they need to be aware of. They also recognized the unfinished nature of the retirement ritual and recommended that pre-retirement courses should help to build links between the retirees and the local community (Phillipson and Strang, 1983, p. 210).

But there are other aspects of which the participants may not be aware nor have considered for their own lives. For instance, are they aware of the positive functions of work for their own lives that may have to be replaced when they retire? I have conducted courses now for many years and few groups have focused on the significance of personal and social identity. Few have examined the place of work in providing for friendship and the opportunities to make new acquaintances; none have focused on the fact that work has shielded them from ontological issues, and so on. In a session that I have conducted on many such courses, I ask the participants to consider what their occupation provides them in their everyday life that they will lose when they retire, so reducing the quality of their lives. The answers have generally been similar and have included the following:

- an activity;
- finance;
- friendships;
- health;
- identity;
- mental stimulus;

- opportunities to continue learning;
- purpose in life;
- structure of time.

This has normally led to a wide ranging discussion about these topics and how we can find other activities that will replace work. Significantly, however, many of these aspects of everyday living are taken for granted, and it is only when opportunity for careful consideration about life is given, that they are discussed in this way. Few courses, however, have focused on the emotional issues of retirement, although Hepworth (1993) pointed to the significance of a social constructivist approach to emotions in older adults. More recently Goleman (1998, pp. 26–27) suggested the following framework for emotional intelligence:

Personal skills

- self-awareness – emotional awareness, self-assessment and confidence;
- self-regulation – control, trustworthiness, conscientious, adaptable and innovative;
- motivation – achievement, commitment, initiative and optimistic.

Social skills

- empathy – understanding, developing others, service, leveraging diversity, political;
- social skills – influence, communicate, manage conflict, leadership, change catalyst bond-building, collaborative and cooperative, team capabilities.

Importantly, these are the types of human value that Hudson (1999) outlines and which we discussed earlier. They are the skills that help individuals develop themselves and that are especially beneficial in retirement – indeed, they are beneficial throughout the whole of life! Skills like these help potential retirees recognize the structural significance of what is happening to them and help them to become agents to build themselves again and make their own way in society.

These are significant curriculum issues in pre-retirement education which need to be fully recognized and included within pre-retirement education curricula. However, the fact that there is not a ritual of incorporation remains a fascinating feature of retirement, one to which a number of organizations, religious and otherwise, might turn their attention. But this need not necessarily be a good thing for everybody, since most people go through their lives imprisoned with the structures of society and to be ritualized out of those structures might be a necessary release and a significant step in their own self-discovery and self-development. Yet the freedom gained by some might be a fearful experience for others, and a complete ritual and a structural framework in which to fit their lives may have helped them.

Conclusion

In a sense, retirement is like throwing somebody into the deep end of the swimming pool – they have to learn to swim. But, as we have seen, it is not always easy. Some people will regard it as a new beginning, others as a disruption, others as merely continuing with their lives with a slight change of circumstances and others as a transition to old age. It is, however, a period in which a lot of new learning occurs and it is to this that we now turn.

References

Atchley R (1993) Critical voices in retirement in Cole T, Achenbaum W, Jakobi P and Kastenbaum R (eds) *Voices and Visions of Aging: Towards a Critical Gerontology* New York: Springer

Davies M (1993) Theories of aging and their implications for pre-retirement education *Educational Gerontology* Vol 8 No 2 pp. 67–74

Erikson E (1950) *Childhood and Society* Harmondsworth: Penguin

Fromm E (1942) *The Fear of Freedom* (1984 edition) London: Ark Paperbacks

Gee S and Baillie J (1999) Happily ever after?: an exploration of retirement expectations *Educational Gerontology* Vol 25 No 2 pp. 109–128

Giddens A (1990) *The Consequences of Modernity* Cambridge: Polity Press

Giddens A (1991) *Modernity and Self-Identity* Cambridge: Polity Press

Goleman D (1998) *Working with the Emotions* London: Bloomsbury

Harvey D (1990) *The Condition of Postmodernity* Oxford: Blackwell

Hepworth G (1983) Ageing and the emotions *Educational Gerontology* Vol 8 No 2 pp. 75–85

Hornstein G and Wapley (1985) Nodes of experiencing and adapting to retirement *International Journal of Aging and Human Development* Vol 21 pp. 281–315

Hudson F (1999) *The Adult Years* San Francisco: Jossey-Bass

Jarvis P (1980) Pre-retirement education: design and analysis *Adult Education* Vol 53 No 1 pp. 14–19

Levinson D and Levinson J (1996) *The Seasons of a Woman's Life* Knorf: New York

Moody (1998) *Aging: Concepts and Controversies* Thousand Oaks: Pine Forge, Calif (2nd edition)

Phillipson C (1998) *Reconstructing Old Age* London: Sage

Phillipson C and Strang G (1983) *The Impact of Pre-Retiremen Education* Keele University: Department of Adult Education

Rosow I (1967) *Social Integration of the Aged* New York: Free Press

Sheehy G (1995) *New Life Passages* Canada: Random House of Canada

Turner V (1974) *The Ritual Process* Harmondsworth: Penguin

van Gennap A (1908) *The Rites of Passage* London: Routledge & Kegan Paul

BOOKS, MONOGRAPHS and JOURNALS

Books: authored

Adult Education in a Small Centre: A Case Study, Surrey: University of Surrey Department of Educational Studies, 1982

Professional Education, London: Croom Helm, 1983

Adult and Continuing Education: Theory and Practice, London: Croom Helm/ New York: Nichols, 1983
Republished London/New York: Routledge, 1988
Second edition London: Routledge, 1995; translated into Estonian (1998), Chinese (2002) and Greek (2004)
Third edition (*Adult Education and Lifelong Learning: Theory and Practice*) London: Routledge, 2004
Fourth edition (*Adult Education and Lifelong Learning: Theory and Practice*) London: Routledge, 2010

The Sociology of Adult and Continuing Education, London: Croom Helm, 1985
Republished London: Routledge, 1989
Translated into Spanish (1989)

Sociological Perspectives on Lifelong Education and Lifelong Learning, Athens, GA: University of Georgia Department of Adult Education, 1986

Adult Learning in the Social Context, London: Croom Helm, 1987
(Awarded the C.O. Houle World Award for Adult Education Literature)

International Dictionary of Adult and Continuing Education, London/New York: Routledge, 1990
Second edition London: Kogan Page, 1999

Paradoxes of Learning, San Francisco: Jossey-Bass, 1992
Translated into Lithuanian (2001) and Chinese (2003)

Adult Education and the State, London: Routledge, 1993
Translated into Japanese (2001)

Ethics and Education for Adults in a Late Modern Society, Leicester: NIACE, 1997
Translated into Russian (2006)

The Practitioner-Researcher, San Francisco: Jossey-Bass, 1999
Translated into Danish (2002) and Estonian (2004)

Learning in Later Life, London: Kogan Page, 2001
Translated into Arabic (2003)

Universities and Corporate Universities: The Lifelong Learning Industry and Global Society, London: Kogan Page, 2001
Translated into Spanish (2006)

Towards a Comprehensive Theory of Human Learning, London: Routledge, 2006
(First volume of the *Human Learning and the Learning Society* trilogy)

Globalisation, Lifelong Learning and the Learning Society: Sociological Perspectives, London: Routledge, 2007
(Second volume of the *Human Learning and the Learning Society* trilogy)

Democracy, Lifelong Learning and the Learning Society: Active Citizenship in a Late Modern Age, London: Routledge, 2008
(Third volume of the *Human Learning and the Learning Society* trilogy)

Learning to Be a Person in Society, London: Routledge, 2009

Books: co-authored

The Teacher-Practitioner in Nursing, Midwifery and Health Visiting, London: Croom Helm, 1985
Republished London: Chapman & Hall, 1989
Second edition (*The Teacher-Practitioner and Mentor in Nursing, Midwifery, Health Visiting and the Social Services*), Cheltenham: Stanley Thornes, 1997

The Human Resource Development Handbook, London: Kogan Page, 1998
Revised edition London: Kogan Page, 2000

The Theory and Practice of Learning, London: Kogan Page, 1998
Second edition London: Kogan Page, 2003

Books: edited

Twentieth-Century Thinkers in Adult Education, London: Croom Helm, 1987
Republished London: Routledge, 1991; translated into Chinese (1999)
Second edition (*Twentieth-Century Thinkers in Adult and Continuing Education*), London: Kogan Page, 2001

Britain: Policy and Practice in Continuing Education, San Francisco: Jossey-Bass, 1988

Perspectives in Adult Education and Training in Europe, Leicester: NIACE/ Malabar, FL: Krieger, 1992

The Age of Learning: Education and the Knowledge Society, London: Routledge, 2001

The Theory and Practice of Teaching, London: Kogan Page, 2001
Translated into Croatian (2003)
Second edition London: Routledge, 2006; translated into Japanese (2011)

Adult and Continuing Education (5 vols), London: Routledge, 2003

From Adult Education to Lifelong Learning, London: Routledge, 2006

The Routledge International Handbook of Lifelong Learning, London: Routledge, 2009

Books: co-edited

Training Adult Educators in Western Europe, London: Routledge, 1991

Adult Education: Evolution and Achievements in a Developing Field of Study, San Francisco: Jossey-Bass, 1991
(An official publication of the American Association of Adult and Continuing Education – the contract was open to competition)

Adult Education and Theological Interpretations, Malabar, FL: Krieger, 1993

Developments in the Education of Adults in Europe, Frankfurt: Peter Lang, 1994

International Perspectives on Lifelong Learning, London: Kogan Page, 1998

Human Learning: A Holistic Approach, London: Routledge, 2005

Learning, Working and Living, Basingstoke: Palgrave Macmillan, 2006

Universities, Ethics and the Professions, London: Routledge, 2009

Research reports: authored

Religious Education Curriculum in the Junior School, 1974
(Submitted to Warley Local Education Authority)

Research reports: co-authored

The Education and Training of District Nurses (SRN/RGN 1976): An Evaluation of the Implementation of the 1976 Curriculum in Surrey (1978–9), 1980
(Sponsored by the DHSS and published by the University of Surrey)

Curriculum Development in the Education of Adults, 1984 (contributor)
(Published by FEU)

The Teacher-Practitioner Course at the University of Surrey, 1986
(Submitted to the King's Fund)

Joint Preparation for Health Visitors and District Nurses: An Initial Evaluation, 1987 (joint author)
(English National Board, London)

The Education of Adults in Europe: England and Wales, 1992 (contributor)
(Interim report to Eurodelphi Project, University of Leuven, Belgium)

Elder Mentoring, 1999 (joint author)
(Published in conjunction with Help the Aged)

Towards the Learning City, 1997 (joint author)
(Corporation of London)

Lifelong Learning: Rhetoric, Reality and Public Policy, 1997 (co-editor)
(Conference proceedings, University of Surrey)

Book series: edited

International Perspectives on Adult and Continuing Education, London:
  Routledge
(Approximately 20 books published)

Theory and Practice in Adult Education in North America, London: Routledge
(Approximately 10 books published)

Journals

International Journal of Lifelong Education, 1981–
(Founding Editor and Co-Editor)

Journal for Adult Theological Education, Vol. 3 No. 1, 2007
(Guest Editor)

Comparative Education, Vol. 35, No. 2, 1999
(Guest Co-Editor)

Comparative Education, Vol. 36, No. 3, 2000
(Guest Co-Editor)

Comparative Education, Vol. 37, No. 4, 2001
(Guest Co-Editor)

Comparative Education, 2005–8
(Chairman of Board of Editors)

Peter Jarvis has served on many other Editorial Boards or as Editorial
Correspondent. He has also published well over 200 chapters and papers in
books and journals.

INDEX